CAMBRIDGE LIBRARY COLLECTION

Books of enduring scholarly value

Music

The systematic academic study of music gave rise to works of description, analysis and criticism, by composers and performers, philosophers and anthropologists, historians and teachers, and by a new kind of scholar - the musicologist. This series makes available a range of significant works encompassing all aspects of the developing discipline.

The Aristoxenian Theory of Musical Rhythm

'Keeping time', along with artistic accentuation and intelligent phrasing, is essential to successful musical performance. Rhythm alone had rarely been the subject of specialised study until the late nineteenth century, when several books on this topic by Rudolf Westphal were published in Leipzig. Westphal's work inspired Charles Francis Abdy Williams's 1911 book which is reissued here. Williams re-examines the classical and romantic repertoire from Handel to Tchaikovsky in the light of ancient Greek musical theory, focusing particularly on the earliest writings by Artistoxenus of Tarentum (fourth century BCE). In Williams's view, the rhythmic forms used by the Greeks are universally intelligible, and appear in all ages and cultures, unlike melodies or scales, which vary hugely. He provides insights into the micro-structure of works including Bach's oratorios, Beethoven's sonatas and Schubert's songs, which will continue to intrigue musicians, Classicists and mathematicians today.

Cambridge University Press has long been a pioneer in the reissuing of out-of-print titles from its own backlist, producing digital reprints of books that are still sought after by scholars and students but could not be reprinted economically using traditional technology. The Cambridge Library Collection extends this activity to a wider range of books which are still of importance to researchers and professionals, either for the source material they contain, or as landmarks in the history of their academic discipline.

Drawing from the world-renowned collections in the Cambridge University Library, and guided by the advice of experts in each subject area, Cambridge University Press is using state-of-the-art scanning machines in its own Printing House to capture the content of each book selected for inclusion. The files are processed to give a consistently clear, crisp image, and the books finished to the high quality standard for which the Press is recognised around the world. The latest print-on-demand technology ensures that the books will remain available indefinitely, and that orders for single or multiple copies can quickly be supplied.

The Cambridge Library Collection will bring back to life books of enduring scholarly value across a wide range of disciplines in the humanities and social sciences and in science and technology.

The Aristoxenian Theory of Musical Rhythm

C.F. Abdy Williams

CAMBRIDGE UNIVERSITY PRESS

Cambridge New York Melbourne Madrid Cape Town Singapore São Paolo Delhi

Published in the United States of America by Cambridge University Press, New York

www.cambridge.org
Information on this title: www.cambridge.org/9781108004879

© in this compilation Cambridge University Press 2009

This edition first published 1911
This digitally printed version 2009

ISBN 978-1-108-00487-9

This book reproduces the text of the original edition. The content and language reflect the beliefs, practices and terminology of their time, and have not been updated.

THE ARISTOXENIAN THEORY
OF MUSICAL RHYTHM

CAMBRIDGE UNIVERSITY PRESS
London: FETTER LANE, E.C.
C. F. CLAY, Manager.

Edinburgh: 100, PRINCES STREET
Berlin: A. ASHER AND CO.
Leipzig: F. A. BROCKHAUS
New York: G. P. PUTNAM'S SONS
Bombay and Calcutta: MACMILLAN AND CO., Ltd.

All rights reserved

THE ARISTOXENIAN THEORY
OF MUSICAL RHYTHM

by

C. F. ABDY WILLIAMS, M.A., Mus. Bac.

Author of *The Rhythm of Modern Music*; *The Story of Notation*, &c.

Cambridge
at the University Press
1911

Cambridge:
PRINTED BY JOHN CLAY, M.A.
AT THE UNIVERSITY PRESS

PREFACE

THE ability to "keep time" must be possessed by every musician if he is to perform intelligently, and to take part in concerted music. In the early days of counterpoint, ere rhythm was thought of, the singers were obliged to "keep time" in order that the various parts might fit each other properly.

When to "keeping time" is added an artistic accentuation and intelligent phrasing, rhythm results.

Musicians give rhythmical life to what they perform, either instinctively, or through the training received from those who have the rhythmical instinct. As a rule, no special study is made of rhythm by itself, and when I met with Westphal's *Allgemeine Theorie der musikalischen Rhythmik*, it struck me as revealing the rhythm of modern music through ancient theory in such a new and interesting light, that I have for many years wished that my English fellow musicians could share in the pleasure and profit that it has given me.

For an opportunity of bringing this ancient theory before musicians I here express my gratitude to the Syndics of the Cambridge University Press.

While correcting the proofs my attention was called to M. Louis Laloy's remarks on certain forms which have long puzzled investigators, owing to the difficulty of reducing them to musical rhythm as understood by us. His views are novel, and so highly suggestive, that one cannot but think that he has discovered the key to the mystery. I have added an Appendix, giving a short outline of these new views: for the arguments by which they are supported I must refer my readers to M. Laloy's *Aristoxène de Tarente*.

C. F. ABDY WILLIAMS

MILFORD-ON-SEA
October, 1911

CONTENTS

PREFACE . . . . p. v

INTRODUCTION . . . . p. x

CHAPTER I. The position of rhythm in Greek music—The reconstruction of its theory by modern philologists—Catalogue of the ancient authorities—Richard Wagner on the work of the philologists—A fundamental error, due to the Graeco-Roman grammarians . . . . p. 1

CHAPTER II. Outline of the history of Greek music—The principles of its scales explained by analogy with the construction of modern scales—The dramatists and their works—Tragedy, Comedy, and Lyric poetry—The instrumental accompaniment to song—The decline of Greek Music . . . p. 9

CHAPTER III. Definitions of rhythm according to Baccheios the Elder—Aristoxenus on rhythm, rhythmizomenon, and rhythmopœia—The musical measure or foot —Thesis and arsis—Ancient methods of beating time—Thetic and anacrusic forms—The chronos protos—Quantity and accent—Greek systems of notation —A recently discovered specimen of Greek notation . . . . p. 24

CHAPTER IV. Errhythm, Arrhythm, and Eurhythm—Time combinations in the measure or foot—The seven differences of foot, according to Aristoxenus—The three species of foot—Aristoxenus on irrational time—Reintroduction of the principle in modern music—Burney on Greek rhythm—Names of the simple feet—Extension and contraction of syllables to suit the musical rhythm—Greek feeling reflected in the ligatures of the plain-song notation—Some Greek rhythmical forms illustrated by quotations from Schubert's songs . p. 34

CHAPTER V. Various significations of the term "rhythm"—The divisions of rhythmical phrases into thesis and arsis—Compound feet—Complexity of rhythm in ancient instrumental accompaniments to songs—Necessity for the limitation of the magnitude of phrases—The Aristoxenian theory of the magnitudes that are capable of rhythmical division . . . . p. 49

CHAPTER VI. The Aristoxenian theory of magnitudes and the music of Wagner and Bach—The grouping of feet in pairs—Pindar's First Pythian Ode—Epitritic rhythms in Handel's "Judas Maccabaeus," compared to those of Pindar—Logaœdic rhythm as exemplified in Pindar, Sophocles, and Bach—Humorous use of logaœdic rhythm by Aristophanes—The employment of quintuple rhythm in ancient comedy and hymnody . . . . p. 70

CONTENTS

CHAPTER VII. Quintuple rhythm in Tragedy—The "Electra" of Sophocles and of Richard Strauss—Glyconic rhythm—Music that is unfettered by rhythmical phrases—Aristides on the ethos of rhythm—The influence of the different forms of rhythm on mind and body, described by Aristides—Cleonides on the ethos of song—The ethos of Italian Opera. Dr Abert's *Lehre vom Ethos in der griechischen Musik* . . . . p. 89

CHAPTER VIII. The Period—Eurhythmy, or balance of periods, in Greek music—The crousis in the Greek strophe—Its modern counterpart in the German Chorale, and in examples of the music of Schubert, R. Wagner, and Hubert Parry—The periodology of a Pindaric ode—The periodology of Bach's B minor Mass and Christmas Oratorio, and of Handel's "Messiah" . . p. 107

CHAPTER IX. The colotomy and periodology of Gluck's "Orpheus," Haydn's "Creation," Mozart's "Don Giovanni" and Requiem, Beethoven's Ninth Symphony . . . . p. 127

CHAPTER X. The colotomy and periodology of Schubert's "Erlking"—Mendelssohn and Schumann—Richard Wagner's adaptation of Greek rhythmical principles to the music-drama—The colotomy of Brahms' songs—The colotomy of Hugo Wolf—Conclusion . . . . . . p. 149

APPENDIX A. Quotations, from original sources, of passages referred to in the text . . . . p. 175

APPENDIX B. Glossary of Technical Terms . . . . . . p. 178

APPENDIX C. Dactylo-epitritic, Logaœdic, and Dochmiac rhythms, and rhythmical modulation. M. Laloy's views . . . . p. 184

INDEX . . . . p. 187

MUSICAL ILLUSTRATIONS

	NO.	PAGE
Aristophanes, "The Knights," Chorus No. 8. Rhythmical scheme	47	85
„ "Peace," Chorus No. 8. Rhythmical scheme	48	86
Bach, Wohlt. Kl. Fugue No. 1	29	62
„ Matthew Passion, Chorus No. 1	30 a	62
„ „ „ „ „	30 b	62
„ Fantasia and fugue in A minor for organ	35	65
„ Motet, "Ich lasse dich nicht"	46	84
„ Chorale, "Du Friedefürst"	53 a	103
„ B minor Mass, Kyrie	59	116
„ „ „ „	60	117
„ Christmas Oratorio, "Bereite dich, Zion"	61	120
Beethoven, "Die Zufriedenheit"	15	50
„ Sonata, Op. 111, Last movement	25	59
„ Sonata, Op. 27, No. 1, Minuet	41	73
„ Sonata, Op. 28, Scherzo	53	94
„ Ninth Symphony, First movement	67	137
„ „ „ „	67 a	138
„ „ „ „	68	139
„ „ „ „	69	140
„ „ „ „	70	140
„ „ „ „	70 a	141
„ „ „ „	70 b	141
„ „ „ „	71	142
„ „ „ Scherzo	72	143
„ „ „ „	73	144
„ „ „ „	74	144
„ „ „ „	75	145
„ „ „ „	76	145
„ „ „ „	77	145
„ „ „ „	78	146
Brahms, Pianoforte Quartet, Op. 25, Intermezzo	26	60
„ "Wie bist du, meine Königin"	85	169
Chopin, Waltz, Op. 42	14	48
„ Nocturne, Op. 15, No. 3	83	158
Delphic Hymn to Apollo	13	47
D'Indy, Pianoforte Sonata, Op. 63, Second movement	31	63

		NO.	PAGE
Franz, "Herbstsorge"		34	64
Gluck, "Alceste," Chorus No. 5		52	92
Grieg, Violin Sonata in F, Op. 8, First movement		51	92
Handel, "Judas Maccabaeus," Chorus, "And grant a leader"		43	79
„ "Messiah," "Behold the Lamb of God"		62	122
„ „ "He was despised"		63	123
„ „ "And with his stripes"		64	125
Mozart, "Don Giovanni," "Là, ci darem la mano"		65	132
„ Requiem		66	134
Parry, "De Profundis"		55	108
Pindar, First Pythian Ode		39	67
„ „ „ „		42	74
„ „ „ „ Rhythmical scheme		42 a	76
„ Tenth Olympian Ode. Rhythmical scheme		44	80
„ Eighth Pythian „ „ „		57	113
„ „ „ „ „ „		58	114
Rheinberger, Organ Sonata, Op. 27		20	56
Schubert, "Des Müllers Blumen"		9	46
„ „ „ „		10	46
„ "Mein!"		11	47
„ "Des Baches Wiegenlied"		12	47
„ "Ungeduld"		32	63
„ Sonata, Op. 42, Scherzo		33	64
„ "Täuschung"		38	67
„ "Pilgerweise"		40	68
„ "Erlkönig"		79	150
„ „		80	150
Schumann, Symphony No. 1, Larghetto		81	156
„ „ No. 3, Scherzo		23	58
„ Novelletten, No. 5		82	157
Seikilos Hymn			31
Sophocles, "Antigone," Chorus No. 3		37	66
„ „ „		45	81
„ „ „ Rhythmical scheme		56	111
„ "Electra," Duet between Electra and Orestes. Rhythmical scheme		49	89
Tschaïkowsky, "Pathetic Symphony," Second movement		28	61
Wagner, "Der Fliegende Holländer"		24	58
„ "Tristan und Isolde," Vorspiel		36	66
„ „ „ Act I, Scene 5		84	165
„ "Meistersinger"		54	108
Wolf, "Jägerlied"		27	61
„ "Im Frühling"		86	171
„ "Agnes"		87	181

INTRODUCTION

IT is often said that the musical art of the present day is so entirely different from that of the Greeks that, fascinating as the study is to many minds, the musician has nothing whatever to learn from the ancient Hellenic art.

This is true of the "melos," *i.e.* that part of music which has to do with melody, scales, intervals, orchestration, vocalisation. Greek melos, with its refinements of modes, genera, transpositions, and modulations, rose, during the classical age, to a very high degree of development, and, in a lesser degree, appealed to the cultured Attic audience much as the music of a Beethoven or Wagner appeals to an audience of to-day. But no sooner had this remarkable manifestation of art arrived at its zenith, than there began a rapid process of decay, in which its most essential features disappeared one by one.

Music, however, does not consist of melos only. More important from the Greek point of view was rhythmos, which gave strength and form to the melos: and it is with this side of music alone that we propose to deal, and to see whether ancient rhythmical theory, like ancient sculpture and architecture, has any message for modern musicians and lovers of music.

The gradual rise of Christianity gave the final blow to the already moribund system of music as understood and practised in Hellas. The Fathers of the Church disdained music as an art, and only utilised it as the "handmaid of religion." They found that the Psalms and certain other Scriptural writings could be brought home to the congregation more forcibly if they were sung than if they were merely recited; hence the words were put to simple melodies, not with any idea of æsthetic pleasure, but merely as a vehicle for their better comprehension and remembrance.

As for rhythm, the old Attic refinements were forgotten at the period of the advent of Christianity, owing to the loss of the feeling for time-measurement in poetry, and the rise of accent or stress in its place. The introduction into the Church of rhythmical hymns in addition to the prose melody of the Psalms was strongly opposed, since the pleasure which the people derived from the musical rhythm did not suit the stern ascetic views of life held by the leaders of the young and still struggling religion, though in the end they were obliged to give way. Instruments were entirely banished, since they were associated with rhythm, and its visible representation in the dance.

In the Eastern branch of Christianity the old modes continued in use, together with the chromatic genus, which is a noticeable feature in the Byzantine music of the present day. It can be heard in the Liturgy of St Basil at the Russian Church in Moscow Road, Bayswater, and in the Greek Uniat Church in the Via Babuino at Rome. The present writer was once privileged to attend a choir practice at the Greek College in Rome. While the language employed was Italian, owing to the singers being of several nationalities, the musical terms were the same as those found in Boethius and in some of the earlier treatises in Gerbert's *Scriptores*. Thus, when the choirmaster required to allude to the modes, he did not speak of Dorian, Phrygian, &c., but of Protos, Deuteros, Tetartos, Plagios. These terms were also used in the Latin Church when it was still under the influence of Greek musical teaching, but in course of time they were latinised, and the whole system was modified to suit western needs. The chromatic genus never entered the Latin Church; it is possible that western ears were not so sensitive as eastern, and could not easily assimilate a succession of semitones.

An easily recognised link between the melos of Greece and that of to-day is to be found in the alphabetical names of our notes. When western musicians began to utilise the Greek scale for teaching purposes, they tried many experiments to find a convenient nomenclature for its different sounds, in place of the Greek terms proslambanomenos, hypate, lichanos, &c. They finally agreed to apply the first seven letters of the Latin alphabet to the seven lowest notes of the Greek scale, and to repeat these letters for each successive octave. This nomenclature has never been altered, in spite of the differences which came in with the general adoption of the major mode; and hence it comes that the alphabetical names of the keys of our pianoforte do not arise from the major or modern minor scale series, but from the ancient Greek scale.

Alongside the practical musical study that was necessary for liturgical purposes, the study of its theory as a branch of mathematics under Pythagorean influence never ceased. The Pythagorean and Neopythagorean doctrines of the mysterious mathematical proportions of musical intervals, their imaginary connection with the movements of planets and the harmony of the spheres, formed the subject of many writings which had not the slightest connection with the art of music. It is, indeed, one of the most remarkable results of monasticism that for centuries men should be found to spend their lives in contemplating imaginary musical theories which could have no moral or practical result of any sort[1].

Perhaps, however, their work was not entirely in vain if it served to keep alive, during the general ignorance of the dark ages, some interest in Hellenic learning, and thus to prepare the ground for the reception of the Hellenic culture that was destined to arise at the Renaissance.

Though many Pythagorean and Neopythagorean authors seem to have been studied in mediæval monasteries, the chief authority for the so-called science of music was Boethius. He wrote about 500 A.D. (when all practical knowledge of Greek music was entirely lost), and seems to have misunderstood much of what he learned from ancient sources. Yet his treatise *De musica* was looked upon, even down to comparatively recent times, as an authority about which there could be no difference of opinion.

The foundation of Universities at Bologna and Paris in the twelfth, and at Oxford and Cambridge in the thirteenth centuries, marked the beginning of the revival of learning. These institutions, though not monastic, were under the wing of the Church, and their teaching was much on the lines of that which obtained in the monasteries. The study of Boethius was compulsory for all graduates of Oxford and Cambridge until the sixteenth century, and down to as late as sixty or seventy years ago it was still demanded of candidates for musical degrees.

Yet Boethius' *De musica* has no connection with the art of music: of beauty of sound its author could know nothing, for he cannot have heard any of the music about which he wrote.

The attenuated remnant of Greek music represented by its diatonic scale had such vitality, that it formed the root from which was destined to grow in course of time the art of polyphony; and out of polyphony was to arise yet another kind of music, capable of still greater expansion and power. To what heights harmony, the

---

[1] The subject has been ably treated by Dr Hermann Abert in *Die Musikanschauung des Mittelalters*, Halle, 1905.

latest phase of melos, is destined to advance, the present generation can never know. It is quite possible that if we had retained the genera, we should not have arrived at polyphony or harmonic effects: the Byzantine system has not done so, and when harmony is applied to it, it is from western musicians that the art has to be acquired. The limitation of music to one genus of scale seems to have made possible the foundation of modern art. For, during the ninth and tenth centuries, taught by Greek theory to make practical experiments with the consonances of the fourth, fifth, and octave, musicians sang the diatonic Cantus Gregorianus in these intervals, with the result that the art of *organum* arose, and out of *organum* grew counterpoint, which eventually led to the polyphonic school.

We have, then, to thank the Church for the process of elimination which made possible the building up of the art of polyphony. This art arrived at its culmination in connection with the modes during the sixteenth century; and now music was to enter on its new phase, in which counterpoint and the young art of harmony were to be used with the major scale (derived, like the ecclesiastical modes, from the Greek diatonic system), and to be brought under the influence of the rhythm of the dance; while the whole of music was to be permeated with the culture that had been acquired through a study of Greek literature.

Greek philosophy had begun to pervade the west, and to become one of the chief motive forces of our modern civilisation. Music shared in the renaissance of learning. Ancient musical treatises were sought, a few remnants of Graeco-Roman musical compositions were discovered and translated into European notation; the Attic drama was studied, and the efforts to reproduce some kind of musical art that should be as expressive as the music-drama of Athens was said to have been, resulted, as is known, in the invention of recitative, and the founding of opera and oratorio.

But there was not, as yet, sufficient knowledge at hand to enable men to understand the real nature of the rhythm that underlay the æsthetic effects ascribed by the ancients to their music. Rhythm had not been cultivated in ecclesiastical polyphony, and only slightly in the madrigal. Time division of the individual notes was, indeed, necessary to polyphony, in order that the various voices should keep their proper connection with one another. But the value of definite rhythmical divisions and varied accentuation, as a means of expression, was scarcely thought of. The study of the metres of the Attic drama, by which their rhythm might have been elucidated, was still under the influence of the rules laid down by the Graeco-Roman grammarians, who knew that there was some occult connection between metre and rhythm, but knew nothing of the melodic rhythms to which the verbal metre had formerly been allied; and their metrical rules could not be made to produce any intelligible musical rhythm. The inventors of recitative thought that they had discovered the ancient Greek idea of dramatic music, but in this they were mistaken. Recitative is an entirely modern art, and seems to have no analogy with anything that was done in the Attic theatre. Its invention is due to a misunderstanding of Greek theory.

Yet, however much the ardent students of Greek in the sixteenth century may have misunderstood the technicalities of Greek rhythm, it is to them that we owe the first attempts to make music express the varying emotions of the drama. Opera and Oratorio, however, quickly became conventionalised in the hands of singers, and it was owing to the study of Greek on the part of Gluck that he attempted certain reforms. In the next century there arose yet another reformer, Richard Wagner, who, making a deeper study of the Greek drama than his predecessors, succeeded in producing the dramatic music that we all know so well.

It can scarcely be said then that we modern musicians owe nothing at all to Greek music: on the contrary, to attempts at its revival we owe our dramatic music, whether under the name of Opera, Oratorio, or Music-drama. Musicians are apt to forget this when, looking merely to the technical details, they say that Greek music has no bearing on the modern art.

During the time that polyphony was developing, there existed alongside it a vast quantity of music, partly sacred, but mostly secular, in which the predominating influence was the rhythm of the dance. From the earliest ages the Church had utilised this element to a certain extent in such parts of its music as were to be sung by the unlearned, while banishing it from the liturgy. Easily grasped dance rhythm was the basis of the litany, the folksong and the ballad, and when instruments began to be used apart from voices, they expressed themselves in this kind of rhythm. The earliest composers of instrumental music emphasised the importance of rhythmical structure by dividing their tablatures into bars, some two centuries before the bar became general in vocal notation; and the verse of poetry laid the foundation of what we now know as the "phrase" of instrumental music. The dance, in fact, had as great an influence on modern music in its early stages as it had on that of

Athens, but there is this difference, that in Athens rhythm was made visible by the corporeal motions of the performer, as well as audible by the melody, while in our music it is audible only, not visible.

The Church has always looked with disfavour on the actual dance, while often using rhythms appropriate to it; and in banishing the dance from ritual music, it unconsciously performed yet another service to the art of music. For by thus forcing rhythm to make its appeal to the mind through the ear alone, without taking the eye into partnership, it certainly raised music to a higher possibility of imaginative and mystical significance than it had had before. The intelligence that can appreciate musical rhythm without the accessories of bodily movements, or the regular pulse of some non-melodic percussion instrument, is of a higher order than that which requires these aids.

It will be seen, then, that the rhythmical side of music has no direct historical connection with that of ancient Greece, while melody has been under Hellenic influence in respect to the Church modes and our minor scale.

When rhythm again entered into the more highly cultivated kinds of music, it had to make a fresh start from the same basis as did that of Greek music, *i.e.* from those forms that were found in the dance. Working up from this basis, musicians gradually developed, and are still further developing, the rhythmical side of music, on lines similar to those of the ancients. The combination of bars into short phrases, of phrases into periods, the use of certain rhythmical figures to express gaiety, solemnity, and other feelings, all have their counterparts in the dactyls and trochees and other "feet" of the Greek theorists, who entered into the signification of these details with an understanding and minuteness such as no writer of modern times has shown.

The melodic side of music varies according to race, temperament, epoch. The melos of to-day in western Europe is founded on scales that differ from those, for example, of modern Byzantine music, those of China, or Japan, or India, and are less highly developed than the chromatic and enharmonic genera of the ancients. Even amongst ourselves there are differences of scale, and hence of melodic means of expression; for the old Scotch pentatonic scale, still to be heard in certain folksongs, differs from the heptatonic scales of musicians, and the bagpipe scale, though heptatonic, is not tuned like that of the pianoforte.

With rhythm the case is different. All the simple forms that we use were used by the Greeks, and are intelligible to other races and other stages of civilisation than ours. The iambuses and trochees, the anapæsts and dactyls of the Greeks reappear in the Hymns of St Ambrose, in the ancient folksongs of Europe, in the litanies of the Roman Church, in the sonatas of Beethoven, in the songs of Schubert, in the modern music-hall ballad, in the music of the South Sea Islanders. While mankind divides its musical scale in ways that are incomprehensible to those who are unfamiliar with them, it divides the time occupied by melody in ways that are comprehensible to all, however they may differ in culture and in race.

The fundamental principles that underlie the art of rhythm, both in the simple forms that appeal to all, and in the more complicated designs that appeal to those of cultivated taste, were investigated by Aristoxenus with a remarkable degree of insight and keenness of perception. Greek musicians developed rhythm in certain directions further than we have done as yet: but there are signs that certain features of their music, such as quintuple measure, the more frequent use of phrases of other than four bars in length, the perception of a thesis and arsis in larger portions of a phrase than the single bar, may, in the future, again take something of the same place as they did in Hellenic music.

The plan of this book is to explain the principles of the Aristoxenian theory, using both ancient and modern examples in illustration of the points to be elucidated, and to apply the theoretical principles thus explained, and the ideas suggested by them, to some of the masterpieces of modern art.

CHAPTER I

The position of rhythm in Greek music—The reconstruction of its theory by modern philologists—Catalogue of the ancient authorities—Richard Wagner on the work of the philologists—A fundamental error, due to the Graeco-Roman grammarians.

To the Greek musician the laws of rhythm were as important as those of harmony and counterpoint are to the modern student. Indeed the Greeks went further than we do, for they considered that the various forms of rhythm had certain definite emotional effects on the mind, and rules were formulated as to what particular kind of rhythm was suitable to express this or that emotion. An appeal was always to be made to the "Aisthēsis," that part of our nature which we vaguely refer to as the "feeling," in German "das Gefühl," the faculty of mental perception, as opposed to bodily sensation.

Modern musicians sometimes attribute a certain tinge of melancholy to the minor mode, but further than this they do not go: no one has yet laid down rules that any particular form of harmony or species of counterpoint is suitable to this or that emotion. It is inconceivable that a modern composer should submit to rules in the matter of expression. Yet the Greek composers of the classical period not only used certain "modes," but moulded their great works according to rule in definite rhythmical forms, that seem to have been understood at the time as expressing the particular appeal to the "Aisthēsis" that was required. These forms can be appreciated by us as rhythmical structures, but apart from the words they do not necessarily connect themselves in our mind with definite emotional effects. They are not the simple forms of the dance, the folksong, the hymn tune, or the ballad: they have a highly artistic construction, complicated in appearance, yet, according to one of the first requirements of Aristoxenus, they must be easy to understand. In other words, however complex were the rhythmical means of expression, the form must be one that could make an immediate appeal to cultivated human feeling.

The theory of Greek rhythm has reached us in a sadly mutilated state. A fragment of a book here, a piece of information there, a quotation somewhere else, have been pieced together and made into a practicable whole, with a patience that amounts to genius, by a devoted band of German philologists. The subject began to attract attention early in the nineteenth century. It had always been noticed that Greek writers laid great stress on the importance of rhythm, and yet the rigid rule of the Graeco-Roman metricists, who made a long syllable always equal to two short ones, produced a chaotic arrangement of Greek and Latin verse that was utterly without meaning to musicians. Burney had already commented on this, and in his first volume he gives examples to prove that the Greeks, with all their theories, could have known nothing whatever about rhythm, unless their ears were entirely different from ours.

But since the discovery of Aristoxenian fragments in St Mark's Library at Venice about a century and a quarter ago, this has gradually been changed, and we now know that the Greeks had rhythmical forms that were, in some respects, more highly developed than ours; and at the same time so orderly and natural are they, that when we fully appreciate the sense of the words to which they are allied they can appeal to our "Aisthēsis" in very much the same way as do the rhythms of our own classical composers.

Amongst the principal investigators were Boeckh, who gave his attention to the metres and rhythms of Pindar's *Odes*, and Hermann, who continued the work begun by Boeckh. To Hermann we owe the useful technical terms, "Anacrusis" and "Cyclical dactyl." Then came Friedrich Bellermann, who published a Greek manuscript of the second century A.D., in which the ancient signs for time-value and rests are shown. After him came Dr J. H. H. Schmidt, who, applying the newly-discovered theory to the extant plays of the Greek dramatists, was able to reconstruct their musical rhythm through the metre of the words; for with the Greeks, whose music consisted of unison or octave singing, musical rhythm adhered to the metre of the words as closely as in a folksong. This has always been known theoretically, and is confirmed in a remarkable manner by the recent discoveries at Delphi.

Rudolph Westphal (1826–1892), a professor of Greek, and an amateur musician of considerable attainments, now began to publish a series of works through which it became evident that there was much in the ancient theory that might be of value to modern musicians. Amongst the most important of his books, from a musical point of view, are *Metrik der griechischen Dramatiker und Lyriker* (with Rossbach), 3 vols. 1854–1865, remodelled, and republished as *Theorie der musischen Künste der Hellenen* (with Rossbach and Gleditsch, 1885–1889): *Die Fragmente und Lehrsätze der griechischen Rhythmiker*, 1861: *Geschichte der alten und mittelältlichen Musik*, 1864: *Plutarch über die Musik*, 1865: *System der antiken Rhythmik*, 1865: *Scriptores metrici graeci*, 1866: *Theorie der neuhochdeutschen Metrik*, 2nd Ed. 1877: *Die Elemente des musikalischen Rhythmus, mit Rücksicht auf unsere Opernmusik*, 1872: *Allgemeine Theorie der musikalischen Rhythmik seit J. S. Bach*, 1880: *Die Musik des griechischen Alterthumes*, 1883: *Aristoxenus von Tarent*, 2 vols. 1883–1893: *Der griechische Hexameter in der deutschen Nachdichtung* (posthumous).

The ancient theory, as reconstructed by the above-mentioned Germans, was condensed into a whole by the late F. A. Gevaert, Director of the Brussels Conservatoire, a musician of great eminence, in the second volume of his monumental work *La Musique de l'Antiquité* published at Ghent in 1881.

The ancient writers on rhythm, in order of date, are:

1. Aristoxenus of Tarentum. Suidas tells us that he was the son of Mnēsios, also called Spintharus, a musician, of Tarentum in Italy. He was educated as a philosopher, but turned his attention to music, in which subject he became a pupil, first of his father, then of Lampros, then of Xenophilus a Pythagorean, and finally of Aristotle. Aristoxenus, after completing his education at Athens, lived at Alexandria. He composed works on every branch of knowledge, to the number of 453. He seems to have written his theory of rhythm from about 335 to 322 B.C. Of his literary output only a few fragments have come down to us. His three books on "Harmonics," *i.e.* scales, were published by Meibomius in 1652[1].

The Harmonics of Aristoxenus were published with an English translation by Macran, at the Clarendon Press, 1902. These books, however, do not concern us here. The fragments of his rhythmical teaching have been collected and published by Rudolph Westphal in

---

[1] Meibomius published at Amsterdam in 1652 *Antiquae Musicae Auctores Septem*. This collection, together with the *Claudii Ptolemaei Harmonicorum Libri tres*, published by Wallis at Oxford in 1682, formed the chief source of research into Greek music up to the time of Hawkins and Burney, and even later. Both works give the full Greek text, with a Latin translation alongside, and copious notes in Latin. When we refer to Meibomius, the above *Septem Auctores* must be understood. Since the days of Hawkins and Burney other Greek fragments have been published, having a more direct bearing on rhythm than those published by Meibomius and Wallis. They will be alluded to in due course.

Die Fragmente und die Lehrsätze der griechischen Rhythmiker, Leipsic, 1861, and there is a translation into German, with a running commentary, in Westphal's *Aristoxenus, Melik und Rhythmik des classischen Hellenthums*, Leipsic, 1883. The rhythmical teaching of Aristoxenus influenced musicians for several centuries after his death, and much of it is only to be gathered from quotations by later writers.

2. M. Terentius Varro, a Latin writer, born in B.C. 116, died B.C. 28, was called by his contemporaries "The most learned of the Romans." Like Aristoxenus, a prolific writer, of his 600 books only a few fragments are extant. They give us technical terms that are not found elsewhere.

3. Dionysius of Halicarnassus, a celebrated Greek rhetorist, came to Rome about B.C. 29, and remained there till his death in A.D. 7. His treatise "De compositione verborum" ("On the putting together of words") is of importance to our subject, as it describes the "cyclical dactyl" (see page 40), and contains the most ancient analysis of simple measures. His references to rhythm are quoted in Westphal's *Fragmente*.

4. Mallius Theodorus, a rhetorist under Augustus and Tiberius, the latter of whom attended his lectures at Rhodes in B.C. 6—A.D. 2. His works are not important.

5. Caesius Bassus, a Roman lyric poet, lost his life at Pompeii when that town was destroyed by the eruption of Vesuvius in A.D. 79. He dedicated a work on metre, which is lost, to the Emperor Nero; it served as a source from which many later writers drew their information.

6. Fabius Quintilianus, a Latin author of the end of the first century A.D., quotes from Caesius Bassus.

7. Aristides Quintilianus lived during the first and second centuries after Christ. His three Greek treatises "Concerning Music" are published by Meibomius, and the rhythmical allusions therein, chiefly quotations from Aristoxenus, are collected by Westphal in his *Fragmente*.

8. The treatise already alluded to by an anonymous Greek writer of the first or second century of our era, which gives the musical time-signs and rests. This important little work was first published by F. Bellermann in 1841 with Latin notes, and again in 1847 by A. J. H. Vincent, with a French translation, in *Notices et Extraits des Manuscrits de la Bibliothèque du Roi, publiés par l'Institut Royal de France*. It is usually referred to as "Bellermann's *Anonymus*."

ANCIENT SOURCES

9. Hephaestion was a Greek grammarian of about A.D. 150. His *Manual on Metres* is said by Gevaert to be the best work in the whole range of metrical literature[1].

10. Philoxenus, an Alexandrian grammarian, who taught at Rome, probably about the same time as Hephaestion. He makes scanty references to rhythm.

11. Heliodorus was also probably contemporary with Hephaestion. Extensive fragments of his teaching remain, and contain portions of the rhythmical teaching of Aristoxenus[2].

12. Longinus, who flourished about A.D. 260, was a commentator of Hephaestion.

13. Terentius Marius, about A.D. 290, and

14. Atilius Fortunatianus, about A.D. 300, are said by Gevaert to be interesting writers.

15. Plotius Sacerdos, a Latin grammarian, who probably lived towards the end of the third century, under Diocletian, wrote a book on metres.

16. Baccheios the Elder appears to have taught music during the reign of Constantine, A.D. 306–337. The *Introduction to the Art of Music* attributed to him is the work of two writers, of the opposing schools of Pythagoras and Aristoxenus[3]. It treats of rhythm on Aristoxenian lines, but only in a cursory manner. It is published by Meibomius and Jan, and quoted from by Westphal in the *Fragmente*.

17. Marius Victorinus, a teacher of rhetoric at Rome about A.D. 350, enjoyed so large a reputation that on his death a statue was erected in his memory in the Forum of Trajan. Many of his works are extant, and the few notices of rhythm contained in them are quoted by Westphal in the *Fragmente*. He is not original but draws upon Varro, Caesius Bassus, and others[4].

18. St Augustine composed a treatise on rhythm about A.D. 375 of no great value.

19. A short passage from Servius, a Latin grammarian of the fourth century, is quoted by Westphal in the *Fragmente*, p. 42.

20. Diomedes, a Latin grammarian, probably of the fourth or fifth century, wrote a treatise on oratory and metre, of which a passage is quoted by Westphal in the *Fragmente*, p. 43.

21. Charisius, a Latin grammarian, lived about A.D. 400. He wrote a treatise on grammar, in which he quotes from earlier writers.

---

[1] Gevaert, *La Mus. de l'Ant.* Vol. II. p. 86.
[2] Westphal, *Fragmente*, p. 12.
[3] Jan, *Musici Scriptores Graeci*.
[4] Gevaert, *La Mus. de l'Ant.* Vol. II. p. 86.

22. Priscianus, a Roman, lived in the fifth century, and taught grammar at Constantinople. Many of his works remain, and have formed the basis of our present knowledge of Latin grammar. Amongst them is one on accents.

23. Martianus Mineus Felix Capella was a native of Carthage, who flourished towards the end of the fifth century. His allegory, entitled the "Nuptials of Philology and Mercury," consists chiefly of a Latin translation of portions of the work of Aristides Quintilianus on music. It is published by Meibomius in his *Septem Auctores*, and Westphal, in the *Fragmente*, prints the original Greek and the Latin translation on the same pages, for comparison.

24. Michael Psellus, a Greek writer, lived at Constantinople in the middle of the eleventh century. He is an important contributor to our subject for the following reason. In A.D. 1785, Morelli, the librarian of St Mark's at Venice, published a little work by him called *Introductory Remarks on the Rhythmical Science*, and in the same volume he included fragments of the rhythmical elements of Aristoxenus. The work of Psellus contains much of the original elements of Aristoxenus, which had been either too fragmentary or considered of too little importance for Meibomius to include in his collection. Morelli added notes to the Aristoxenian text, and quoted the parallel places in Psellus: and this is practically all that survives of the original teaching of Aristoxenus[1]. The publication came under the notice of Westphal, who was struck with the interest that the theory here expounded might have for modern musicians; and this was the origin of his investigations. In his *Fragmente* Westphal quotes those parts of Psellus that are derived from Aristoxenus.

Of Byzantine metricists, the brothers Tzetzes in the twelfth century have preserved to us some fragments of the ancient teaching[2].

Rhythm is slightly referred to by the author of the Nineteenth Problem formerly attributed to Aristotle, but now believed to have been of Alexandrian origin[3]. These, then, are the original sources from which the ancient theory of musical rhythm has been reconstructed. With the exception of Bellermann's *Anonymus* (No. 8), the writers give no musical examples, and rhythm is generally referred to in a manner that presupposes a familiarity with it on the part of the reader, and, in some cases, the later authors quote from the earlier without always understanding them.

[1] Westphal, *Aristoxenus, Melik und Rhythmik*, pp. xii, xiv.
[2] Gevaert, *La Mus. de l'Ant.* Vol. II. p. 86.
[3] Compare C. Jan, *Musici Scriptores Graeci*, Leipsic, 1895.

The work of reconstruction has entailed immense labour. Richard Wagner, who was so deeply impressed with the Greek drama as to lay the foundations of his "Music of the future" upon Greek ideals, knew that the technicalities of Greek rhythm were being explored, but when he wrote his *Oper und Drama* it was too early for him to be aware of the significance of the investigations that were being carried on. Like most of those musicians who learn Greek at school, he had been struck with the impossibility of obtaining a recognisable rhythm from Greek poetry on the scholastic assumption that a long syllable was equal in time-value to two short syllables. Speaking of the Greek manner of intoning speech, in which certain syllables were really pronounced relatively longer than others, not merely accented, as in the modern European languages, he says[1]:

"Nevertheless there is something at the root of this tendency towards an extension in pronunciation, where it is not merely a dialectic custom, but an involuntary result of increase of agitation, which our prosodists and metricists will have to observe carefully, if they wish to explain Greek metres. They had only our rapid speech-accent in their ear, when they invented the measure by which two shorts invariably equal one long. The explanation of Greek metres would easily have occurred to them if they had had in their ear for the so-called long the sustained notes of musical measure, by which the length of words can be varied in melody."

Wagner is mistaken when he attributes the invention of the rule of "two shorts equal one long" to "our prosodists and metricists." It goes back for nearly eighteen centuries, having been invented by Latin grammarians of early imperial times, who knew little of, and cared less for, musical rhythm. It has been persistently taught in the schools from the renaissance of Greek literature to the present day. But through the publication of Bellermann's *Anonymus* we have learned that syllables, when sung, were extended or shortened by the ancients to suit a musical rhythm, just as they are by present-day composers, the only difference being one of degree. For the ancients did not, as far as we are aware, extend a syllable so as to embrace a whole musical phrase, but only as far as was necessary to make the time-divisions recognisable.

Oper und Drama was written in 1851, before the full significance of Bellermann's *Anonymus* could have been recognised: for it would take more than ten years to uproot a tradition of so many centuries standing. Eighteen years after *Oper und Drama* there appeared

[1] *Oper und Drama*, Gesammelte Schriften, 2nd Ed. Vol. IV. p. 124.

the second volume of J. H. H. Schmidt's *Antike Compositionslehre*, in which the lyrical portions of many Greek dramas were set out in recognisable musical rhythms, based upon a better understanding of the subject than was possessed by the Latin grammarians. To this followed the remarkable series of works by R. Westphal.

Not a note of the melody of the Greek theatre remains, but its rhythm, being based on the metre of the words, can be reconstructed through the theory of Aristoxenus with reasonable certainty; and when thus reconstructed, and set out in musical notation, it shows several features that may be at least interesting, and perhaps suggestive, to modern musicians. In any case we can gain valuable hints from the theory alone, even without the verbal examples.

But before discussing the theory we propose to give our readers a slight sketch of the rise of the art of music in Greece, with special reference to the notices about the gradual introduction of new rhythmical forms, as mentioned by Plutarch.

CHAPTER II

Outline of the history of Greek music—The principles of its scales explained by analogy with the construction of modern scales—The dramatists and their works—Tragedy, Comedy, and Lyric poetry—The instrumental accompaniment to song—The decline of Greek music.

ANCIENT Greek music was a branch of the system in vogue throughout the Babylonian and Egyptian civilisations. This system still exists in a modified form under the name of Byzantine music, and can be heard, not only in many of the oriental Christian churches, but in the folksongs of Greece, and, strange to say, Brittany[1].

Both in melody and rhythm, Greek music became more highly developed in certain directions than modern western music, while in others it remained behind, notably in that it never arrived at anything analogous to what we know as harmony and counterpoint. Where we use harmony as a means of expression, the ancients made use of subtle divisions of the octave, foreign to our ear, and melodic intervals forbidden by our theorists. In rhythm they largely employed the quintuple species, which as yet is scarcely known to us, and subtle combinations of time-values, demanding a highly trained rhythmical sense for their due appreciation.

Music undoubtedly has a mysterious power over the mind, and to this must be attributed the fact that the ancients credited its supposed founders with miraculous gifts. To the mythical Thracian Orpheus, called by Pindar the "Father of Song," Apollo presented a lyre, by whose sounds not only men and wild beasts, but even trees and rocks were so fascinated that they followed the player, and the powers of Hades were moved by it to restore to Orpheus his dead wife Euridice[2].

Historically the first systematic cultivation of the art of music took place at Sparta. Aristoxenus divides its early history into a

---

[1] Bourgault-Ducoudray, "Trente mélodies populaires de Basse Bretagne."
[2] But the Greeks were not the only people that attributed miraculous power to music. The legend of the "Pied Piper of Hamelin" is a case in point, and others might be cited.

first and second archaic period. The chief musicians of the first were Olympos, who used the diatonic tetrachord, and had not learned to divide the semitone into the quartertones of the enharmonic genus, and Terpander, who established certain alterations in the tuning of the tetrachord. Glaucus, one of the speakers in Plutarch's *Dialogue on music*, refers to the two archaic periods as, respectively, the first and the second musical institution at Sparta.

Here, as in the other Greek states, art and religion, and the public games in which they were exercised, were regulated by the government. The periodical Spartan festival in honour of Apollo, called the Karneia, was largely connected with the development of music, especially with kitharody, or vocal music accompanied by the kithara. He who sang the best kitharode in praise of Apollo won the prize.

Terpander came to Sparta as a stranger. He so enchanted the Spartans that not only did they give him the prize, but ordained that his system should be adopted as the state music. The compositions of both Olympos and Terpander were still known in the time of Aristoxenus, under the name of kitharodic *nomoi*. They were considered to have a noble simplicity of character which could not be imitated in after ages, and they were handed down by verbal tradition, not by writing. Their rhythm was usually that of the epic hexameter. Terpander would set a melody to some portion of the Homeric epos, and perform it in the public games, with a prelude of his own composition, and the prelude now became an important part of the structure[1].

Besides hexameters, he would sometimes use the orthios and trochaios semantos[2]. The word nomos was equivalent to our word "form" in music, as we should say, sonata-form, fugue-form, &c. The Terpandrian nomos was an ode, in a certain definite form, addressed to a god. It had seven distinct sections, or, as we should say, movements, all of which, like our early suite movements, were in the same key, and in the same mode, while the rhythm was for the most part in hexameters. Westphal gathers from Plutarch that the instrumental accompaniment of the Terpandrian nomoi, and in other early compositions, was not always in unison with the melody, but that it sometimes played intervals of a second, a fourth, a fifth or a sixth with it; and from Aristotle we learn that such intervals were

---

[1] Pindar speaks of "Dance-leading preludes."

[2] Orthios $\frac{3}{2}$ ♩ | ♩ ♩. (arsis thesis) Trochaios semantos $\frac{3}{2}$ ♩ ♩ ♩. (thesis arsis) For details see p. 42.

played above and not below the melody. This is apparently a very elementary kind of harmony, but too little information is at hand for us to get an idea of its effect.

Terpander used two principal scales, an octachord (represented by the white notes of the pianoforte from E to E), *i.e.* the Dorian mode or Dorian octave species, and a heptachord (represented by E, F, G, A, B flat, C, D).

Westphal considers that Olympos was a semimythical person who gave his name to a school of aulos playing that came from Asia into Greece about this time[1]. "Aulos," a kind of oboe, is often translated as "flute."

The school of Olympos introduced two new modes, the Lydian, practically our C major, and the Phrygian, our D to D without black notes. A nomos to Pytho the dragon, in the Lydian mode, and one to Athena in the Phrygian, are ascribed to Olympos. The two new modes, called by Plato barbaric, owing to their external origin, were well received by the public, and quickly incorporated into the Spartan system.

Plutarch tells us that the second musical institution of Sparta was brought about by Thaletas, Xenodamos, Xenocritus, Polymnastos, and Sacadas, all of whom were foreigners. The first three composed pæans, the name given to choral songs of thanksgiving to Artemis, or Apollo, for deliverance from evil. The pæan was also a song of victory after battle, or any solemn chant was thus named; the song with which soldiers advanced to battle was also called a pæan. The word must not be confounded with *pæon*, a rhythmical form, to be described later.

Polymnastos composed aulodic nomoi, songs in certain forms accompanied by the aulos. He and his successors were composers also of orthioi, compositions in slow, solemn, triple measure. Sacadas and his pupils wrote elegies, accompanied by the aulos. At that time an elegy was a poem, on any subject, in hexameters and pentameters. Later on the word was applied particularly to lamentations in verse.

Sacadas was an excellent composer of auletic nomoi (pieces for the aulos), and was victor in three Pythic contests. He also invented a new form of song in three strophes, the first being in the Dorian mode, the second in the Phrygian, the third in the Lydian. To this form of composition was given the name of *trimeres*.

---

[1] Analogously the Italians at the present day speak of what we know as the Polyphonic school as "Palestrina-music."

Xenodamos composed hyporchemata, choral hymns to Apollo of a lively character, and in quintuple rhythm. Thaletas is said to have introduced, as new rhythms, the pæon epibatos (slow quintuple measure), and the cretic (a form of quick quintuple measure)[1].

The second Spartan institution differed from the first in that it introduced choral music, in addition to solo singing, and a special form of dance suitable to the pæan and hyporchema. A new festival was established called gymnopaidæa, in honour of those who fell in the battle of Thyrea. In this festival the chief feature was, as the name implies, the dancing of naked boys, and the choral songs and dances of the gymnopaidæa soon spread throughout the other Greek states[2].

These compositions, then, together with the pæans and hyporchemata, were looked upon as the product of the second Spartan musical institution. The words *orchēsis*, dancing, *orchēstikos*, suitable for dancing, *orchēstēs*, a dancer, *orchēstra*, a place for dancing, now came into general use, together with *choros*, Latin *chorus*, the band of dancers. It will be seen how large a place dancing took in the state music[3].

The choral music was rendered, according to Aristotle, either in unison, or, when men and boys sang together, in octaves. Solo music, however, also took a large place in the second Spartan institution in the nomoi orthioi of Polymnastos, in the aulos odes, and aulos playing of Sacadas. To this period also belong three important innovations: the introduction of quartertones into the scale, the construction of an instrumental notation, and an increase of available compass in the scales.

Later on, we know not when, the chromatic tetrachord came into use. It had several forms, the only one of which that is possible to our ear being that which proceeds upwards by semitone, semitone, minor third; *e.g.* E, F, F sharp, A. Musicians such as Archytas,

---

[1] For further details see Westphal, *Die Musik des griechischen Alterthumes*, p. 144, &c.

[2] The dancing of naked boys as a religious thanksgiving after victory was not uncommon in antiquity. Sophocles, at the age of sixteen, was chosen, on account of his beauty and musical powers, to lead the gymnopaidic chorus after the victory of Salamis. Outside Greece, even men danced for the same object: it will be remembered that David, when King of Israel, "danced before the Lord with all his might" on bringing the Ark in triumph back to Jerusalem, and that Michal taunted him with having danced "uncovered." II Sam. vi. 14 and 20.

[3] Religious dancing survives in the west at one place only, in Seville Cathedral, where splendidly dressed choir-boys dance before the high altar on certain festivals, and sing at the same time, being accompanied by an orchestra. Thus, strange to say, is preserved in one corner of Christian Europe the old Greek ideal of religious music, a combination of choral song, dance, and instruments.

Eratosthenes, Didymus, and others, modified the two lower intervals by tuning them in thirds of tones, three-eighths of tones, and in other minute intervals that have now a mathematical interest only. These intervals seem to have represented various attempts at obtaining new sources of expression in music that was entirely melodic. The tuning of our modern intervals is regulated by the necessities of harmony, and harmony will tolerate nothing smaller than the semitone. From earliest infancy we are accustomed so to associate melody with harmony that it is impossible for us to imagine the effect of any music without it. But the intervals of melody will admit of many modifications that can gratify the ear of those to whom harmony is an entirely unknown feature, and, as a matter of fact, we ourselves, when we sing without instrumental accompaniment, or play a string quartet, do not employ the artificially tempered intervals that the use of harmony renders necessary for the pianoforte and organ.

We do not propose to follow in detail the gradual development of the complete system of keys and modes out of the few we have alluded to in our account of the two Spartan institutions. Suffice it to say that, at its zenith, Greek music made use of seven octave species (which afterwards became the seven "modes" of the Roman Church, with certain modifications and complete alteration of nomenclature) and of two "Perfect Systems." The "Greater Perfect System" consisted of two octaves of notes corresponding to our descending melodic minor scale; the "Lesser Perfect System" consisted of the lower octave of the Greater System, with the addition above it of the notes B flat, C, D. The Greater System gave us the nomenclature of our notation, the founders of which placed A, the first letter of the alphabet, on the lowest note of the two Greek systems, and the Lesser Perfect System gave us our B flat, which allowed of modulation, and from which began the application of flats and, afterwards, of sharps to each note of the scale.

The two Greek systems, like our scales, could be "transposed," that is to say, they might start from A, or B flat, or B natural, or C, and so on through the complete semitonic scale, as far as the voices and instruments extended. The octave species consisted of certain arrangements of the tones and semitones within the compass of an octave: the materials being selected from one of the "Perfect Systems." And since the systems could be transposed, it follows that the octave species could be transposed also. Each octave species contained two tetrachords, either "conjunct," as we shall show in our minor scale, or "disjunct," as the two tetrachords of our major scale. For practical purposes the lower tetrachord of an octave might differ from the upper in form, and since each tetrachord could be modified by more than one diatonic, at least four chromatic, and one enharmonic tuning, it will be seen that the possibility of variety in the scales was practically inexhaustible.

For those to whom the subject is new, perhaps we can make it clearer if we explain our own system on similar lines: and it will not be out of place to do so, since our musical scale is a direct lineal descendant of that of ancient Greece.

Modern music makes use of four octave species (instead of seven), each of which can start from any semitone of, say, the familiar pianoforte; *i.e.* it can be "transposed" to any pitch required, and its transposition during the course of a given composition by the device known as modulation, is, in itself, a means of æsthetic effect. But as we use no interval smaller than a semitone, we have not the wealth of melodic material implied by the enharmonic and chromatic and diatonic genera in their various forms.

Our first octave species is called the major scale: it consists of two similar tetrachords, not joined, and therefore, in Greek parlance, "disjunct."

$$\underbrace{\text{C D E F}}_{\text{tetrachord}}, \underbrace{\text{G A B C}}_{\text{tetrachord}}.$$

Our second octave species is the ascending melodic minor scale; it consists of two dissimilar tetrachords, the upper of which corresponds to the major tetrachord. A B C D, E F sharp G sharp A. It would be called a "mixed" octave species by the Greeks, for its two tetrachords are not alike.

Our third octave species is the descending form of the minor scale. It is particularly interesting in this connection, for it is the fundamental octave species of the two Greek systems. They looked upon it as containing two "conjunct" tetrachords, with an "added" note below, to complete the octave, thus,

$$\text{Added note } \text{A}, \underbrace{\text{B C D E}}_{\text{tetrachord}} \underbrace{\text{E F G A}}_{\text{tetrachord}}$$

the two tetrachords forming a junction at the note E.

Our fourth octave species is the harmonic minor scale, which like no. 2 is of the "mixed" variety, the upper tetrachord containing an augmented second, and being in this respect analogous to the Greek chromatic genus.

What we have lost in variety of scale we have more than made up for by the use of harmony and counterpoint.

The ancient scales and modes and genera, the greater and lesser systems formed the melodic material to which the Greeks applied their rhythmical laws. They looked upon melody without rhythm as raw material, without form; the application of rhythm to this material produced a satisfactory work of art.

In the early days of Greece it had been the custom to celebrate the gathering of the vintage by dancing and singing choral lyrical compositions round the altar of Dionysus, or Bacchus, the god of wine. Between the songs the leader of the chorus recited the story of the sufferings that the god and his adherents underwent before his worship was accepted in Greece. The choral songs were called dithyrambs, and they first began to take artistic shape at the hands of Alcman of Sparta (B.C. 660) and Stesichorus of Himera (B.C. 620). About B.C. 600 Arion of Lesbos still further improved their form, which was now that of the strophe and antistrophe, though sometimes the antistrophe, so essential a part of the later drama, was omitted.

The members of the dithyrambic chorus were dressed as satyrs, half goat, half man, and their song was the "goat-song," *tragœdia*, our tragedy. The contents of the dithyramb were of a joyful and elevated character. The poem was set to music in the Phrygian mode, and was accompanied by auloi.

Contemporary with the dithyramb was another form of the cult of Bacchus, connected with the earlier phallic worship. Its ritual consisted of the chorus running through the roads, dancing and singing, with their faces smeared with wine lees. This was the song of the revel, *comœdia*, our comedy.

In order to give a rest to the chorus during the celebrations around the altar of Bacchus, Thespis, who flourished about B.C. 536, introduced an actor to carry on a dialogue with the coryphæus, the leader of the chorus. This brought in a certain amount of dramatic element, and Thespis was called by some, the "Father of Greek Tragedy"; but of the details of his scheme nothing is known, and the ancients themselves were divided as to whether he was the actual inventor of tragedy, or an improver on ancient tradition.

Under the Peisistratides, about B.C. 560–510, Athens became the chief seat of art and literature. The Dionysiac festival now no longer confined itself to the story of Bacchus, but brought in other subjects, while retaining the form of a series of songs and dances round an altar which stood in the centre of the orchestra; but the dances were now interspersed with dialogues. Thus Choerĭlus, an Athenian, is said to have gained a dramatic victory in B.C. 523 with a drama on a maiden called Alope. Other composers of tragedies were Pratinas, about B.C. 497, and Phrynicus, who attained immense popularity about B.C. 476.

The next improvement was brought about by the famous Aeschylus (B.C. 525–456). He introduced a second actor, made the dialogue of more importance than the chorus, used scenery, imitated the elaborate vestments of the Eleusinian mysteries; and under his auspices the drama became a splendid spectacle, while still retaining its religious character[1].

Aeschylus wrote 70 tragedies, the subjects of which were the ancient legends of gods and heroes; he invented the trilogy, or series of three plays dealing with some one legend, to be performed on three days, and, in one case at least, he added a satyric drama to the trilogy, thus making a tetralogy. Like all Greek dramatists, he was not only the writer of the words, but the composer of the music. Musicians will recall that in these respects he is imitated by Richard Wagner, who, writing his own words, took the old Norse legends of the Nibelungen-Ring as his subject, made a trilogy thereof, and, by adding a "preludial drama," converted it into a tetralogy.

Sophocles (B.C. 495–406), when he was 27 years old, brought forward a play to compete with Aeschylus. Political feeling was running high, and those to whom fell the duty of appointing the judges had not ventured to do so, when Cimon, the successful admiral and general, entered the theatre with his nine colleagues. They were at once led to the altar, and, the proper oath having been administered,

---

[1] The tendency to make religious ceremonies ever more æsthetic is innate in human nature. The early Christian Church, which began in Asia Minor, developed an elaborate ritual, imitating in this respect the rituals of the Jews, of Isis, and others of the pagan cults which it eventually supplanted. The Roman Church followed suit in this respect, but it has never attained to the magnificence of vestment and ceremony used in the eastern Churches. The Roman ritual of to-day falls far below that of the present-day Armenians, for example, and the Russo-Greek Church. Other instances might be cited in the magnificence of Solomon's Temple, and, in our own days, in the constant craving for more elaborate "vestments" and ceremony, in the Church of England. A young Siamese prince once said to the writer, "If ever I thought of becoming a Christian, I should prefer to join the Church of Rome, because its elaborate ceremonies remind me more of my own Buddhist worship than your Church does." The innate love of splendid ceremonial, that led to the elaboration of Christian ritual, led Aeschylus to elaborate the æsthetic significance of the theatre, *i.e.* of the worship of Dionysus.

they acted as judges, and gave the first prize to Sophocles, the second only to Aeschylus, who thereupon left Athens in disgust.

Sophocles, though occasionally defeated by others, had the field practically to himself for many years. He introduced various developments. Early in his career he brought in a third actor, and afterwards increased the number of actors. He raised the tragic chorus from twelve to fifteen performers, the new members being respectively a coryphæus, or leader of the whole, and leaders of the two halves into which, for antiphonal purposes, the chorus was divided. He reduced the importance of the chorus, which now took no part in the dramatic action, but merely commented on the events and sentiments of which the actors were the exponents. In his choice of material, and in its working out, Sophocles is more human than Aeschylus. In place of the inexorable destiny to which man and gods have to submit, Sophocles makes the faults of human beings recoil on themselves, and at the same time he teaches the wisdom of that moderation in all things which formed so large a part of Greek philosophy.

He wrote 130 plays, of which seven are extant. He won about 20 first and several second prizes.

Euripides was born on the day of the battle of Salamis, 480 B.C. He was on intimate terms with Sophocles and Socrates, the latter of whom would never enter the theatre except when a play of Euripides was performed. His innovation on Sophocles consists of representing human nature, not as it ought to be, but as it is; and under the names of ancient heroes are exhibited the characters of his own time. Aristotle calls him the most tragic of poets. Comparing him with Aeschylus, it has been said, "Aeschylus has an element of Hebrew grandeur; Euripides has a strong element of modern pathos and romance."

He made constant use of the *deus ex machina*, and other mechanical devices, by which gods appeared to descend and ascend before the audience. His characters speak in the language of conventional everyday life, but indulge in philosophical discussions, while the subject-matter of the chorus is often detached from that of the play. Of his more than 70 tragedies, 18 are extant. His "Alcestis," one of the best known, was originally the last play of a tetralogy. Of his final work, "Orestes," a minute fragment of the musical notation was discovered recently, and is published in the *Mittheilungen aus der Sammlung der Papyrus Erzherzog Rainer*, Vol. V. Part 3, August 1892.

Contemporaneously with the development of tragedy, and equally supported by the State, there grew up Comedy, of which the chief representative for us is Aristophanes (about 444–380 B.C.). Comedy was submitted to contests like tragedy, and the performance of the latter was frequently preceded by a comic drama.

Into the history of comedy it is unnecessary for us to go, the works of Aristophanes being the only ones of interest to us here. Attic comedy was a satire or burlesque on the political and religious movements of the hour, on innovations in music and the other arts, on topics of the day, and personal matters. But the aim of Aristophanes was not merely to amuse; he pointed out defects in the administration of affairs, and the evils of the times. Thus, the Peloponnesian War, which he attributed to the influence of Pericles, is satirised in his "Peace." In other places he points out the wickedness of the lawyers, who encouraged litigation. He also satirises the education of his day, which, in view of the intellectual development of the age, aimed at substituting free-thought and philosophy for the old religious belief in gods.

Besides being a humourist, he was a poet and musician of the highest order. Of his 54 plays we possess 11.

In form, comedy was the same as tragedy; actors carried out the drama, and a chorus, fifty in number, commented on it. But in some of Aristophanes' later works there was no chorus[1].

The drama, whether Tragedy or Comedy, was set to music throughout. The choruses took the form of a series of strophes and antistrophes, and the dialogue was carried on in melody, accompanied by the instruments. For very intense effects the actor spoke his words, while the instruments continued to accompany, as in the "melodrama" of German opera. A modern analogy may be found in the part of Samiel in the Finale of the second act of "Der Freischutz": but there is this difference, that the Greek actor always maintained the musical rhythm while speaking, whereas Samiel speaks "rhythmically" in one place only.

The whole of the drama, in fact, whether spoken or sung, was uttered in rhythmical measure: there was nothing equivalent to our recitative, with its freedom from formal construction. The Greek play was absolutely a "music drama," that is, a real drama, enhanced by the magic influence of music; and in this respect it differed from Italian opera, in which dramatic requirements were subordinated to

---

[1] Wagner's "Tristan und Isolde" has no regular chorus.

the demands of musical form, to the display of vocal dexterity, or the possible jealousy of rival singers.

Besides the drama, lyric poetry, *i.e.* poetry intended to be sung to the accompaniment of the lyre, was equally cultivated. Its chief exponent was Pindar, who lived from about 522 to 400 B.C. He was a member of one of the noblest families of Thebes, where his father carried on the profession of an aulos player. Pindar studied at Athens under Lasos of Hermione, the founder of the Athenian school of dithyrambic poetry. Returning to Thebes at the age of twenty, he won prizes in the musical contests, and, becoming rapidly known as a poet of the first rank, was employed all over the Hellenic world to compose choral songs in praise of the winners in the public games. This was his chief life-work, and in return for it he received both money payment, and the highest honours that could be bestowed on him. Of his innumerable poems only four books of his Epinicia, songs of victory composed for winners in the Olympian, Pythian, Nemean and Isthmian Games, have reached us. A victory gained in any one of these contests conferred honour on the winner, his family, and his city. It was celebrated with religious ceremonies and choral music. A few bars of music, which bear strong evidence of dating from Pindar's time, will be discussed in a later chapter.

Another poet and musician, a rival of, and contemporary with, Pindar, was Simonides of Ceos (556–467 B.C.). Educated at Athens, he perfected the form of the Elegy, and Epigram (a short poem on some one thought, or a sepulchral inscription in verse), besides composing dithyrambs and epinician odes. He conquered Aeschylus in 489 B.C., in a contest for the prize offered for an elegy on those who fell at Marathon; and in his eightieth year he gained a victory at Athens with his dithyrambic chorus, this being his 56th prize. His powers of expression and poetic conceptions made him the most popular poet of his time, but he was inferior to Pindar in originality and fervour.

We learn from Plutarch that in the classical epoch of Greek music, the instrumental accompaniment was treated with considerable variety, though he does not enter into details, merely saying that Pindar and his contemporaries excelled in their treatment of the instruments. Westphal suggests that the "instrumental conversation," as it is called by Aristoxenus in Plutarch (Westphal's Ed. p. 16, line 1), which was "more complex" with the "ancients," *i.e.* the classical musicians, was some kind of polyphonic accompaniment of a *fugato* nature. In the XIXth Problem, allusion is made to the playing together of two instrumental parts, the lower of which sustained the melody, the upper the accompaniment, but it does not appear whether the two parts were played on one instrument or on two. Amongst the Pompeian frescoes there is a picture of two men, crowned with bay leaves, apparently playing a duet on two kitharas. Perhaps the complexity consisted, as in our music, of the accompaniment enhancing the effect of the melody by the addition of more elaborate rhythmical figures. But until, if ever, we recover some fragments of the actual instrumental notation, all suggestions as to its characteristics must be mere speculation. With the melody and instrumental music of the time of Pindar and Sophocles we have, at present at all events, no practical acquaintance: with the greater part of the rhythmical developments and theory, we can become well acquainted.

As in our own time, so with the Greeks, there were not wanting writers on theory as well as composers and executants. Lasos of Hermione, as head of one of the music schools of Athens, wrote a book on Melos, to which Aristoxenus alludes, and Suidas tells us that he was the first of a succession of musical authors[1].

With the epoch of Alexander the Great (356–323 B.C.) classical Greek art began its decline, and what we know of its theory is chiefly due to Aristoxenus and his successors.

"Krexos, Timotheus, Philoxenus, and their companions," he says, "strove in an unworthy manner after novelty, giving themselves over to a style which pleased the great public, and is now called the 'Contest-prize style.' The result is that limitation of compass, simplicity and dignity, are confined to the older period[2]."

"We do the same as the dwellers in Paestum on the Tuscan Sea: once Greeks, they are now sunk in barbarism, and become Tuscans or Romans, and have given up their old Hellenic speech and culture. Only one of the Hellenic festivals do they still celebrate: at this the old national names and customs come back to them, and they

---

[1] The series of authors who wrote on music in the Greek language was a long one. Beginning with Lasos in the latter half of the sixth century B.C., it extended to at least the fourth century of the Christian era, to which period Alypius is assigned. By this time political power was getting more and more into the hands of the rival Churches of the east and west, which gradually separated on lines of their own. Henceforward we are only concerned with the writings of the western branch of civilisation, which are all in Latin. Boethius (about 475–524 A.D.) wrote his book on Greek music in Latin, and thus began the long series of Latin treatises on music. But Greek music was by that time a lost art in the west, and all succeeding theorists confine their attention to the music of the Latin Church, which, in the liturgical form known as Gregorian, is an attenuated offspring of the music of ancient Greece.

[2] Aristoxenus, in Plutarch, p. 10 (German translation on p. 42), Westphal's Edition.

separate in sorrow and tears. Even so will we, now that the theatre is sunk in barbarism, and the music of the great vulgar public has come to so low an ebb, here in our small circle, think of the ancient music as it once was[1]."

"What shall I get if I put aside the new and pleasing music, and cultivate the old diligently?" "You will sing less in the theatre, for art cannot be at the same time both pleasing to the multitude and in the old style[2]."

A curious instance of an attempt on the part of a musician to change his style from the old to the new is related in Plutarch, p. 23. "Amongst his (Aristoxenus') contemporaries was Telesias of Thebes, who, in his youth, had been taught the noblest music, and was familiar with the works of the most celebrated masters, especially those of Pindar, Dionysius of Thebes, Lampros, Pratinas, and the other lyric poets. He was a splendid aulos player, and well versed in other branches of his art. Now this man was, in his riper years, so enchanted with the variegated music of the stage, that he despised the excellent masters on whose works he had been brought up, and dedicated himself to the style of Philoxenus and Timotheus, and to the most sensational novelties. But when he set to work to compose in the two manners, that of Philoxenus and that of Pindar, he found that he could produce nothing in the style of Philoxenus, so strongly did the good education of his youth influence him[3]."

Further quotations showing the decline of music will be found in the occasional remarks of Aristoxenus collected by Westphal at the end of his *Aristoxenos*. That Aristoxenus' views were not merely those of a *laudator temporis acti* is proved by the fact that no Greek work of art of the post-classical period, having any connection with music, as had the Dramas and Pindaric odes, was found of sufficiently lasting interest to cause copyists to preserve it for the benefit of posterity.

Greece became a Roman province in 147 B.C., and thenceforward her musicians, who were still the foremost in the world, were carried to Rome, generally as slaves, to adorn the festivals of the wealthy. A terrible catastrophe for a conquered nation! The profession of music, which had in its palmy days been confined to the members of aristocratic families, and was employed in carrying out the highest ideals of art and morals, was now turned to servitude in the houses and festivals of an ostentatious plutocracy.

[1] Aristoxenus, in Athenaeus, 14, p. 623. Quoted in Westphal's *Aristoxenos*, p. 473.
[2] Themistius, *Orationes*, 33. Quoted in Westphal's *Aristoxenos*, p. 473.
[3] Westphal, *Aristoxenos*, p. 474.

The Romans being unable to appreciate the fine distinctions of the genera, musicians gradually eliminated all except the one kind of diatonic genus which still subsists in the music of the Latin Church, though the chromatic genus was never lost in the east. As to rhythm, both the Greek and Roman languages, during the early centuries of our era, gradually lost their quantity, and poetry became marked by accent, as with us. Music then had to adopt its own rhythm independently of the words; an accented syllable being, however, generally sung to a long note, an unaccented to a short. In addition to this, Latin prose translations of the Bible were set to music, in which musical rhythm was of course non-existent. Where the Church used rhythm at all was only in the simple trochees and iambuses of the early hymns, suitable for a musically uncultured society: and since the feeling for measure in the words had by now practically given place to accent, the instinctive feeling of the singers gave a time-value to the melody which was not given by the words, as in more ancient times. Complexity of rhythmical structure, so dear to the classical Greeks, disappeared, to reappear in some of its old manifestations in the classical music of modern Europe, though without any historical or theoretical connection between the two arts.

From what has been said it would seem that, during the time of Hellenic greatness, the whole of Greece looked upon music as a noble and elevating art, capable of practical use for religion and the inculcation of virtue. But, as with us, so with the Greeks, there were always found men who could not appreciate the emotional effects of music, or, if they could, resisted them and were indifferent, or actively antagonistic to the art.

It has long been known that Philodemus of Gadara, in Syria, whose book on music was found amongst the Herculanean papyri, was one of these; but so much have we been accustomed to look upon the whole of the Greek nation as "musical," that Philodemus' work has generally been alluded to as "a musical treatise of no great importance."

Attention has, however, recently been given to this writing, and the results are discussed at considerable length by Dr Hermann Abert in his "Die Lehre vom Ethos in der griechischen Musik[1]." It would appear that the Sophists and the Epicureans, to the latter of which sects Philodemus belonged, endeavoured to show that music had not the ethical significance that was claimed for it by great writers such as Plato and Aristotle; that it merely consisted of a sensuous

[1] Leipzig, 1899, p. 27, &c.

combination of sounds and rhythms, to which the illusions of the ancients gave a meaning that it did not actually possess. That which really moved the audience was the significance of the words, while the music to which they are allied has just as little effect on the soul as, for instance, the art of cooking. Philodemus endeavours to support these views by examples from experience, from the difference of taste in music from time to time, and the different effects that the same melody may have on different persons. He argues that the public are moved by music merely through the ideas that have been put into their heads in the course of time.

And in religious songs, music has very little significance compared with the words. The general idea that music has any connection with piety is entirely erroneous. Music is merely an article of luxury, having no useful object, and serving only for pleasure, like the enjoyment of meat and drink, though he allows that labour can be lightened by it.

The account given by Abert of Philodemus' arguments is very interesting reading, since it shows that even in artistic Greece there were opponents of the art of music, just as there were in England in the eighteenth and nineteenth centuries. But no amount of logical arguments by learned men will stem the tide of human nature, and the general public and the musicians, of Athens in the fifth century B.C., and of London in the eighteenth century A.D., went their own way, cultivating their music without troubling themselves about the opinions of a small body of opponents. It is only with the exponents of music that we have to do here, with those who, by means of its mysterious influence, have contributed to the elevation and joy of mankind.

CHAPTER III

Definitions of rhythm according to Baccheios the Elder—Aristoxenus on rhythm, rhythmizomenon, and rhythmopœia—The musical measure or foot—Thesis and arsis—Ancient methods of beating time—Thetic and anacrusic forms—The chronos protos—Quantity and accent—Greek systems of notation—A recently discovered specimen of Greek notation.

"WHAT is rhythm?" asks Baccheios the Elder, in his catechism (Appendix A, 1), and answers the question thus. "A measuring of time by means of some kind of movement. According to Phaedrus, rhythm is some measured thesis of syllables, placed together in certain ways. According to Aristoxenus, it is time, divided by any of those things that are capable of being rhythmed. According to Nicomachus, it is a well-marked movement of 'times.' According to Leophantus, it is a putting together of 'times' in due proportion, considered with regard to symmetry amongst them. According to Didymus, it is a schematic arrangement of sounds. Sound, schematised in some way, produces rhythm, and rhythm arises in speech, or melody, or movements of the body."

Movement is essential to rhythm. The ancients, who liked to systematise everything, divided the arts into two triads, of which the first consists of those which depend on repose and space, that is to say, Architecture, Painting, and Sculpture, while the second triad contains those which employ movement, namely, Music, Poetry, and the Dance. In the first triad the element of form produces symmetry, in the second, rhythm[1]. "We delight in rhythm," says the author of the XIXth Problem, "because it has a recognisable and regulated number, and moves us regularly. The regular movement is more easy to us than the unregulated, since it is more in accordance with nature."

The idea of rhythm being number and regulated movement is frequently alluded to by the Greek theorists. The number and movement do not necessarily refer to the body, or to any object, but to words or syllables or musical notes. Rhythm is something that

[1] Westphal, *Allgemeine Theorie der musikalischen Rhythmik*, 1880, p. xlviii. See also Gevaert, *La Mus. de l'Ant.* Bk. I. Ch. II.

occupies time, and can only be exhibited by some kind of movement, and the movement itself is regulated by numbers, in the way that we teach children to "count their time" in playing on an instrument. The idea of music being motion must have suggested itself to our forefathers, when they gave to the various divisions of the sonata the names "first movement," "slow movement," and so on.

According to Phaedrus, rhythm has to do with the "thesis[1]" of syllables placed together in certain ways. In every word of two or more syllables, one syllable is made more prominent than the rest by means of stress, or, as we generally say, accent. Accent has not to do with time-value, though in music the thesis is more often placed on a long than a short note. In prose the accented syllables, the theses, occur at no regular intervals, while in poetry their occurrence is regulated so as to produce a satisfactory sense of order: and when this order is further regulated by definite time-values, rhythm arises. The difference between rhythm and metre is tersely described by Servius. "The rhythmicists subject syllables to time measurements, the metricists subject time to the syllables" (Appendix A, 2). Poetry must not be read as it would be sung; the theses certainly recur at regular intervals, but they are syllabic intervals, not time intervals. When they are subjected to time, rhythm arises, whether the poetry is read or sung.

With the Greeks, the rhythmical figures of a vocal melody arose out of the long and short syllables to which it was set. Poetry was the predominant partner. With us the opposite is the case; music itself gives the rhythmical scheme, to which the syllables must conform, and thus we are able to set half a dozen different rhythmical schemes to one poetic text. Extension and contraction of syllables were used for purely rhythmical purposes, but long melodic passages on a single syllable, as in our Italian opera, would have no meaning to a Greek audience. The first consideration was that the words and rhythm should be easily understood and appreciated by the audience. This does not mean that the bars were to be all alike, or that there was to be rustic simplicity about the rhythm. On the contrary, the forms were in some respects more complicated than anything that our composers use, and yet the cultivated Athenian audience delighted in understanding and appreciating their intricacies. There was, of course, no polyphony, no orchestration and no harmony (in the modern sense); all being in unison, more special attention was given to rhythmical expression than is the case with us.

[1] Aristoxenus calls the thesis *Basis*.

The definitions of Nicomachus, Leophantus, and Didymus, are practically the same as that attributed to Aristoxenus, but in his own writings Aristoxenus distinguishes between rhythm, rhythmizomenon, and rhythmopœia.

"We must imagine," he says, "two different natures, that of rhythm and that of the rhythmizomenon, having the same relations to one another as a plan has to the object that is planned" (Appendix A, 3). The rhythmizomenon is the raw material, which is subjected to rhythm; and there are three kinds of rhythmizomenon, namely, music, poetry, and dancing. Melody alone consists of a succession of intervals, without meaning. Only when it is subjected to rhythm does it take shape and form. Ordinary speech consists of a succession of accented and unaccented syllables, in no definite order; when, however, these are subjected to rhythm, the speech becomes poetry. The steps of a person walking or running are continuous, but if they become ordered in some recognisable arrangement by rhythm, the dance arises. Intervals, speech, and steps are the three *rhythmizomena*, the respective materials to which rhythm is applied.

This is the Aristoxenian theory. The material itself, whether melody, speech, or bodily movement, is not rhythm, but when subjected to rhythm, it becomes the "rhythmizomenon," the "thing rhythmed."

And rhythm arises through the division of the time occupied by the thing rhythmed (App. A, 4).

Rhythmopœia is the art of applying rhythm to the rhythmizomenon. This art was carefully studied, and more attention was given to it in theory than is the case with us. It has to do, not only with the construction of the phrases, but of the measures themselves. Thus, the four measures of Ex. 1 all differ from one another in their

Ex. 1. [musical notation in 3/8]

rhythmopœia, whereas in Ex. 2, while the rhythmopœia of the

Ex. 2. (a) [musical notation in 6/8, with "accent" marked]

(b) [musical notation in 6/8, with "accent" marked]

measures is the same throughout, that of the whole phrase (a) differs from that of the phrase (b) by the position of the chief accent. Aristoxenus calls the rhythmopœia of the complete phrase, as opposed to that of the single measures, "continuous rhythmopœia"

Like the modes of melody, each rhythmical form was supposed to induce some particular emotional effect on the mind. For example, the spondee (𝅗𝅥 𝅗𝅥) was suitable for solemn hymns to the gods; the anapæst (♪ ♪ 𝅗𝅥), used specially for marches, induced energy and vigour. Hence the construction of the individual measures was of importance.

The measure itself was called the "foot" (*pous*), and it will be convenient to apply this term to it, since modern bars are sometimes called measures. The foot performed the same function in some respects as our simple bar, but while our bar must always begin with an accented note, the Greek foot might begin with either its accented or unaccented portion. The accented portion was called thesis, meaning a downward movement of the foot, or of the hand of the conductor, and the unaccented portion, called arsis, represented the raising of the foot or hand. The Latin equivalents are *positio*, and *levatio*, or *elatio*. In modern German the two portions of the foot are called, respectively, *Hebung* and *Senkung*. Since there is no English equivalent for these terms (down-beat and up-beat do not express them closely enough), we shall adopt the Greek terms Thesis and Arsis. Under certain circumstances a thesis or arsis may occupy a whole foot, as we shall see in due course.

Q. "What do we call arsis?" asks Baccheios. (App. A, 5.)

A. "When the foot is raised from the ground as if we intend to step. *Q.* And what is thesis? *A.* When it is put down."

Time was, as a rule, audibly beaten. In the XIXth Problem reference is made in Sections 21, 22 to the difficulty that the Hegemon, or leader, had in keeping his singers together in the rhythm. He seems to have marked the theses by snapping his finger and thumb, but sometimes the foot was put down "with noise," according to Marius Victorinus; or the hands were clapped together. In flute playing the performer sat, and marked the theses with a piece of wood fastened to his foot. The beat of the bar thus audibly expressed by the conductor or performer was called semeion, or sign. Aristides (Meibom. p. 31) describes thesis and arsis as "ψόφον καὶ ἠρεμίαν," "noise and stillness." In modern music the drum has taken the place of the noisy movements of hands and feet. In Italy many years ago we noticed in the opera at Bologna, and also in one of the churches in Rome, that the conductor had a sonorous piece of metal fastened to his desk, on which he tapped the rhythm when the orchestra or singers wavered: a curious instance of the reintroduction of a very ancient custom.

The feet and phrases which commence with the thesis have been conveniently termed by Hermann "Thetic" feet or phrases, and those which commence with the arsis are called by him "Anacrusic." The anacrusic form (Ex. 2 a, page 26) was of more importance than the thetic (Ex. 2 b); it is practically the only form recognised for modern music by Dr Hugo Riemann, in his *Agogik und Dynamik*. Greek theorists nearly always allude to the arsis before the thesis, the implication being that the anacrusic was of more importance than the thetic form.

The whole of the Aristoxenian theory of rhythmopœia is founded on the various uses of the *chronos protos*, a term which can conveniently be translated as "primary time." The primary time is theoretically indivisible; it is described as the smallest time-division that is perceptible to the senses. Aristides Quintilianus calls it the *Unit* of Time. It is the smallest time that is used in a given composition, and therefore that is perceptible in that composition (App. A, 6). It is the short syllable in poetry: a long syllable occupies two or more primary times. It is the time of a single short note in ancient melody, since the length of the notes depended on that of the syllables to which they were allied. The primary time practically corresponded to the single beat in a modern bar of moderate *tempo*. In very rapid music the conductor will embrace several primary times in a beat, and in very slow movements he will sometimes give more than one beat to a single primary time. In applying the theory of the primary time, as we shall have to do, to modern music, it will be found that our primary value may be the quaver, the crotchet, or the minim, according to the particular scheme of notation employed by the composer; there is no rule about it. In this work we shall follow the continental precedent, by using the quaver as the primary time in all examples that are not drawn from actual compositions.

Modern languages make no distinction between long and short syllables. Our poetry is founded on the distribution of accents, whereas Greek poetry was based on time, or "quantity," as it is generally called by the grammarians. That is, the long syllable occupied, as a rule, twice the time of the short syllable, not only in poetry, but apparently also to some extent in ordinary speech. The rules for distinguishing between the long and short syllables of Greek verse are well known[1]. Thus, the opening words of Pindar's

---

[1] The difference between the Latin teaching and the Aristoxenian theory as to length of syllable is simply this; the Latin grammarians knew, and modern schoolmasters know from

third Olympian Ode would be sung, and perhaps said, as follows:

Τυνδα - ρί-δαις   τε   φι - λο-ξεί - νοις   ἀ - δεῖν   καλλι-πλο-κά-μῳ   θ' Ἑλένᾳ.

The primary time or "short" syllable has the value of a quaver, the "long" that of a crotchet. According to the grammarians, there must be no exception to the rule of "one long equals two shorts," and the line is rhythmically impossible. By the Aristoxenian teaching one syllable in the above example is given the value of a dotted crotchet, that is, three "shorts," and by the alteration of this single note from "two time" to "three time" value the whole line obtains a satisfactory musical rhythm.

Theoretically the primary time, as we have said, is indivisible: yet it will be found that this rule is occasionally broken, as in the Choreic dactyl (♩ ♫). Probably it was given to beginners merely to explain the matter. We all know that musical students are forbidden under any circumstances to write consecutive fifths: the rule is strict, yet every competent composer knows how and when to dispense with it. May it not have been the same with the rule about dividing the primary time?

The Aristoxenian teaching with regard to the *chronos protos* appears to have lasted almost into the age of mensural music, for Hieronymus de Moravia, writing about A.D. 1250, says, "*Instans* is the smallest and indivisible portion of time in which sound can be heard clearly and distinctly, and this is what the ancients called *tempus*."

Having explained the theory of the primary time, the Greek writers generally proceed to show how it is combined in various ways to build up, first simple feet, equivalent to our bar, then compound feet, equivalent to our phrases. It is explained that the actual time occupied by the short syllable is not definitely fixed, but varies according to whether the movement is slow or fast. This is easy enough to understand; it merely means that a melody may be sung *adagio* or *allegro*, as with us, in which case the primary time, like all other values, will be longer or shorter respectively.

To indicate musical intervals in writing, the Greeks made use of two systems of alphabetical letters, one nominally for instruments, and the other for voices[1], though both seem to have been employed indifferently for either vocal or instrumental music. The letters,

them, *which* syllables are long and which short, while the Aristoxenian theory shows *how* long and *how* short they should be in relation to one another.

[1] It will be remembered that down to about A.D. 1600 our musicians used the staff notation for voices and the tablatures for instruments.

placed upside down or obliquely, mutilated and altered in various ways, were called *semeia*, or signs. For time-values other signs were added above them, as was the case in the tablatures, and in the modern tonic sol-fa system. The melodic signs are given in their entirety by Alypius, a writer of unknown date, whose book is printed by Meibomius and by Jan in the *Scriptores*. There is no necessity here to go into their details, which are somewhat complicated. More important for us are the signs which were occasionally, not always, added to indicate values. They are given by Bellermann's *Anonymus*, and have been of great assistance in the elucidation of rhythmical doctrine. We learn from *Anonymus* that a primary time was indicated by a note with no time-sign over it, and other values were shown as follows:

A "two-time long," *i.e.* a note of the value of two primary times, was indicated by — equivalent to ♩

a three-time long¹ by ⌐ „ „ ♩.
a four-time long by ⊔ „ „ ♩
a five-time long by ⊔⌐ „ „ ♩♪

Further than this he does not go; but he shows that "empty times" existed, that is, times devoid of sound, equivalent to our rests. They were indicated thus:

An empty primary time ∧ equivalent to 𝄽
„ „ two-time ⊼ „ „ 𝄼
„ „ three-time ⌐∧ „ „ 𝄼 𝄽
„ „ four-time ⊔∧ „ „ ▬
„ „ five-time ⊔⌐∧ „ „ ▬ 𝄽

According to Aristides (Meibom. p. 40), "An empty time is that which exists without sound, for the completion of a rhythm." It is one of the most ordinary features in modern song, but the "empty time" of the voice is usually filled in by the accompaniment. We shall have to refer later on to an unfortunate filling in by Mozart of an "empty time" in Handel's "Messiah."

These signs were usually omitted from vocal notation, since the values of the notes were understood from the syllables, and rests occurred only at the ends of verses.

To indicate accent a dot, called *stigma*, or in Latin *ictus*, was placed above or alongside a note. It seems not only to have

¹ The vertical portion of the sign for the three-time long is on the left of the horizontal portion in *Anonymus*. In the Seikilos hymn quoted below it is on the right.

performed the same function as our bar-line, but also to have been used for syncopation, or any artificial displacement of accent, though we are not yet in possession of a sufficient number of examples to be sure on this point. The *ictus* was not so necessary in vocal as instrumental music. The early musicians of our own system also found this to be the case, for they did not introduce bars into vocal notation till about the year 1600, while all the instrumental tablatures were carefully barred from the first.

Of the few fragments of original Greek music that have come down to us, one vocal composition shows not only the time-signs, but the *ictus*. It is a hymn, composed by one Seikilos, and engraved on a marble pillar. It was discovered by Professor Ramsay in 1883, but not till 1891 were the letters between the lines of the hymn discovered to be musical characters.

We quote this short piece, and give its translation into modern notation. The inverted gamma on the last syllable, representing the

note E, differs from the usually accepted versions. It was kindly supplied to the author by the late Mr D. B. Monro, after a "squeeze" had been taken from the stone.

Dr Wessely of Vienna was the first to point out that the letters were musical notes, and he published the result of his investigation, with M. Ruelle, in the *Revue des Études grecques*, V. 1892, pp. 265–280. Dr Otto Crusius discusses the rhythm in the *Philologus*, Vol. LII. pp. 160–200. Although the translations into modern notation agree with one another, the versions of the Greek notation published by Jan in the *Scriptores*, and Monro in *The Modes of Ancient Greek Music*, differ in an important particular with regard to the *ictus*. In the Monro version there is no duplication of the *ictus* on two successive notes. From what we have read of the Aristoxenian theory, we think that the Jan version is more likely to be the correct one with regard to the *ictus*. Spitta suggests that where the dot occurs on two adjacent notes, syncopation is implied, or that the passage is similar to those mixtures of 3/2 and 3/4 that our early musicians frequently used, and that Brahms has revived in the form of 2/4, 3/4, 6/8. Syncopation consists of the anticipation of an accent: its use is common in all nations. That it is a spontaneous and natural means of expression is proved by the frequency with which an illiterate singer will introduce it where it does not occur in the written version of what he sings[1].

The Greeks, with their sensitive ear and their keen appreciation of rhythmical subtleties, would certainly notice the telling effect of syncopation, with its displacement of accent, and as they did not divide their music into definite time portions by any equivalent to our bar, it was natural that they should place an *ictus* on the note that was to have an unexpected accent[2].

[1] An untaught singer would, for example, be very likely to sing as follows, in Braham's "Death of Nelson" although the notes under the asterisks are crotchets.

Ex. 3.

We scorned the foreign yoke; For our ships were British Oak

[2] All musicians are aware of the different effects that would be produced by "bowing" the above passages on the violin in two different ways, thus:

Ex. 4.

It will be observed that one of the notes near the end of the Seikilos melody has a dot by its side instead of above it. This was given me by Mr Monro. If it is not a defect in the stone, it may perhaps be a lesser *ictus*.

This, then, is the only vocal example that contains the *ictus* definitely marked. In some of the later hymns the class of rhythm is indicated by words, such as "iambic," or "dactylic." In some of the instrumental exercises given by Bellermann's *Anonymus* the *ictus* is marked, but the manuscripts are so variable in this matter that it is difficult to make out any precise arrangement of the accents.

CHAPTER IV

Errhythm, Arrhythm, and Eurhythm—Time combinations in the measure or foot—
The seven differences of foot, according to Aristoxenus—The three species of
foot—Aristoxenus on irrational time—Reintroduction of the principle in modern
music—Burney on Greek rhythm—Names of the simple feet—Extension and
contraction of syllables to suit the musical rhythm—Greek feeling reflected in
the ligatures of the plain-song notation—Some Greek rhythmical forms
illustrated by quotations from Schubert's songs.

ARISTOXENUS says that not every possible division of a rhythmizomenon is rhythmical. Only when times are arranged in due proportion with one another is this the case. Certain combinations are condemned by our æsthetic feeling. There are fewer methods of grouping tones in melodious than in unmelodious succession, and this is also the case with regard to time-divisions. Hence a rhythmizomenon can be arranged rhythmically or unrhythmically, "errhythmically" or "arrhythmically." And not only in these two ways: for the rhythmizomenon may be "eurhythmical," *i.e.* "beautifully rhythmical[1]."

A phrase is errhythmical when its times are arranged in due proportion to one another, so that its rhythm becomes clear and convincing. Errhythm may, however, be inspiring or the reverse; it may express something, or nothing particular. A performance in which all the rhythmical details are brought out clearly and intelligently is errhythmical, but so also is the monotony of the mechanical perfection induced by a too frequent use of the metronome.

Similarly, any phrase that is correctly written as to its barring and accents, however monotonous it may be in effect, is errhythmical; but so also are the inspired phrases of a Mozart or a Beethoven.

Arrhythm arises if a phrase is barred or a composition phrased in such a way as to offend the aisthēsis, or to be incomprehensible. Under modern conditions arrhythm does not often arise, for our stereotyped phrase, the conventional four-bar rhythm, is so easily

[1] Paraphrase from Aristox. *Rhyth. Elements*, in Westphal's *Fragmente*, pp. 29 and 30.

constructed, and so familiar, that every beginner can soon master it sufficiently to write it errhythmically, however wanting it may be in expression. But arrhythm very often takes place in the performances of incompetent executants : bars are deprived of their full value, notes are unduly shortened or lengthened, accents are misplaced, phrasing is ignored.

Eurhythm is exemplified in the works of the great masters, and can be heard whenever these are adequately performed. Moreover, a composition which is merely errhythmical to the eye in print may sometimes become eurhythmical in the hands of a skilful performer. Everyone knows how a common-place song may be transformed by a well trained singer in such a manner as to "hit the popular taste": in this transformation the beauty of voice is undoubtedly the principal element, but the management of rhythm has something to do with the popularity of the kind we contemplate, for with mere uninspiring, cold, and correct errhythm such a song would scarcely be able to take a hold on the popular imagination, however fine the voice might be.

By various combinations of primary times the ancients constructed a limited number of measure-forms, or feet, called most of them by special names, and attributed to them certain "characters" (ethos). The single primary time is called a "simple" time, or "simple" note. Any note longer than the primary time is "compound." Thus

♪ is a simple time, represented by a short syllable,

♩ is a compound time, called a "two-time," or "two-note" (dichronos, disēmos).

♩. is a compound time, *i.e.* a "three-time note" (trichronos, trisēmos[1]).

"That by which we mark the rhythm, and make it perceptible to the sense, is the foot[2] or more than one foot. Of the feet, some are made up of two times, an up and a down,

---

[1] The Germans and Americans describe notes by their relative arithmetical values, but instead of starting from the smallest, like the Greeks, they commence with the semibreve, which is called a whole note, while a minim, crotchet, &c. are respectively the half-note, quarter-note, and so on.

[2] The technical terms "foot" and "measure" mean the same thing. The "foot" of poetry is the counterpart of the "measure" (not necessarily the "bar") of music. Aristoxenus has only one term for this rhythmical section in all three of his rhythmizomena, music, poetry, and the dance.

In America the musical bar is called a measure. Musicians have been accustomed, from the time of the introduction of bars into vocal music, to consider the bar as a rhythmical unit. But a bar may contain a value equivalent to two or more poetic feet, and unless we adopt

Ex. 5. (*The Greek "measure" or "foot" is indicated by the inverted brackets.*)

(a) 2/8 [musical notation with ar th ar th ar th]

some of three, in which there are two up and one down,

(b) 3/8 [musical notation] (c) 3/8 [musical notation]

or one up and two down,

(d) 3/8 [musical notation]

and some of four times, of which two are up and two down,

(e) 4/8 [musical notation] (f) 4/8 [musical notation]

It is evident that a foot cannot consist of one time alone, for one note cannot make a division of time; and without a division of time a foot cannot exist." (App. A, 7.)

Modern musicians hold that rhythm is not perceptible unless at least two accents are heard, and this implies a minimum of three notes, for to produce accent there must be non-accent as a contrast. Our readers will probably be able to recall instances in which a composer has purposely puzzled his audience at the outset of a movement, by an indefinite rhythmical construction of the first motive.

If a two-time arsis in a triple foot consists of a single compound time, it is evident that syncopation will arise, as in Ex. 5 c. That rhythmical measure cannot be produced by one note alone, however long, is plain enough. For example, the note held by the oboe for the orchestra to tune, may be of the most beautiful quality, but it makes no measurement of time, and is, therefore, not rhythmical.

There are seven differences of foot[1]:

1. Difference of value, for example,

    Ex. 6.   (a) 3/8 [notation] and 6/8 [notation]

2. Difference of species, as

    (b) 3/8 [notation] and 4/8 [notation]

---

the Greek term "foot" as a musical technical word, we must, in a scientific investigation of the nature of a rhythmical phrase, use "measure" in a sense differing from that of "bar." But a satisfactory technical terminology for rhythm in the English language has yet to be invented.

[1] Westphal, *Fragmente*, p. 35.

3. Difference of proportion and unproportion. See page 39.

4. Feet may be simple or compound, like our bars; but Aristoxenus calls a whole rhythmical section a compound foot containing a number of simple feet.

5. Difference of diæresis, or distribution of accent: as

(c) [musical notation in 3/8]

6. Difference of scheme, as

(d) [musical notation in 3/8]

7. Difference in the order of parts, whether the foot begins with the arsis or thesis, as

(e) [musical notation in 3/8 with ar th / th ar markings]

"Three species of foot can be used in rhythmopœia, the iambic, the dactylic, and the pæonic. The iambic is in uneven proportion, the dactylic in even, and the pæonic in the ratio of three to two. The smallest of the feet contains the value of three times, for a two-time foot would have its notes packed too closely together[1]."

In two-time rhythm the syllables following one another rapidly without variety might, according to Greek ideas, easily become ineffective or monotonous. Instruments must, however, have been capable anciently, as with us, of rapid passages of equal notes, but vocal music reigned supreme, and the laws of rhythm, at any rate the elementary laws (and Aristoxenus only treats of the elements), were formulated for it alone. We find a certain analogy to this in the present day, if we consider that the modern teacher of elementary harmony confines his attention to rules that are more suitable for voices than instruments.

The two-time foot was, however, used in practice, for Aristides Quintilianus (App. A, 8) tells us that it was called the pyrrhichius because it was employed in the war-song known as the *pyrrhichē* and in the contests connected therewith. Martianus Capella says that it also occurred "in a certain boyish game[2]."

The first recognised species of rhythm, then, is iambic, or triple rhythm, so called from the three-time poetic foot known as the

---

[1] Westphal, *Fragmente*, p. 36, line 9.
[2] The song and contest are said to have been invented by one Pyrrhichos, but other derivations of the word are given. Liddell and Scott's *Lexicon*.

iambus. The iambus consists of a one-time arsis and a two-time thesis, the arsis coming first[1].

Ex. 7.   (a) ♪ | ♩ ♪ | ♩ (ar th ar th)

According to Aristides, the word iambus comes from *iambizein*, to lampoon, to threaten, to abuse, because satiric verses were in iambic metre. It will be noticed that the iambus is an anacrusic form: but the iambic species embraces every kind of foot that contains the value of not more or less than three primary times. It is the generic term for what we call triple measure.

The second or even species is called dactylic, from the dactyl, a poetic or musical foot consisting of a compound two-time thesis followed by a "dissolved" arsis, of equal value to the thesis. This seems perhaps a somewhat roundabout description of the rhythmical figure which musicians will recognise as forming the basis of the slow movement of Beethoven's Seventh Symphony, and of many other classical movements; but it is advisable to accustom our readers to these descriptions, as they will be necessary later on for more complicated forms. The dactyl derives its name from *dactylus*, the

Ex. 7.   (b) | ♩ ♫ | ♩ ♫ | (th ar th ar)

finger, which has one long joint and two short ones: hence schoolboys know the dactyl as a "long and two shorts." It is a thetic form, but all feet containing four primary times are classed as dactylic.

The third species has five primary times in its foot, divided into a three-time thesis, followed by a two-time arsis, or *vice versa*. Hence it is said to be in the ratio of three to two. It is called the pæonic species from the poetic foot pæon, the simplest form of which is shown in Ex. 7 *c*.

Ex. 7.   (c) | ♩ ♪ ♩ | ♩ ♪ ♩ | (th ar th ar)

It was called "two-limbed," owing to its triple-duple form. "In the pæonic genus there are two simple feet, the *pæon diaguios*, consisting of a long thesis and a short, and a long arsis (as in Ex. 7 *c*), and the *pæon epibatos*, of a long thesis and long arsis, and of two long theses and a long arsis (from what follows we know the 'two long

---

[1] Aristides Quint., in Westphal, *Fragmente*, p. 56.

theses' should be 'a twofold long thesis' $\genfrac{}{}{0pt}{}{5}{4}$ 𝅘𝅥 𝅘𝅥 𝅗𝅥 𝅘𝅥). The *diaguios* has been so called because it is, as it were, *diguios*, jointed, two-limbed; it is used with two *semeia* (down beats by the conductor). The *epibatos* is so called because it consists of four notes, namely two arses and two theses differing in value[1]."

Quintuple time was far more commonly used by the Greeks than by us, though there are evidences that this beautiful form of rhythm is again coming into vogue. Probably the chief difficulty in dealing with it is the idea that it is a single measure, in which there is to be no secondary accent: whereas if we look upon it as "two-limbed," and give each limb its thesis and arsis, most of the difficulty will disappear. The conductor will then, of course, give two down beats in each bar.

The pæonic species was used for solemn hymns and invocations to the gods: a Hymn to Apollo, found at Delphi in 1893, is in this species of rhythm.

It must not be imagined that any iambic or dactylic or pæonic composition contained respectively an iambus, a dactyl, or a pæon in each bar. The monotony of this would have been more felt by the Greeks than by us, for we have the resources of harmony to help us, which they had not. Thus, the *allegretto* of the "Moonlight" sonata is in pure iambuses throughout, but by means of chord-suspensions all monotony is avoided. The fifth song of Beethoven's Liederkreis "An die ferne Geliebte" (Es kehret der Maien) is almost entirely in pure anapæsts (inverted dactyls), but as the harmony changes in the middle of each foot the lively anapæstic rhythm has its full force without any monotony. The Greeks were compelled to vary their rhythm more than this, as they were more dependent on its effect than we are.

To obtain variety by means of rhythm alone demanded considerable skill.

The third difference alluded to on page 37 has to do with proportion and unproportion, called rationality and irrationality. There is, in Greek theory, a time-value called irrational, namely, in the words of Baccheios, "that which is longer than the short, and shorter than the long." It is represented in our examples by the dotted quaver. Aristoxenus explains the matter thus[2], "Every foot is defined by some ratio, or by an irrationality which has a middle

---

[1] Aristides Quint., in Westphal, *Fragmente*, p. 58, Meib. p. 58.
[2] See App. A, 9.

value between two values that are perceptible to the aisthēsis. We can make this clear by taking two feet, one of which consists of a two-time arsis and a two-time thesis, | ♩ | ♩, (ar, th) and the other of a two-time thesis and a one-time arsis, | ♩ ♪ | (th, ar). Then let us add a foot having a two-time thesis, and an arsis with a value that comes midway between the values of the above-mentioned arses, ♩ ♪. (th, ar) (the dotted quaver is midway between the crotchet and quaver). This foot will have the up beat *irrational* to the down. The irrational will be midway in value between two ratios that are perceptible to the senses, namely, between the equal and the two-to-one ratios. And this foot is called the irrational choree."

Irrational time on an arsis seems to have been a slight pause, long enough to be noticeable, but not to break the rhythmical flow. It was evidently much used as an element of expression. It is coming into favour with our own composers, and is variously indicated in the notation. Brahms, for example, places the sign ⌢ over a bar-line, Strauss the sign ', and Vincent D'Indy ⌐•⌐.

The last named composer, in his sonata op. 63, explains the use of the sign in much the same terms as we explain the Aristoxenian unproportional time, viz. as " a slight pause, not so important as ⌢ ." It can be used with good effect in certain church hymns, where it enables the congregation to take breath, and so gives additional vigour to the rhythm, whose flow it does not break. In ballad singing it has always been used, though never written.

But the Greeks used it more freely than we do. Its employment in the thesis of a triple foot gives rise to the cyclical or three-time dactyl, ♩♪♩. Before the teaching of Aristoxenus was known, a dactyl occurring in the midst of three-time rhythm would be expressed in notation by a change of time-signature, thus:

Ex. 7. (d) 3/8 ♩ ♪ | 2/4 ♩ ♫ | 3/8 ♩ ♪ | ♩. |
                    dactyl

Burney, in the chapter on ancient rhythm in Vol. I. of his "History," after giving examples, says (p. 84), "The most striking circumstances in all these examples is the perpetual change of time, occasioned by the mixture of unequal feet.......I believe the best modern band would find it difficult, if not impossible, to keep exactly together in the execution of a Greek chorus, though assisted by all the clatter of an ancient coryphæus." This was written under the old impression that a long syllable was invariably equal to two shorts. But with an understanding of the unproportional or irrational measure, Ex. 7 *d* would now be written as Ex. 7 *e*. The second

Ex. 7.   (*e*) [musical notation: cycl. dact.]

measure, having an irrational thesis, is the "cyclical" form described by Dionysius of Halicarnassus, the text of whose description is quoted in App. A, 10.

Aristides (Westphal, *Frag.* p. 59) alludes to irrational chorees, consisting of a long arsis and two theses. (He means a long thesis and two arses.) He calls them "like the iambus," "but the division of the words is dactylic." This would produce Ex. 7*f*, in which a

Ex. 7.   (*f*) [musical notation]

long thesis is followed by an arsis of two shorts, as in the dactyl, but the foot is triple, *i.e.* iambic, as to its species.

The simple feet were,

1. The pyrrhichius, called by Baccheios the hegemon, not admitted by Aristoxenus, and described, under the name of proceleusmaticus, as mean and vulgar, by Aristides, [musical notation: th ar / ar th]

In the Iambic or Triple species.

2. The iambus, [musical notation: ar th]

3. The iambus with dissolved thesis[1], [musical notation: ar th]

4. The reversed iambus[2], [musical notation: th ar]

5. The three-time foot with a two-time arsis, [musical notation: ar th]

6. The same dissolved[3], [musical notation]

---

[1] Psellus, in Westphal, *Fragmente*, p. 76, ἄρσει καὶ διπλῇ βάσει. See also Gevaert, *La Mus. de l' Ant.* Vol. II. p. 106, where this foot is called the iambic tribrach.

[2] Gevaert, *La Mus. de l' Ant.* Vol. II. p. 65. Examples occur in Greek notation in Bellermann's *Anonymus*.

[3] Psellus, in Westphal, *Fragmente*, p. 77.

7. The trochee or choree, 3/8 [th ar notes]

The word trochee, from *trochos*, a wheel, denotes something that runs swiftly and smoothly. Trochaic measure was usually in quick *tempo*. The word choree alludes to the dance, *choros*.

8. The semantic trochee, 3/2 [th ar notes]

9. The orthios has a four-time arsis and an eight-time thesis,
3/2 [notes]

The last two have a religious character.

10. The tribrach, or dissolved trochee. This had a light and somewhat trivial character, 3/8 [th ar notes]

11. The molossus, a weighty and solemn form of tribrach, whose single "times" had the value of two primary times,

3/4 [th ar notes]

12. The cyclical dactyl, with an irrational thesis, 3/8 [th ar notes]

13. The cyclical anapæst, 3/8 [ar th notes]

14. The choreic dactyl described by Aristides (see p. 29),
3/8 [th ar notes]

In the Dactylic or Even species.

15. The dactyl, 4/8 [th ar notes]

16. The double proceleusmaticus, 4/8 [th ar notes]

17. The spondee, 2/4 [th ar notes]

The spondee is derived from *spondai*, libations, owing to the solemn hymns that were sung during the ceremony of pouring out drink offerings to the gods. The spondee has always been more or less associated with religious music, and forms the rhythmical basis of most modern church hymns.

18. The major spondee[1], 𝄵 $\stackrel{th}{\d}\stackrel{ar}{\d}$

The solemnity associated with the simple spondee is intensified in the major spondee. Handel uses it with overpowering effect in the chorus of "Judas Maccabaeus," "We never will bow down to the rude stock and sculptured stone," where he changes from triple to spondaic measure at the words "We worship God, and God alone."

19. The anapæst, $\frac{4}{8}$ $\stackrel{ar}{\eighthrest\eighthrest}$ | $\stackrel{th}{\d}$

The anapæst is the reverse of the dactyl, and is thus alluded to by Dionysius of Halicarnassus, App. A, 10. It has a lively and energetic character, and was specially used in choral marches and processions. The songs composed by Tyrtaeus for the Spartan army in the second Messenian war were in anapæstic rhythm.

The Pæonic or Quintuple species.

20. The simple or "two-limbed" pæon, $\frac{5}{8}$

This is also called the cretic. It may begin with a three-time arsis, $\frac{5}{8}$

21. The bacchic pæon, $\frac{5}{8}$

22. Another form is, $\frac{5}{8}$

23. Yet another is, $\frac{5}{8}$

But according to Hephaestion, the cretic is the only one of the above five-time feet that is suitable for melody.

24. The pæon epibatos, $\frac{5}{4}$

This is a grand form of pæon, in which each beat has the value of two primary times.

25. The compound pæon, $\frac{5}{8}$

---

[1] Aristides Quintilianus. See Gevaert, Vol. II. p. 36.

This is really not a "simple" foot, since it is supposed to be made up of a trochee and a pyrrhichius. The pæon, says Aristoxenus, can be divided in the proportion of 4:1, but this arrangement is unrhythmical.

Amongst the *Oxyrhynchus Papyri*, published in 1898, there is a newly discovered fragment of the Rhythmical Elements of Aristoxenus, from which we learn that the pæon "may consist of five component syllables, and therefore, evidently, of five primary times also. A continuous use would not be made of such a rhythm; for its character is quite alien to the pæon, and the feet previously mentioned. It might, however, be used, if its especial appropriateness in combination with other feet should commend it, though, as a general rule, owing to the difficulty previously raised, it is perhaps better to leave untried uses which exhibit mixed rhythms not approved by common taste. Else why should not this form be employed (? by the dactyl) and anapæst[1]?" The reason that Aristoxenus objects to giving five primary times to the pæon is that the ancients considered a succession of short notes mean and vulgar, as we have seen, by Aristides' reference to the proceleusmaticus (p. 41). There are, however, examples of this form of pæon in the Delphic Hymn to Apollo, and it will be noticed that Aristoxenus, as a true artist, allows the rule to be broken where it can be done effectively. Would that we might recover yet more of his work!

Simple feet could occasionally be represented by a single note; *i.e.* the triple species by a three-time long, ♩·, the even species by a four-time long, 𝅗𝅥, and the quintuple by a five-time long, 𝅗𝅥♪. This extension of syllables is called τονή, and in analysing the rhythmical construction of Greek verse the investigators have been able, by means of these long notes, whose positions are found by the context, to carry out Aristoxenus' law that rhythm must be easily understood, and agreeable to the aisthēsis. Aristides and his translator Capella call these notes "peripleo[2]," *i.e.* "very full," since they are greater than the normal two-primary-time value; and "rhythmoeides," *i.e.* "peculiar to the rhythm," since they help to maintain the flow of rhythm. Another "rhythmoeides" note is the semiquaver in the cyclical dactyl and cyclical anapæst. This is called by Aristides "strongulos," *i.e.* "compact," or "terse." He adds that such notes "are hurried more than is proper."

---

[1] Grenfell and Hunt, *Oxyrhynchus Papyri*, Part I. p. 18.
[2] Westphal, *Fragmente*, p. 50.

It will be noticed that the feet numbered 8, 9, 18, and the pæon epibatos described on page 38, contain the values of, respectively, 12, 8, and 10 primary times, instead of the 3, 4, and 5 associated with the simple feet of the triple, quadruple and quintuple species. This lengthening of the individual notes is merely a method of producing a very slow movement, and corresponds to our *tempo*-expression "*Largo*."

Let us see how the above simple forms are applied in modern music. But first we must explain that if a two-time thesis is divided into two separate notes in the melody and sung *legato*, the effect is almost the same as if the thesis had only a single note, as far as the rhythmical force is concerned. The foot remains the same, but there is a difference of scheme, as explained on page 37.

The idea may perhaps be best shown by an example of the bowing of the violin. The passage

Ex. 8.   (*a*)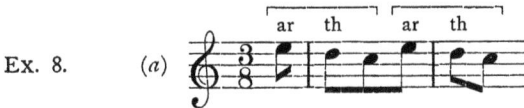

played with three separate bows in each foot consists of two tribrachs.

The same played thus,

(*b*)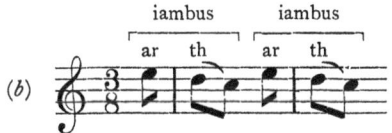

has the effect of two iambuses, and thus,

(*c*)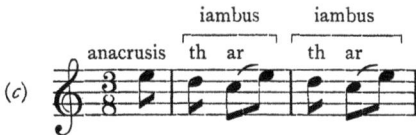

of two reversed iambuses, preceded by an anacrusis.

So strongly was this effect of the singing of one syllable to several notes felt at the period when Plain-song was first being noted down, that two or more sounds joined together on the same syllable in what we call the *legato* manner, were, in many cases, not considered as so many separate notes, but a compound "note" which varied its pitch. This "note" was therefore represented by a single "*figura*" in the neumes, and when mensural music arose such "figurae," "figures," or compound "notes," were represented by ligatures (Italian, *legatura*). The complicated rules about ligatures took their rise from the idea that notes thus bound together were one sound only. It is true that the Greeks did not look upon them thus, but considered that the rhythm was divided in one way in the words and another in the melody. But as the poetry was the predominant partner, the foot took its name from the words, not the melody, and an iambic combination of syllables sung to a tribrach of notes would remain iambic.

Schubert's song, "Des Müllers Blumen," is an example of iambic rhythm.

Ex. 9. Schubert, "Des Müllers Blumen."

The opening phrase of the song, shown in Ex. 9, consists of four iambuses, or, if we prefer it, *quasi*-iambuses, as explained in Ex. 8 *b*, and this form continues throughout the first four lines of the poem. These lines refer to the flowers and the stream. In the next two lines, which complete the stanza, there is a change of idea, the singer referring more directly to his own personal feelings. This change is subtly and beautifully conveyed by a change in the melody from iambuses to trochees. It is No. 7 of the Aristoxenian "differences" explained on page 37.

Ex. 10.

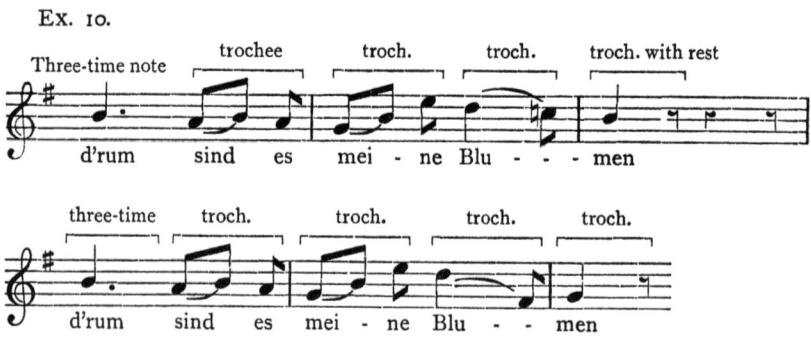

An example of dactylic rhythm may be quoted from Schubert's "Mein!"

Ex. 11. Schubert, "Mein!"

The form of the words might suggest spondees. But if the melody were in spondees a certain heaviness would result, out of keeping with the lively character of the sentiment. The composer, by "dissolving" the alternate arses into two notes, and thus forming dactyls, gives the melody a lightness of movement which seems exactly to express the sentiment of the singer. The effect is still further lightened later on by the use of the proceleusmatic form

Anapæstic rhythm occurs throughout Schubert's "Des Baches Wiegenlied." Not only the words, but the melody and the accompaniment are anapæstic.

Ex. 12. Schubert, "Des Baches Wiegenlied."

Examples of quintuple rhythm are rare in modern music. But we have an actual Greek example, words, melody, and rhythm, in the Delphic Hymn to Apollo, from which we select a few bars as an example of this rhythm.

Ex. 13. From Gevaert, "La Mélopée Antique," p. 402. Hymn to Apollo discovered at Delphi in 1893.

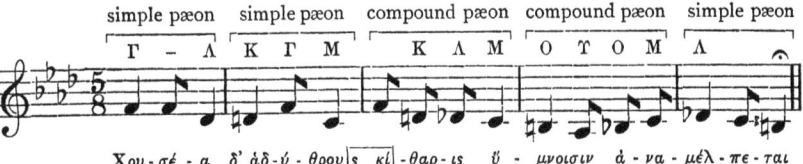

Our capacity for hearing several melodies at once, an outcome of centuries of familiarity with counterpoint, enables us to combine the species simultaneously. Thus, in one of the most beautiful of Chopin's Waltzes, spondees (even measure) are combined with the uneven measure of the molossus and ionicus, to be described in the next chapter.

Ex. 14. Chopin, Waltz, op. 42.

What a graceful and imaginative rhythmical effect! and how easily destroyed by the slightest misunderstanding on the part of the performer, who out of the "eurhythm" of the composer might produce the "arrhythm" alluded to by Aristoxenus.

CHAPTER V

Various significations of the term "rhythm"—The divisions of rhythmical phrases into thesis and arsis—Compound feet—Complexity of rhythm in ancient instrumental accompaniment to songs—Necessity for the limitation of the magnitude of phrases—The Aristoxenian theory of the magnitudes that are capable of rhythmical division.

THE word "rhythm," like most other musical terms, is used by the Greeks in more than one sense. This would cause them no more difficulty than our own terms give us. For example, when we meet with the word "note" in a modern musical treatise, we know by the context whether it signifies a particular sound, or the sign by which that sound is indicated in writing, or the key of the pianoforte that corresponds to the sound and written sign. All three things are equally designated as "note" by us, and it is conceivable that when, in some two thousand years time, English, German or French shall have become dead languages, and the then living people wish to learn something of our musical art from fragmentary treatises, they may find words with more than one technical signification a little perplexing.

The term rhythm is applied in three ways: (1) in the sense already explained in Chapter III; (2) a single foot is sometimes called a rhythm; and (3) a whole phrase or sentence is called a rhythm.

Likewise the two words *chronos* and *pous*, meaning, respectively, time and foot, are each applied in several ways. Primary time is by now familiar to the reader. But Aristoxenus and Aristides apply the word *chronos* to the thesis and arsis, respectively, of a foot, and again to a group of feet, and, further, to the whole phrase. The thesis and arsis are called *chronoi podikoi*, "foot-times"; the time occupied by a group of feet is *chronos rhythmopœias idios*, "time appropriated to the rhythmopœia," and the whole phrase is called an "eight-time," "sixteen-time," &c., phrase or foot, analogously to the way in which the verse-lines of our hymns are often described by the number of syllables they contain.

In Example 15 we have four iambuses. The iambus, as our readers know (p. 41), is divided into two portions, in the ratio 1 : 2. These portions are the *chronoi podikoi*, "foot-times," and the iambic *chronoi podikoi* are therefore in the relation 1 : 2.

Ex. 15. Beethoven, "Die Zufriedenheit."

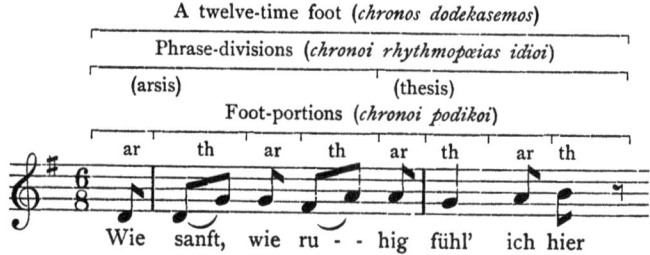

The *chronoi rhythmopœias idioi*, "times peculiar to the rhythmopœia," divide the complete phrase into two parts, one being arsis and the other thesis. We propose to call these two parts "phrase-divisions." They are shown in Ex. 15 by the barring, but, contrary to the Greek method, modern musicians do not consider these larger divisions as having the relation of thesis and arsis.

Thus, according to Greek theory, Ex. 15 is in triple rhythm, but duple phrase-division. We moderns look to the foot only, not to the phrase-division for our arsis and thesis.

Aristides[1] speaks of "Pairs of rhythms" (syzygies), that is, "pairs of feet." Amongst them is the compound foot called Ionicus:

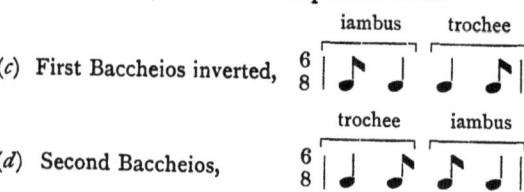

that is, the ionicus which commences on a greater note. For convenience we will anglicise the technical term as "First ionicus."

(*b*) Ionicus a minore commencing with a lesser note, "Second ionicus,"

and the Baccheios, another compound foot:

---

[1] Westphal, *Fragmente*, pp. 55 et seq. A syzygy is a pair of feet, one of which is a thesis-foot, the other an arsis-foot.

It will be noticed that in these examples the foot contains six primary times in each case, but that the diæresis, or distribution of accents and values, differs, thereby producing different æsthetic effects.

Aristides also describes a species of rhythm called "mixed[1]." Amongst the mixed rhythms are two dochmiacs, the first of which is a combination of the iambic and pæonic species,

Ex. 17. (*a*) First dochmiac, $\frac{3}{8}$ ♪ ♩ | $\frac{5}{8}$ ♩ ♪ ♩ | (iambus, pæon)

and the second is a combination of all three simple species,

(*b*) Second dochmiac, $\frac{3}{8}$ ♪ ♩ | $\frac{2}{4}$ ♩ ♫ | $\frac{5}{8}$ ♩ ♪ ♩ (iambus, dactyl, pæon)

iambic, dactylic, and pæonic. "Even more clever mixtures than these," says our author, "are used."

A succession of first dochmiacs is perfectly gratifying to the æsthetic sense, and fulfils Aristoxenus' condition, if we imagine a rest or rests between them. Westphal believed that this should be the case, and the recent discovery of a few notes of the music of Euripides' "Orestes" seems to confirm his view in a remarkable manner. In this fragment an instrumental note frequently occurs between the dochmiacs, making the rhythm of the passage work out somewhat as follows[2]:

(*c*) $\frac{6}{8}$ ♫♫ | ♩ ♪♩ ᛍ | ♩ ᛍ (iambic species, pæon, rest, instrument)

According to Aristides, the word *dochmius* means aslant, oblique, and the term *dochmiac* refers to the varied nature of the rhythmopœia, which "cannot be considered as straightforward[3]."

The prosodiacs are compounded of a pyrrhic, an iambus, and a trochee:

Ex. 18. (*a*) First prosodiac, ♫ ♪♩ ♩♪ (pyrr. iamb. troch.)

---

[1] Westphal, *Fragmente*, p. 59.

[2] For a fuller discussion of this question we may perhaps be allowed to refer to an article by the present writer entitled "Notes on a fragment of the music of Orestes," in the *Classical Review*, July 1894.

[3] Westphal, *Fragmente*, p. 59. For a more recent view see App. C.

or the same group preceded by an iambus:

(*b*) Second prosodiac,

Since the triple takes a larger place than the duple species in the prosodiacs, it is natural to consider them as compound feet in triple rhythm. In this case it seems difficult to express them in modern notation in a way that will satisfy the æsthetic sense easily enough to be of practical use. But if we express them in duple time, a satisfactory rhythm results:

Ex. 19.

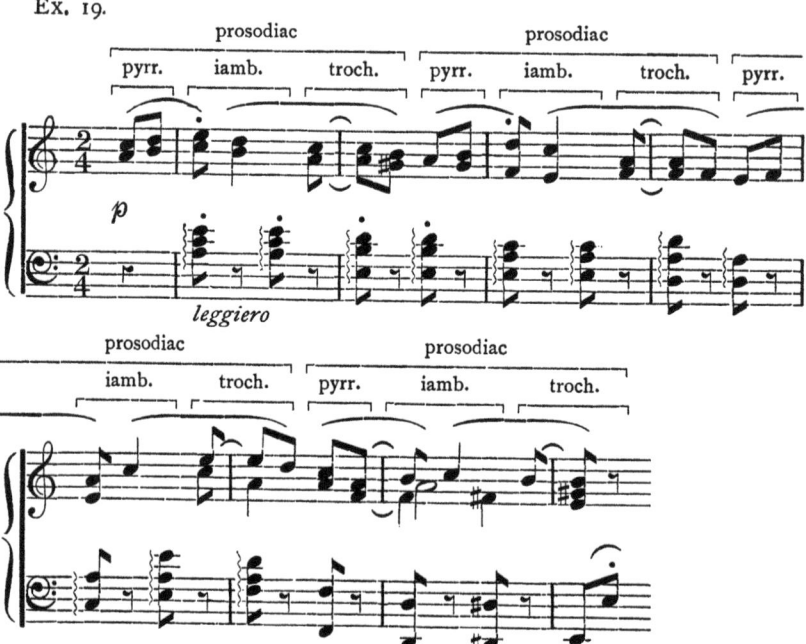

The second prosodiac becomes satisfactory with a quaver rest:

Ex. 19 *a*.

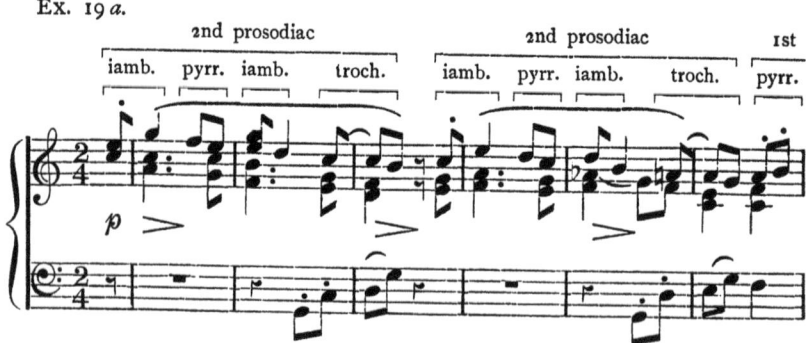

THE ENOPLIUS

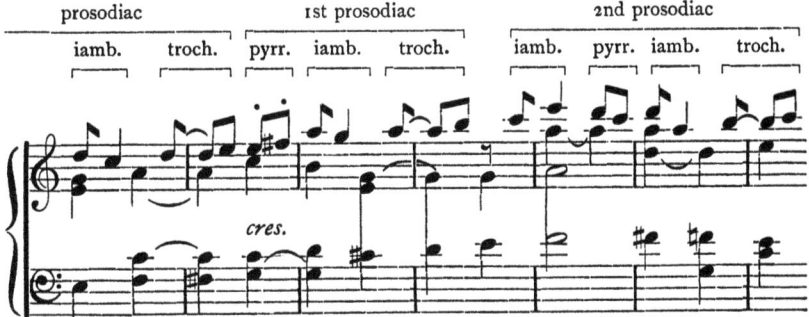

The word "prosodiac" applied to rhythm must not be confounded, as is frequently the case in ancient MSS., with "prosody," a song sung to music, hence, the accents placed over words that were to be sung, to indicate where musical inflections should occur.

It will be noticed in the two foregoing examples that the melody alone takes the prosodiac form, while the accompanying parts are free. This is natural to all modern music: any melody may be accompanied by a part that differs from it in scheme, though the principal accents of both coincide. A passage in Plutarch seems to infer that some similar kind of complexity was not unknown to instrumental music in Greek classical times. "In the rhythmopœia," says Plutarch, "the ancients (*i.e.* the classical musicians) employed a greater variety than at present. Indeed, they used considerable complexity of rhythm, and even greater complications in instrumental music." (App. A, 11.)

A passage in Plato's "Republic" objects to boys being taught to accompany themselves on an instrument when singing, "by playing a melody differing from that of the song as do the professional musicians." This is what every singer does now-a-days; but how far it extended with the Greeks we cannot know. Possibly, like the lute players of the sixteenth century of our era, they extemporised their accompaniments on the kithara, and like our musicians, used the instrument to complete the rhythm when the verse was catalectic.

Baccheios describes yet another compound foot, the Enoplius, which, he says, consists of an iambus, a pyrrhic, a trochee, and an iambus. Like the prosodiac, this cannot be represented in modern notation with a triple time-signature; but with 2/4 it works out in the following energetic rhythm:

Ex. 19 *b*.

Its name comes from *enoplos*, meaning armed, and it was especially adapted to war-tunes. If we are right in representing the prosodiac and enoplius in even, instead of uneven measure, it would seem that the Greeks were fully alive to the value of syncopation for giving energy to music especially adapted to action. The *prosodios* was a processional song, the *enoplios* a war-song. Both were, according to our suggestion, in syncopated rhythms, and everyone who is familiar with the national music of the Magyars knows the intensity of energy that can be expressed by a strongly marked syncopation.

We now come to the consideration of the complete rhythmical phrase. A melody, however varied, if continued too long without a break, or some kind of close, produces insupportable weariness. The rhythmical feeling is incapable of continuous exertion: hence it is found necessary to break a melody into short sections called phrases, or rhythms, or periods, by what an old German writer calls "resting-places for the mind." A melody that is carried on too long without landmarks is like the utterances of an incompetent public speaker, who pours out a stream of words, the meaning of which, owing to the unbroken flow, we have a difficulty in following, and a sense of weariness soon becomes perceptible.

It is for this reason that written prose is broken into sentences by punctuation signs. In poetry, the lines, technically called verses, answer the same purpose as the sentences of prose and the sections of melody.

In modern music these sentences or phrases are indicated by various forms of harmonic close, and the closes, in ordinary cases, occur at intervals of from two to four feet.

It seems strange that the length of time occupied by a whole movement of a symphony or sonata or a chorus in an oratorio should be broken into short phrases, occupying a few seconds each: yet such is the constitution of the rhythmical sense, that this is necessary if we are to understand and enjoy a work of art. The space of time that we can appreciate is extremely limited, and cannot be extended by cultivation. The phrases of the songs by which the uncultured "folk" expresses its feelings are as long as the longest in cultivated music.

The Greeks were naturally cognisant of this limitation, and Aristoxenus lays down its laws. To him, any rhythmical combination of two or more notes is a "foot," simple or compound; and a compound foot may extend to what we call a whole phrase.

"The smallest of the feet, having a size that is easily embraced by the sense, are understood at once, by means of their two portions (arsis and thesis). With the greater feet the contrary is the case: having a magnitude difficult to be grasped by the sense, they need many notes, so that the magnitude of the whole foot, being divided into many parts, becomes more easily understood[1]."

This sentence of Aristoxenus explains why in our slow movements the feet are often more broken[2] into notes of smaller value than in quick movements. The mind only with difficulty grasps comparatively large intervals of time, and the effort leads to weariness. In a slow movement the feet occupy relatively large portions of time, but when these are broken up by means of small notes, all difficulty and heaviness disappear.

It is not necessary always to break the time by actual sounds, for it may be done by the bâton of the conductor if necessary. To put the matter to a practical test, let a conductor endeavour to make an amateur choir sing, for example, Dowland's madrigal "Awake, sweet love," in which the *tempo* is slow, and the notes mostly minims (semantic trochaic, page 42), with three beats to the bar. He will soon find a strong desire on the part of the choir to get faster than his beat. Owing to the cause explained by Aristoxenus, the long notes are difficult to sustain at their proper value, and, unless the choir is very experienced, it may fall to pieces.

Now let the conductor break the time into smaller sections by beating six crotchets in the bar, and all difficulty will at once vanish. The movement of the bâton calls upon the eye to aid in measuring the time into smaller values than the notes, thus making the rhythm easier to grasp by the performers. And, as we already know from Aristoxenus (see p. 24), time may be divided by the movement of a body as well as by sound.

To the ancients, a simple foot consists of two portions only, the arsis and thesis, though these may be divided, so that there can be three, four or five notes in a simple foot[3]. A compound foot may have a great many more notes, and these have to do with the rhythmopœia. "We must," says Aristoxenus, "distinguish between the values that are natural to the foot, and those that are brought

---

[1] Aristox. *Stoicheia*, Westphal, *Fragmente*, p. 33, line 11.

[2] In this connection it may be worth while to notice that mensural music was anciently sometimes called "*musica fracta*," "broken music," in allusion to the breaking up of the time occupied by the lengthy plain-song notes by means of figuration in the accompanying parts.

[3] Westphal, *Fragmente*, p. 33. Aristoxenus here limits the number of notes in a simple foot to four, but there are five notes in several of the bars in the Delphic Hymns.

about by the rhythmopœia." A simple fugue theme with its counter-subject will serve to show the distinction.

Ex. 20. Rheinberger, Organ Sonata, op. 27.

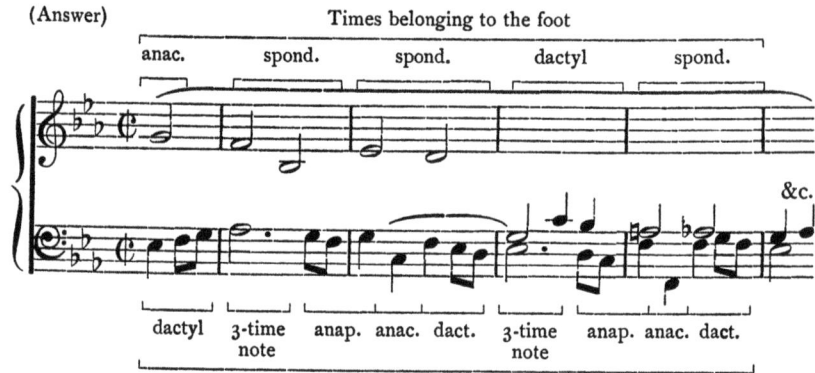

In this fugue the subject is given out in grand major spondees, with plenty of organ tone. The answer, which we quote, begins with the anacrusis[1]. The counter-subject, by its smaller notes, produces movement against the dignified spondees. The principle is exactly the same as that which we applied to Dowland's madrigal. In Greek parlance, the theme divides the time of the whole into the unbroken thesis and arsis of the simple feet, while the counter-subject breaks these into smaller portions by a varied rhythmopœia, as our imaginary conductor broke up the long "times" with his bâton. The importance of the rhythmopœia, "the art of constructing rhythm," is shown by this example. It is comparatively easy to write a melody in simple spondees; it requires more skill to accompany the spondees with a striking rhythmopœia, and when that skill reaches the height attained by a Beethoven, a Bach or a Brahms, it becomes a manifestation of genius.

Aristoxenus looks at the phrase, not from the modern point of view of how many bars or feet it contains, but how many primary times. To him, as we have said, a phrase is only an enlarged form of foot. "The smallest foot that can be used in rhythmopœia is that of three times. A two-time foot would require too many beats. The three-time foot belongs to the iambic species, that is, to the ratio of 2 : 1."

---

[1] Contrast is produced in the rhythmical feeling by the fact that while the subject is thetic, the answer is anacrusic. Aristoxenus' 7th "difference," p. 37.

" In the second place stand the feet of four-time value. These are in the dactylic or even species. In the third place stands the foot of five-time value. This can have two ratios, either 4 : 1, or 2 : 3 ; but the ratio 4 : 1 is not rhythmical[1]."

Ex. 21 a.

In Ex. 21 a the feet are divided in the ratio 4 : 1, which Aristoxenus says is arrhythmical. It sounds halting and unsatisfactory.

Ex. 21 b.

In Ex. 21 b the same passage is divided in the ratio 3 : 2, and becomes easily comprehensible to those who are familiar with quintuple rhythm.

"In the fourth place is the six-time foot. This is capable of two kinds of division, for it can be even or uneven."

Ex. 22 a.   Even species.

In this example the arsis and thesis of the six-time foot each contains three primary times, and they are therefore in even ratio to one another.

Ex. 22 b.   Uneven species.

Here the six primary times are divided into an arsis of two and a thesis of four times : hence the foot belongs to the uneven species.

" The ratio 5 : 1 is arrhythmical[2]."

---

[1] Westphal, *Fragmente*, p. 36.   [2] Westphal, *Fragmente*, p. 37.

But Schumann uses the ratio 5:1 with beautiful effect in his Third Symphony:

Ex. 23. Schumann, Symphony No. 3, Scherzo.

The fundamental scheme here is the stately molossus, 𝅗𝅥 𝅗𝅥 𝅗𝅥 while we are charmed with the unusual phrasing of the melody, by which the time is broken into smaller fragments than those of the molossus, on the principle described on p. 56.

"The seven-time magnitude (*megethos*) has no diæresis, for of the three ratios of which the number seven is capable, 3:4, 2:5, and 1:6, none is of rhythmical power."

But the moderns occasionally use a seven-time bar, or, what is the same thing, an alternation of four-time and three-time bars. In Brahms' "Variations on a Hungarian theme," op. 21, No. 2, the seven-time phrases are divided in the ratio of 3:4.

"The eight-time foot is of the even species, for of the possibilities of dividing 8, namely, 4:4, 1:7, 2:6, 3:5, only the first is available for rhythm[1]."

The eight-time foot can only be divided into thesis and arsis in the ratio 4:4. This is our two-bar or two-foot phrase in even rhythm, of which examples are to be found in nearly every large composition. But do we divide it into thesis and arsis? Yes, when we write it in a compound even-time bar, but not when we distribute it over two bars as in Ex. 24.

Ex. 24. R. Wagner, "Der Fliegende Holländer."

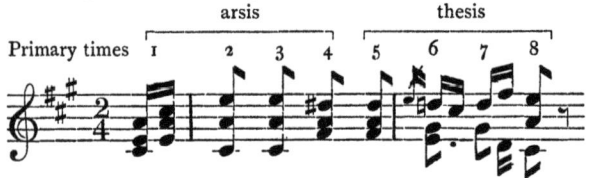

Mein Schatz ist auf dem Meere draus

We have divided this phrase into thesis and arsis in the Greek method. Modern musicians, as a rule, look no further than the thesis and arsis of the bar, and do not recognise the fact that they often

[1] Westphal, *Fragmente*, p. 37.

ARSIS AND THESIS 59

divide a two-bar phrase into these parts by means of the notation. They do it instinctively and unconsciously. On the other hand they just as often do not divide it thus, and it is quite possible that to many it will seem far-fetched to suggest the above division of Ex. 24.

But if we consider that every group of notes, however small, has its thesis and arsis, and that a bar in slow *tempo* may contain a very large number of such groups for its own thesis and arsis, we shall see that it is merely carrying the principle to its logical conclusion if we apply it, in the Greek manner, to the whole of a short phrase. An example from Beethoven's last sonata, though not in four-time, has all its divisions so clearly produced in the notes, that we use it to explain the matter more closely.

Ex. 25. Beethoven, Sonata, op. 111.

The two bars quoted in Ex. 25 exhibit no less than four series of theses and arses simultaneously. Those numbered from 1 to 3 are recognised by musicians, but those numbered 4 are in accordance with the Greek theory of extending the idea of thesis and arsis to the whole phrase. It is probably on account of our use of harmony and counterpoint that we do not feel such rhythmical divisions so acutely as the ancients.

We can conceive the theme of Ex. 25 written in *tempo moderato* with two feet in the bar, thus,

Ex. 25 a.

in which case the Greek idea of phrase accentuation would be realised; and this idea was carried still further, as we shall show later.

With the description of the eight-time foot the fragment of Aristoxenus' work breaks off, and the rest is lost. But this loss can, to a great extent, be repaired, as Westphal has shown. He has reconstructed the missing portion of Aristoxenus' treatise by analogy with the above quoted part, and explains his method thus: " This is one of the most important parts, but the loss is not absolutely irreparable. For what remains gives us a safe guide by which we can restore the remaining 'magnitudes' from the eight-time onwards, and can then continue the broken course of the manuscript to its end, through what is known to us from the quotations of Psellus, the Paris Fragment, Aristides, and his translator Martianus Capella. A mistake here is practically impossible, since the course which the restoration must take is clearly indicated by what has gone before[1]."

We paraphrase the description of the remaining magnitudes from Westphal's *Aristoxenos*, p. 47 onwards.

Ex. 26. Brahms, Pianoforte Quartet, Op. 25.

[1] Westphal, *Aristoxenos*, Vol. I. p. 36.

In the sixth place are the feet of nine-time magnitude. Of the various ratios by which the number nine can be divided, only that of 3 : 6 is rhythmical. The nine-time foot is therefore of the iambic or triple species.

In Ex. 26 the nine primary times are distinctly heard in the violoncello part, while the violin and viola play an iambic-natured melody above them. Westphal himself quotes several examples from the works of J. S. Bach in illustration.

The ten-time magnitude is divisible into the pæonic and the dactylic species. In the first case the ten-time measure is a pæon epibatos (page 43, No. 24), whose five "times" are each of two primary values, and the ratio of the thesis to arsis is as 6 : 4.

Ex. 27. Hugo Wolf, "Jägerlied."

Zierlich ist des Vogels Tritt im Schnee,

In Ex. 27 the ten-time phrase is contained in a single bar, and the same construction is repeated in the succeeding bars, while the musical phrasing corresponds exactly to that of the words. The analysis shows the arsis and thesis of the above-mentioned pæon epibatos.

Or the ten-time phrase may be divided into two pæons having the ratio 5 : 5, in which case it will belong to the even or dactylic species, as in Ex. 28.

Ex. 28. Tschaïkowsky, "Pathetic Symphony."

A magnitude of eleven primary times is incapable of rhythmical arrangement.

The possible divisions of the twelve-time magnitude for rhythmical purposes are 4 : 8 (iambic), and 6 : 6 (dactylic).

Ex. 29. Bach, "Wohlt. Kl." No. 1.

Ex. 29 shows a fugue-subject containing twelve primary times, divided in the ratio 8:4.

Ex. 30 a. Bach, " Matthäus-Passion."

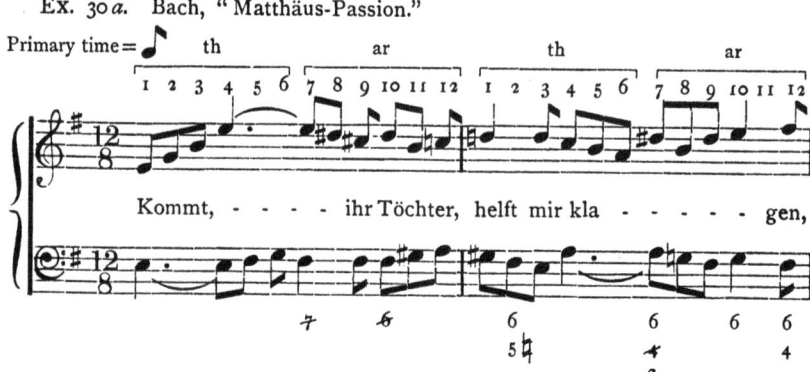

Here the twelve-time phrase is divided in the ratio of 6:6. The arsis is marked off from the thesis by a change of harmony on a sustained note, a construction which is several times repeated. In other places in this wonderful chorus the second choir enters with interjections on the arsis, never on the thesis. Towards the end, where the words "Sehet ihn aus Lieb und Huld," which refer to the object of compassion, rather than to the personal feeling of the speaker, the composer makes the same musical theme re-enter with a change in the order of its thesis and arsis. (The seventh "difference" of Aristoxenus.)

Ex. 30 b.

The "difference" may be merely the result of chance, but we prefer to think that the composer was so keenly sensitive in his rhythmical feeling that he deliberately chose the 12/8 rather than the 6/8 signature, in order to give effect to the thesis and arsis of the phrase, and that he instinctively changed the order with a change of sentiment, just as the Greeks might have done.

Magnitudes of thirteen and fourteen times are incapable of rhythmical division.

Magnitudes of fifteen times can be iambic or pæonic. In the first case the division will be in the ratio 5 : 10, equivalent to the simple iambic measure 1 : 2. In the second the division will be 6 : 9, which is equivalent to 2 : 3, the pæonic simple-measure ratio.

A rhythmopœia so complicated as 5 : 10 would seem almost impossible to modern feeling. Yet Vincent D'Indy has used it very effectively in several places in his pianoforte sonata, op. 63, one of which we quote.

Ex. 31. Vincent D'Indy, Pianoforte Sonata, op. 63.

The *tempo* is very rapid, and the "iambic" nature of the phrase is brought out by the stronger accentuation of the bars which we have allotted to the thesis. The phrase here quoted is preceded and succeeded by "dactylic" or even phrases of two bars each.

In the 6 : 9 division the phrase has a two-fold, followed by a three-fold group of simple triple feet, or *vice versa*. A very beautiful example occurs in every phrase of Schubert's song "Ungeduld," in which the melody has the pæonic, or 3 : 2 construction, while the accompaniment fills in the time between the phrases, as described

Ex. 32. Schubert, "Ungeduld."

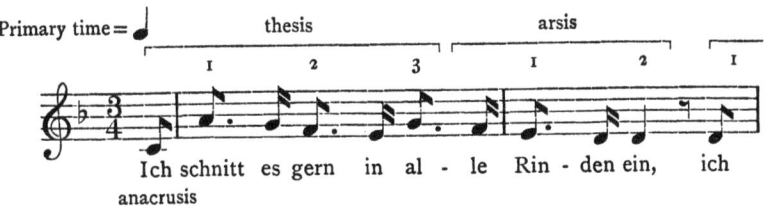

64 ARSIS AND THESIS

in the account of the dochmius, page 51, thus obviating any halting effect which such quintuple phrasing might have to modern ears.

We have considered the first bar here to be the phrase-thesis, because it contains the highest, and therefore the most prominent note in the melody; a construction which is followed in all the succeeding phrases of the song. It will be noticed that the musical rhythmopœia exactly coincides with the metre of the words, which are in iambic pentameters.

The fifteen-time magnitude is used several times in succession in Schubert's first pianoforte sonata, without any complementary times between the phrases.

Ex. 33. Schubert, Sonata, op. 42.
Scherzo. Allegro vivace.

Here the repetition of the forcible accentuation of the opening notes seems to suggest that the first nine times are the phrase-thesis, and that the diæresis should be in the ratio 6:9, *i.e.* 2:3, pæonic. If we are right in thus dividing the passage, it will be a pæonic phrase in triple rhythm. The division can easily be made appreciable by a very slight augmentation of tone at the tenth "time." Of the æsthetic value of this *nuance* we must leave our readers to judge by practical experiment on a good-toned pianoforte.

Fifteen-time magnitudes also occur in the Trio of Schubert's sonata in E flat, op. 122.

The sixteen-time phrase can only be divided in the proportion of 8:8, *i.e.* 1:1. It is therefore of the even species. It is the greatest magnitude of this species, for we cannot grasp anything greater in even rhythm. "Even rhythm begins with the two-time, and ends with the sixteen-time. Beyond this we cannot perceive the nature of rhythm," Aristides. See App. A, 12. It may be exemplified by a four-bar phrase thus:

Ex. 34. R. Franz, "Herbstsorge."

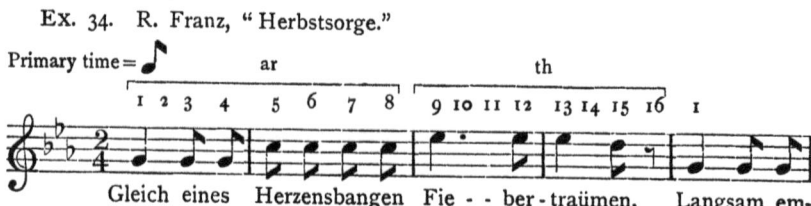

Here we have tentatively allotted the last half-phrase to the thesis, because the melody rises to a high note in it: but the succeeding phrases do not, as in the Schubert song, Ex. 32, follow the same melodic construction, and this is a case in which we moderns do not feel the phrase-divisions in the same way as did the Greeks.

Ex. 35. J. S. Bach, Fantasie und Fugue.

This example shows an instrumental sixteen-time phrase.

The rhythmopœia consists of broad major spondees, lightened by occasional subdivisions, and the end of the phrase is clearly marked by the half-close. Much of the rest of the movement is divided by closes into phrases of four bars, as in the above quotation, but the divisions are more or less deftly concealed, so as to make as little break as possible in the continuity. In dividing the phrase we have been led by the rise of melody to assign the latter half to the thesis: but that is a matter of opinion, and many musicians will perhaps be unable to recognise a difference of this nature between the two halves of the phrase.

A seventeen-time magnitude is incapable of rhythmical division.

A phrase of eighteen times can be divided into even portions, 9:9, but this would overstep the limit of perceptibility for even portions; therefore this magnitude cannot be used in the relation of 9:9. It is available in that of 6:12, in which case the phrase-diæresis is iambic. This is the largest magnitude in iambic division that is appreciable by the æsthetic sense, as we learn from Aristides, who says, "The uneven species begins with the trisemos and goes as far as the eighteen-time magnitude: beyond this we do not perceive the nature of rhythm[1]." App. A, 12.

Two eighteen-time phrases occur at the beginning of the Vorspiel

---

[1] Westphal, *Fragmente*, p. 53.

to "Tristan und Isolde." They are separated by rests, which make an "empty" portion of no less than six primary times in duration.

Ex. 36. R. Wagner, "Tristan und Isolde."
Langsam und schmachtend.

The opening *crescendo* notes, in unison, of which the rhythmical form is inappreciable unless we watch the conductor, lead to a *sforzando* discord, which is dwelt on until it resolves on a new discord. The vagueness of the rhythm, the dwelling for apparently indefinite times on the discords before resolving them, fully realise the word "schmachtend," "longing," "yearning."

The eighteen-time foot was represented in ancient poetry by the Iambic Trimeter, which had many varieties of detail, and was looked upon as one of the most important of metrical forms. It consisted of six simple feet, acatalectic or catalectic, sometimes divided by a cæsura into two unequal portions. Four of the simple feet formed the thesis, and two the arsis, of the trimeter. A great number of rules for its construction are to be found in school books, which seem to complicate the matter, but all are primarily based on æsthetic considerations, apparently unknown to the grammarians, and perhaps too advanced to be given to school boys.

Ex. 37 is an eighteen-time foot from Sophocles' "Antigone," with the melody used in the Bradfield College Greek Theatre in June 1898.

Ex. 37. Sophocles, "Antigone," *v.* 582. As sung at Bradfield College, 1898.

This chorus contains a considerable number of eighteen-time phrases in various forms, intermingled with those of four and three simple feet. We shall have occasion to recur to it again later on.

Modern vocal examples are rare. Schubert, one of the greatest masters of rhythmical effects, certainly uses a number of eighteen-time melodic phrases in his "Täuschung," but the form being a little difficult to the modern perception, he satisfies our feeling by adding a fourth bar in the accompaniment as a sort of echo, making the whole into a "four-bar" phrase. This kind of division of the rhythmical phrase between the voice and pianoforte is a favourite device with Schubert, who obtains some of his most exquisitely imaginative effects from it. We have seen (p. 51) that it is probable that the Greek musicians used the same device.

Ex. 38. Schubert, "Täuschung."

Ein Licht - - tanzt freundlich vor mir her - -

The nineteen-time magnitude has no rhythmical diæresis.

The twenty-time magnitude is only capable of division in the proportion of 8 : 12, *i.e.* 2 : 3. It is rare, both in ancient and modern music, except with Brahms, who has frequently founded compositions on it with excellent effect. It is the even-time Pentapody, the five-foot phrase, found in Brahms' Rhapsody, op. 119, the principal subject of which consists largely of phrases of twenty quavers in length.

The pentapody occurs several times in Pindar's First Pythian Ode. We quote one of them in Ex. 39, with the well-known melody to which it is supposed to have been sung in ancient times.

Ex. 39. Pindar, First Pythian Ode.

ἀμ - - βο - λὰς τεύ - χῃς, ἐ - λε - λι - ζο - μέ - να

Its companion phrases consist of two-, three-, and four-feet phrases, *i.e.* dipodies, tripodies, and tetrapodies.

Of the remaining magnitudes the twenty-one- and twenty-four-time are too large, in the Aristoxenian sense. In the following example a verse of four feet is set, by "extension" of its syllables, to a musical phrase of twenty-four primary times.

Ex. 40. Schubert, "Pilgerweise."

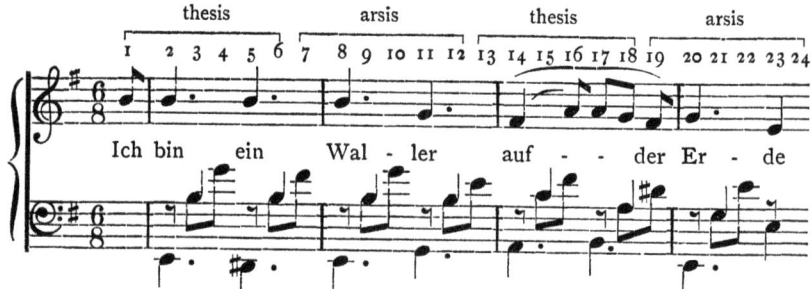

But if we examine it closely we shall find that it seems to divide itself into two half-phrases by the harmony; hence it is, in the Aristoxenian sense, a period of two members, each of which has its own arsis and thesis, as shown in our example.

Magnitudes of twenty-two and twenty-three times are incapable of rhythmical division, but the twenty-five time can be divided in the pæonic ratio of 10:15, equivalent to 2:3. "The twenty-five-time magnitude," says Aristides, "is the greatest length of phrase that can be grasped by our æsthetic feeling[1]."

It would certainly be a highly developed æsthetic sense that could appreciate a single phrase consisting of five quintuple feet, unbroken by any kind of cæsura. We know of no instance in modern music. Tschaïkowsky's well-known movement in the Pathetic Symphony is divided throughout into pairs of feet (ten-time phrases, according to Aristoxenus). In Paderewski's "Chants des Voyageurs" No. 4, the quintuple section falls into phrases of single feet (monopodies). Vincent D'Indy's quintuple movement in op. 63, perhaps the boldest that has yet appeared, falls for the most part into two-feet phrases with occasional three-feet, or fifteen-time phrases.

In the very beautiful quintuple movement of Chopin's Sonata, op. 4, the phrases are for the most part of two bars, or if they are of four, the harmonic construction makes them easy to grasp. There is no case of a five-bar phrase in quintuple rhythm, and we doubt if one could be found in any classical composition.

May it not be that the Aristoxenians, like all the ancients, loved to systematise everything that had to do with figures, and that their

---

[1] Westphal, *Fragmente*, p. 53.

limits of length were merely theoretical? Thus, for the four-time measure, four times four *ought* to be theoretically the limit, and hence the sixteen-time phrase must be the largest in this species. For the five-time, five times five *ought* to be the limit, to round off the theory, though it may not have been a possible magnitude in practice. But we only throw this out as a suggestion.

CHAPTER VI

The Aristoxenian theory of magnitudes and the music of Wagner and Bach—The grouping of feet in pairs—Pindar's First Pythian Ode—Epitritic rhythms in Handel's "Judas Maccabaeus," compared to those of Pindar—Logœdic rhythm as exemplified in Pindar, Sophocles, and Bach—Humorous use of logœdic rhythm by Aristophanes—The employment of quintuple rhythm in ancient comedy and hymnody.

THE Aristoxenian theory of magnitudes with their limitations may appear somewhat laboured; yet music, as we have seen, can only be made comprehensible by some kind of limitation of its rhythmopœia.

But, the reader may say, what about Wagner's music? If we look through the score of "Tristan und Isolde," for example, we find not a single harmonic close, not a musical punctuation, or "resting place for the mind," until the middle of the second scene of the first Act.

It will be remembered that Aristoxenus says of the greater feet that "having a magnitude difficult to be grasped by the sense, they need many notes, so that the magnitude of the whole foot, being divided into many parts, becomes more easily understood."

Wagner's method of making his music understood without the regular recurrence of periodic closes is the same in principle as that of Aristoxenus: there runs throughout it a constant recurrence of short striking rhythmical figures, which take the place of the "many notes" of Aristoxenus. By their means the composer is able to follow every phase of the dramatic feeling without hindrance, and at the same time to make his music acceptable to the "aisthēsis." Wagner, therefore, unconsciously applied the Aristoxenian principle on a large scale.

He was not, however, the first to feel the hindering effect that too pronounced a periodic construction might have in certain cases, for Bach felt it before him, and frequently smoothed over the junctions of phrases, making them weld into one another, as it were, by his treatment of the harmony, while short rhythmical figures make his music acceptable.

The appeal to the imagination by the avoidance of well-defined cadences in much of Bach's music made this composer difficult and impossible to audiences nurtured on Italian methods, and Wagner's more imaginative methods may have helped towards a better understanding of Bach. A comparison of a chorus of Handel with one of Bach is instructive on this point. Handel drives his cadences home with every harmonic device, while Bach uses harmony for just the reverse process. The one strove for immediate popularity, and attained it, the other spoke from the inmost recesses of his religious and imaginative soul to those who could, and still can, feel with him : and this is why his greatest music is so "modern" in character. Yet in his dance music, and in other places where it is appropriate to do so, Bach could make his cadences just as forcible and easy to understand as those of Handel.

With regard to the Aristoxenian theory of an arsis and thesis in the whole phrase, we ourselves feel that passages of small notes naturally divide themselves into pairs or threes, as the case may be, each little group having its arsis and thesis, and that these groups fall into larger groups, till we arrive at the complete bar, as already explained by Ex. 25, page 59. Here, as a rule, we stop, and consider that each of the two or four bars in an ordinary phrase is of equal accentuation. The Greek system of melody, being all in unison, and all for voices, did not make use of the very small notes that are found in our music, and it seems that there was nothing equivalent to the "divisions" in our old operatic bravura songs. Ornaments there were, several of which passed into the neumes of the Church. Their names are given by Bellermann's *Anonymus*, and what little can be gathered about them is collected in Gevaert's *La Musique de l'Antiquité*, Vol. I. pages 386–392. But they seem to have been all subject to the rules of the primary time, and hence were not analogous to our shake, or turn, or the *tremolo* of the violin. The attention of the audience was not divided, as with us, between rhythm, melody, harmony, orchestration, but was concentrated chiefly on rhythm, and being thus more free than we are from other considerations, it is natural that the ancients should be able to carry on their rhythmical sense to the appreciation of the larger thesis and arsis of the phrase to an extent which would be impossible for us.

But there are certain cases in modern music in which, by grouping the bars in pairs, and looking upon each pair as containing an arsis and a thesis in the Aristoxenian sense we can give a greatly enhanced interest to the music. Anyone can try the experiment for himself with movements containing simple bars. With compound bars, such as 6/8, 9/8, &c., the composer himself indicates the arsis and thesis of the pairs of feet.

Let the reader experiment on the following movements of Beethoven. The bars are to be arranged in pairs, of which one is to be looked upon as thesis and the other as arsis, or, what is the same thing, it may be imagined that the music is written in compound instead of simple bars.

Sonata No. 5 in C minor. First movement. Thesis, arsis. The first g of bars 10 and 12 should be considered as the ends of rhythms. The modulating motive, commencing with the key of A flat, is also in the order thesis, arsis, as indicated by the *fp* on the first note. The second subject in E flat is in the same order.

Sonata in F, No. 6. The opening bars in the first movement should be accented in the order thesis, arsis, but the second subject seems to gain in vigour if played in the order arsis, thesis, owing to the rise of melody in its first two bars.

Allegretto. To us it seems that the minuet should be in the order arsis, thesis, while the trio makes a contrast by reversing the order to thesis, arsis.

The *presto* seems to be a subject of sixteen-time "magnitude," divided into arsis of two feet and thesis of two. In this case the chief accent would be on the first note of the third bar. In the course of the movement there occur phrases of two and of one foot.

Sonata No. 7 in D. First movement. The feet seem to demand the order arsis, thesis. The second phrase contains six feet; it is a hexameter, and should have a hardly perceptible cæsura between the D and D sharp of bar 8. In the *pp* minim subject the order should be arsis, thesis.

Minuet. Here again we seem to have a series of twelve-time tetrapodic phrases, divided into an arsis of two and a thesis of two feet, the chief accent occurring on the third bar of each phrase. After the double bar the order is reversed by the *sforzandos*.

In the opening of the *allegretto* of the Sonata in E, No. 9, the first two *crescendo* bars lead to a *sforzando* on the third bar, producing the effect of a division of the phrase into a two-bar arsis followed by a two-bar thesis. Afterwards the theme is broken into pairs of bars, of which the first is arsis, the second thesis (*sforzando*).

The *scherzo* of Sonata in G, No. 10, opens in the same way, the effect of thesis on the second half of the phrase being produced by the entrance of the harmony, as opposed to the unaccompanied melody of the first half. On the repetition of the opening phrase the thesis is enhanced by *sforzando*.

The effect of arsis and thesis applied to pairs of bars is very striking in the *allegro molto* of the Sonata in E flat, No. 13. This movement gains greatly in intensity by being played as in Ex. 41

Ex. 41. Beethoven, op. 27, No. 1.
Allegro molto e vivace.

rather than with an equal accent on each bar; and the same is the case with the *scherzo* of op. 28 and Nos. 15 (in D), 18 (in E flat) and the *allegro molto* of No. 31, op. 110.

It is now time to examine how the various forms of foot and phrase were combined into an artistic whole, which should be characteristic of the ideas to be expressed.

We have one very small fragment of the melody of the great Attic epoch, which is preserved by Athanasius Kircher in his *Musurgia*, and said by him to have been copied from an ancient MS. in the library of the monastery of San Salvatore near Messina. He affirms that the book contained other melodies of the same kind, but, in spite of all search, it cannot be found. The melody obeys a certain rule with regard to the acute accent, which is not hinted at by any of the ancient writers, and is only known from the careful analysis to which recently discovered fragments of Graeco-Roman melody have been subjected. The rule could not possibly have been known to Kircher or his predecessors, and, that the melody almost invariably obeys it, seems to be a very strong proof in favour of its genuineness[1].

The Odes of Pindar, as is well known, were composed to order, in celebration of the victors in the national games. The games consisted of racing, leaping, running, wrestling, and so on, as well as of musical contests, to which the Welsh Eisteddfod perhaps offers the nearest modern analogy. The Pythian games were specially famed for their musical competitions, and the first Pythian Ode commences with a strophe in praise of the lyre, whose patron was Apollo, the god of song and music. The games were part of the worship of the gods, and as victory was the gift of a particular god, the *epinikion*, or song of victory, is more or less a hymn of thanksgiving or praise to the deity who gave the victory.

---

[1] The rule is explained in Monro's *Modes of Ancient Greece*, pp. 90–91.

Expression was kept within bounds by the dread of Nemesis, who would punish any overpraise or presumption on the part of the poet. Moreover, Pindar was an aristocrat, and he wrote for aristocrats; hence there is always a dignified reserve in his style[1].

Ex. 42. Pindar, First Pythian Ode. From Gevaert's *La Mus. de l'Antiquité*, Vol. I.

[1] See Gildersleeve's "Pindar, The Olympian and Pythian Odes," Introductory Essay. (New York, Harper.)

Translation:

"Golden Lyre! Joint possession of Apollo and the black-haired Muses.

"The step of the dancer follows thy festive joy. The singers are guided by thy notes, whensoever thy melodies lead the dance.

"Thou preparest Preludes on thy quivering strings, and disarmest the sharp thunderbolt."

The poem was written to commemorate the winning of the chariot race by Hieron, the Tyrant of Syracuse, in the Pythian games of 474 B.C.

It will be noticed that the prevailing kinds of foot are the spondee and dactyl, with an occasional use of the anapæstic spondee and anapæst proper. The dactyl and spondee are associated with dignity of movement and religious solemnity. The bars marked *t* would formerly have been called trochees, but we now know that a trochee is always a three-time foot. We cannot, in a solemn hymn, mix three- and four-time measures; hence the apparent trochee must, by τονή, receive the form shown, in order to bring it into line with the four-time rhythm[1].

The combination of the so-called trochee with the spondee, as in the first four bars of our example, is called *epitritos*, which means the ratio of 3 : 4. For the Roman grammarians looked upon the first two pairs of bars here as seven-time feet, with an arsis of three and a thesis of four times, thus ♩♪ | ♩ ♩ |, whereas we now know that the Greek rhythmicists rejected the seven-time measure as being incapable of rhythmical division. Rhythms containing this combination are called by the grammarians epitritic; and when dactyls occur, as here, the poem is called dactylo-epitritic[2].

The only bars on which some doubt might be raised are in the second and third verses, where the notes lengthened by τονή to the minim value seem to drag. They might be crotchets, but the rhythm would, perhaps, slightly lose in dignity in this case. The version we give is accepted by Gevaert as being probably the nearest to the true interpretation.

The first verse consists of a period of seven feet, divided by the comma after φόρμιγξ, as well as by the shape of the melody, into two phrases, technically called cola, *i.e.* members, of respectively three and

---

[1] See p. 44.

[2] The *epritritos* is used with great effect in Pindar's Third Olympian Ode, where it occurs singly in the first three verses, and ends by dominating the last two entirely.

four feet[1]. The admiration the Greeks had for their national instrument is expressed by addressing it in the two words "Golden Lyre!" set to a simple rhythmical phrase.

Verse 2, according to the arrangement shown, consists of a period of three members, containing respectively $4 + 5 + 2$ feet. The metrical arrangement of this verse given by Gildersleeve corresponds with the musical barring in Gevaert.

Between verses 2 and 3 there stand the words χόρος εἰς κιθάραν, "Dance with the Lyre," and the notation changes from vocal to instrumental. It is evident that the first two verses were sung without action, and that the dance commenced with verse 3. This verse is in two members of, respectively, four and two feet.

In verse 4 there is *metábolē*[2] of ethos. Instead of pure dactyls and spondees the verse commences with an anapæstic spondee, and goes on with pure anapæsts; the transitory use of anapæstic rhythm would perhaps have a reference to the dance just commencing, but the rhythm quickly returns to the more solemn thetic form, in which it remains to the end of the fragment.

The Odes of Pindar, like the Choruses of Greek Plays, consist of a series of triads, each triad being formed of a strophe, antistrophe and epode. The antistrophe is rhythmically, and was melodically also, the exact counterpart of the strophe, while the epode takes a new form. A poem may have one such triad or several; if there are more than one, the rhythmical scheme of every succeeding triad is almost note for note the same as that of the first.

The First Pythian Ode contains five triads, whose rhythmical scheme is as follows:

Ex. 42 *a*. The Rhythmical scheme of Pindar's First Pythian Ode, expressed in notation.

Strophe and Antistrophe.

---

[1] A "period" contains one, two, three, or more "cola." It will be discussed later on.
[2] Metabolē means change. There could be metabolē of rhythm, of ethos, of rhythmical scheme, of mode, of key, the last being equivalent to our "modulation."

We have written out this example in Common time, *i.e.* with two measures in the bar, in order to show clearly the grouping of the feet by pairs, one of which is an arsis-foot, the other a thesis-foot. By this means the principal ictus-syllable of a pair of measures falls on the first note of a bar. This is a common practice with modern composers, though probably not one in a hundred knows why instinct leads him to use C rather than 2/4 in certain movements, and 2/4 rather than C in others[1].

The frequency of the intermediate 2/4 bars will strike the musician. This apparent irregularity does not appear when the whole is written in 2/4 time to give a bar to each foot or measure, as is generally done in translating Greek metre into musical notation. The ear perceives nothing unusual when the melody is sung in a dignified *tempo*, neither too fast nor too slow, as required by Aristides[2].

There are several instances of irrationality. If it were not for the very careful explanation of irrational time given by Aristoxenus, we should be disposed to take no notice of the slight pauses indicated in the notation, and to consider that the occurrence of a long syllable where there should be a short, or *vice versa*, was a licence, enabling the poet to use a more expressive word than he otherwise could. But as Aristoxenus is so very explicit in stating that such syllables are to be given a value longer than the short, and shorter than the long, we must abide by his rule, and look upon the bars in which it occurs as being sung in a sort of *tempo rubato*. But we confess to having a sort of half belief that occasionally, at any rate, the so-called irrational syllables were poetic licences, in spite of our faith in Aristoxenus.

The phrasing, or "colotomy," as indicated by the slurs is that given by Gildersleeve, who follows J. H. H. Schmidt. The actual colotomy practically used by the ancients is a debateable point, which cannot be settled definitely until, if ever, we recover considerable portions of the melodies. In this case the melodic construction would be a great help towards a more precise knowledge of the colotomy.

The prevailing rhythmical form is the *epitritos* of the first two bars. Verse 5 of the strophe is wholly made up of it, and no verse is without one or more examples. An effective modern use of the form is found in the chorus "And grant a leader bold and brave" in Handel's "Judas Maccabaeus."

[1] That is, assuming that the primary time is the quaver in each case.
[2] "Rhythmical *agogē* is quickness or slowness of times, since, while preserving the ratios of theses and arses, we can make differences of magnitude in each. But the best *agogē* for rhythmical expression is when theses and arses occupy a medium space of time" (Meibom. p. 42). *Agogē* is therefore exactly equivalent to our *tempo*, and Aristides recommends a *tempo moderato* as best suited to rhythmical expression.

EPITRITIC RHYTHM

Ex. 43. Handel, "Judas Maccabaeus."

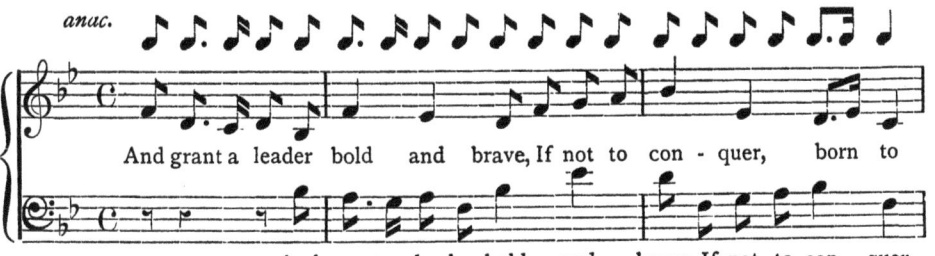

Here the epitritic character (𝅘𝅥𝅮𝅭 𝅘𝅥𝅮𝅘𝅥𝅮) of the rhythm is even more in evidence than in the Pindar Ode, but in order that frequency of use may not entail revulsion of feeling, Handel produces a contrast by eliminating the *quasi*-trochees towards the end of the chorus, and using only even notes. A lesser composer would probably have retained the dotted notes to the end. Both Pindar and Handel knew how to give the epitritic character to their respective compositions without wearying their audiences by overdoing it[1].

Gildersleeve's remarks on the style of Pindar's rhythms are so clear and concise that we venture to quote them at some length. He says, on page lxxiii. of the Introduction, "About half the extant odes of Pindar are composed in these (epitritic-dactylic) rhythms, which are also called Dorian. They are elevated, well-balanced, equable,

---

[1] In rhythmical matters, as in most manifestations of art, genius may be as much in evidence through restraint as through effort. Any ordinary healthy musician can, if he wishes, express himself in tolerably vigorous rhythms; the difference between the great and the mediocre is that the one, by carefully considered restraint, appeals to the imagination, while the other, by overloading, or overdoing his rhythms, in order to impress them, may make an immediate appeal to a public that does not want to think, but his work is unlikely to have an enduring value. Musical achievement that will appeal to generations to come is the product of an instinct so profound, a power of concentration so great, as to be inconceivable to the ordinary mind.

and present a marked contrast to the lively, lilting, excited logaœdic measures, and the still more stirring cretic....The logaœdic rhythm is a 3/8 rhythm, the basis of which is the trochee, but not the trochee with the ordinary ictus. This trochee has a stronger secondary ictus on the short (note), admits irrationality (♩ ♪), and takes as a substitute the so-called cyclical dactyl (♩.♪♩). The apparent jumble of dactyls and trochees, as in prose, gave rise to the name logaœdic[1]....The logaœdics are much used in the lyric portions of the drama, and are familiar in the Odes of Horace.......The logaœdic rhythms are lighter, more airy, than the epitritic. They have a festal glitter rather than a steady light, a rapid flitting rather than a compassed march."

The following is an example of logaœdic rhythm:

Ex. 44. Pindar, Olympian Ode, No. 10. Written for Agesidamos, winner of the Boys' Boxing Match in B.C. 484.

Τὸν Ὀ - λυμ - πι - ο - νί - καν ἀ - νάγ - νω - τέ μοι
Ἀρ - χεσ - τρά - του παῖδα πό - θι φρε - νὸς
ἐ - - μᾶς γέ - γραπ - ται. γλυκὺ γὰρ αὐ - τῷ μέ - λος ὀ - φεί - λων
ἐ - πι - λέ - λαθ'. ὢ Μοῖσ', ἀλ - λὰ σὺ καὶ θυ - γά - τηρ
Ἀ - λά - θει - α Δι - ός, ὀρ - θᾷ χε - ρὶ
ἐ - ρύ - κε - τον ψευ - δέ - ων
ἐ - νι - πὰν ἀ - λι - τόξ - ε - νον.

Translation:

"Read me the name of the Olympian winner, Archestratos' son, that I may know where it is written on my heart: for I had forgotten that I owed him a sweet strain.

"But do thou, O Muse, and thou Truth, daughter of Zeus, put

[1] This word means something between poetry and prose, prose-like poetry.

forth your hands, and keep from me the reproach of having wronged a friend by breaking my pledged word[1]."

The same rhythmical form is, of course, taken by the antistrophe, while that of the epode makes a contrast, though it retains the logaœdic character. It will be seen that this is much more dance-like than that of Ex. 40, and seems more suitable to the winner of a boys' contest, while the dignified rhythm of the 1st Pythian would be suitable to the governor of an important city.

Our next example is from one of the Greek dramas, and as this work was actually performed at Bradfield with an adherence to the Greek rhythmical schemes and colotomy, we venture to include the melody which we composed for it, in which we made use, as far as possible, of the little that is known of the Greek theory and practice of melody. Between the verses short "crouseis" are introduced, in accordance with ancient practice, and as a means of giving relief to the singers as well as the audience.

Ex. 45. Sophocles, "Antigone," Chorus No. 3 (vv. 582 &c.). Music composed for Bradfield College by C. F. Abdy Williams. Translation by G. G. Freeman, adapted to the Greek rhythm by C. F. A. W. Published by Breitkopf and Haertel.

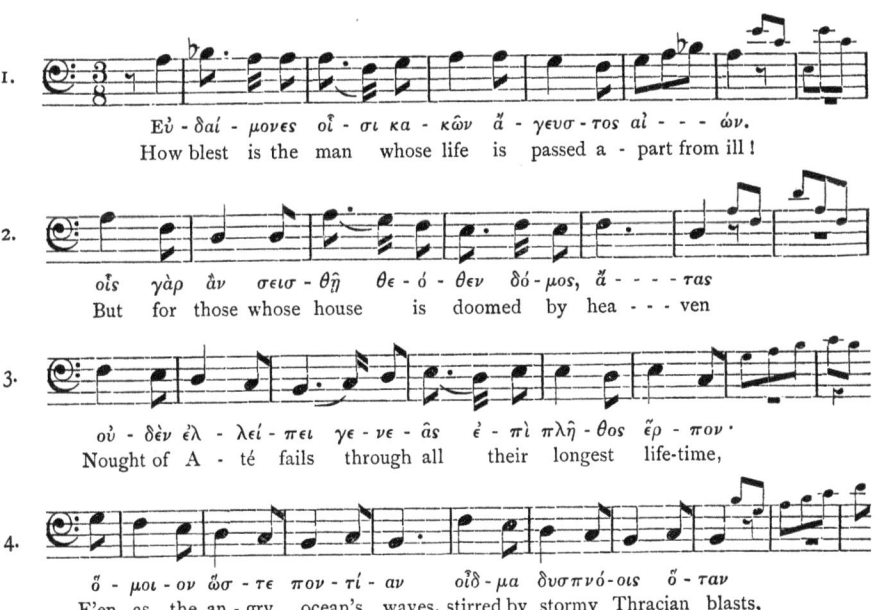

[1] From "The Extant Odes of Pindar, translated into English," by Ernest Myers, M.A., 1892. The allusion to wronging a friend has reference to the fact that Pindar had long promised this ode.

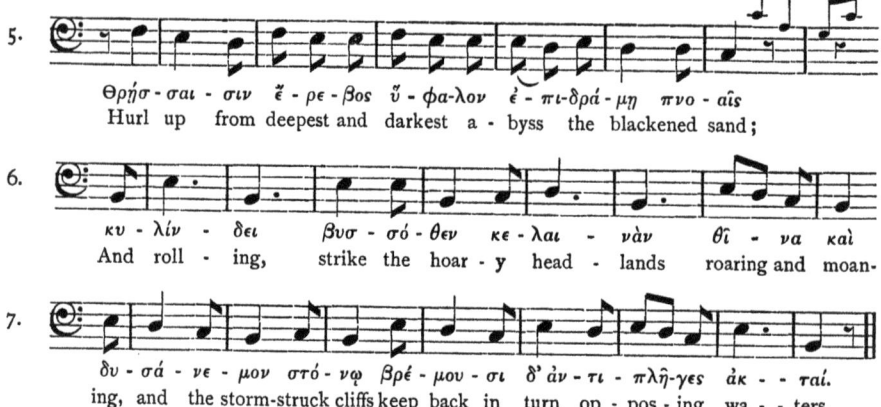

Creon, King of Thebes, has decreed death to any who should perform funeral rites over the body of his conquered enemy Polyneikes. Antigone, the sister of Polyneikes, and the betrothed of Creon's son, dares to brave the decree, is discovered, and brought before Creon, who condemns her to die. The Chorus of Theban Elders, aghast at the wickedness of punishing a pious action with death, prophesy stormy and evil days to his house. The analogy between the angry waves and the anger of the gods is continued in the antistrophe.

The rhythm is logaœdic, the form generally used to express a tragic situation. To give effect to the irrational notes, which are here undoubtedly of great importance, crotchets are written instead of quavers bearing a pause. The music was composed for a practical purpose, and the minute time-division involved in the Greek idea of irrationality is not only foreign to modern experience, but would be impracticable by a chorus whose members are only accustomed to modern rhythm[1].

At first sight it would appear as if triple rhythm, with the dotted notes, was hardly suitable to the tragic sentiment that has to be expressed here; nor would it be, if sung in the gay and dance-like manner usually associated with the figure of the first two bars. But *tempo* and accent play a large part in rhythmical effect. The cyclical dactyls (♩ ♪ ♪) in the Folksong, "Come lasses and lads," sung at a fairly fast pace, and without strong accent, give an effect of gaiety and light-hearted joy: the same form, repeated over and over

---

[1] It will be remembered that the ancient chorus was very dependent on its conductor, especially on his audible methods of marking the rhythm.

again, driven into the soul as it were, at a *presto* rate, with powerful accentuation, in the Scherzo of the Ninth Symphony, can be productive of an almost terrific emotional force.

The rhythm in our example is to be treated in neither of these ways, but taken at a slow and dignified march *tempo*, and the Greeks gave it, in addition, the special accentuation mentioned on page 80. This is hardly appreciable to moderns, but perhaps it can be nearly expressed by the musical term *pesante*; and it certainly could be rendered effective by an appropriate use of harmony.

With regard to the translation, those of our readers who are familiar with Greek will naturally prefer to read the rhythmical effects in their full force in the original language: to those who are not, we must mention that a translation from Greek drama into any modern language that shall convey at once the dramatic, emotional, linguistic and rhythmical effects of the original, is an impossibility, and that we only give one here in order that such readers may have a general idea of what the Greek text is describing.

It will be noticed that the cyclical dactyl always occurs in pairs, and that it is only used in the first four verses, the tribrach (three equal notes), more or less occupying its place in the remaining portion of the strophe. This is analogous to the contrast used by Handel in the chorus alluded to on page 79.

Analysis of the remaining choruses of this play (except the last) shows that all the rhythms are logaœdic, that the occurrence of the cyclical dactyl does not take place by hazard, but differs in each strophe, apparently according to some well thought out scheme. The first three choruses conclude with what musicians would call a Coda, in which the triple rhythm gives way to the livelier anapæstic form, ♫ | ♩ ♫ | ♩: æsthetically this finds its analogy in the quickening of *tempo* that frequently occurs at the end of a modern composition, *e.g.* in Beethoven's "Fidelio" and "Egmont" Overtures. In the latter case the rhythm actually changes from a dignified triple to quadruple, as in the Greek drama, and for the same æsthetic reason, though Beethoven does not use the anapæstic form.

Bach employs logaœdic rhythm for intensely emotional words in his seventh motet; and, except for the regularity of his four-bar phrases, his use of this rhythm is, in principle, exactly the same as that of Sophocles. In both artists we find cyclical dactyls at the beginning of the movement, giving way to even notes at the end.

In both the cyclical dactyls occur sometimes singly, sometimes in pairs. Bach marks his motet to be sung *un poco lento* and harmonises it in such a manner as to make each note impressive; thus he produces a modern equivalent to the weighty accentuation described on page 80.

We quote the first two phrases in Ex. 46.

Ex. 46. Bach, Motet No. 7.

The music being homophonic, the rhythmical effect is exactly similar to that of a Greek Chorus, in that the purity of the cyclical dactyls and trochees is not disturbed by any contrapuntal accessories. The use of a rhythmical form generally associated with the dance, or with light music, to express deep religious emotion, by two of the greatest composers, in artistic epochs twenty-four centuries apart is not mere chance. It is rather an evidence of the unchanging character of human nature and of the capacity of genius of the highest order to probe the depths of that nature by the means of materials that, to the ordinary man, would appear inappropriate. In the one case the emotion of the chorus is stirred by indignation at wrongdoing; in the other by a sense of love and blessing. The logaœdic rhythm expresses the emotion in both cases.

But logaœdic rhythm was also used very largely in Comedy as well as Tragedy. Here, however, its treatment differed entirely, and it evidently went at a brisker pace. Aristophanes frequently uses it in what Schmidt calls a "Folksong" manner, as in Ex. 47.

EX. 47. Aristophanes, "The Knights," Chorus No. 8, *vv.* 1111 &c.

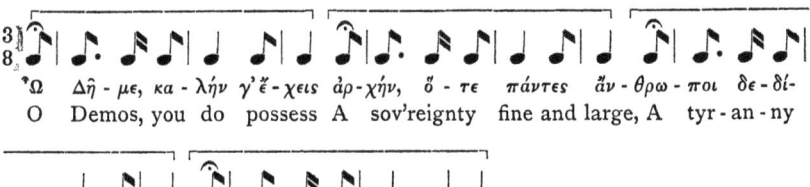

Ὦ Δῆ - με, κα - λήν γ' ἔ - χεις ἀρ - χήν, ὅ - τε πάντες ἄν - θρω - ποι δε - δί-
O Demos, you do possess A sov'reignty fine and large, A tyr-an-ny

α - σί σ' ὥσπερ ἄν - δρα τύ - ραν - νον.
feared by all. Yet you can be ca - joled,

ἀλλ' εὐ - πα - ρά - γω - γος εἶ, θω - πευ - ό - με - νός τε χαί - ρεις
For flattery's your de-light, you listen with o - pen mouth, to

κἀ - ξα - πα - τώ - με - νος πρὸς τόν τε λέ - γοντ' ἀ - εὶ κε-
any who speaks you fair, to any who fools you well. Your

χη - νας· ὁ νοῦς δέ σου πα - ρὼν ἀ - πο - δη - μεῖ.
mind may be present in-deed, Your thoughts are in cloud - land.

The translation, adapted to the rhythm, is founded on that of W. J. Hickie in Bohn's series. The Chorus of Knights sarcastically addresses Demos, who typifies the Democracy of Athens. The rhythm, it will be seen, consists of a series of logaœdic tripodies, all exactly alike, except for the last phrase of each group, in which there is a three-time note. Each phrase starts with an irrational time, followed by a cyclical dactyl. The slight pause on the first note of the phrase, the democratic simplicity of the phrase itself, the constant repetition, all seem to concur in the sarcastic character of the words. If the science and feeling for rhythm were as well understood by modern as by ancient audiences, one could easily imagine the composer of a comic opera making a hit by imitating the rhythm of some low-class song; and this is what Aristophanes does here.

Demos defends himself by sneering, in his turn, at the long hair of the Knights, a sign of birth and opulence. He uses exactly the same rhythmical form, which would, of course, be natural to him, and the scene is carried on by further bandying of sarcasm between the

86   RHYTHM OF COMEDY

chorus and him, the rhythmical form never changing, till a third person comes on the scene.

The monotony of such a succession of similar rhythms would strike the cultivated modern hearer, even if it were disguised by the resources of harmony. To the Greek, accustomed to greater variety of phrase-construction than ourselves, it would probably be even more striking. But this is evidently part of the composer's sarcasm: an ignorant democracy likes repetition *ad nauseam*, or, at any rate, is not bored by it to anything like the same extent as the alert mind of the cultured man. And there is after all something humorous about the eternal irrational note at the beginning of every phrase: it seems like a stammerer, who, after hesitating over his first syllable, once having found his voice brings out the sentence in a sort of run. A similar pause at the beginning of a phrase might have a comic effect in modern times.

Our next example, No. 48, shows how quintuple rhythm, which

Ex. 48. Aristophanes, "Peace," Chorus No. 8, *vv.* 1127 &c.

was associated with religious rites, could also be used with humorous effect in comedy. The passage is from Aristophanes' "Peace." Trygaeus, weary of the Peloponnesian War, ascends to heaven on the back of a huge beetle, to remonstrate with Jupiter on the mischief he is allowing to take place. But Jupiter is away from home, and the demon of war occupies his seat, while the goddess Peace is shut up in prison. Trygaeus manages to liberate her and restore her to her ancient honours. The chorus here quoted from gives expression to the satisfaction felt by the soldiers at this *dénouement*.

The first four verses consist of dipodies, short exclamations, expressive of rustic pleasure. The favourite irrational time occurs on each anacrusis. Then there follow some of the long periods of absolutely similar bars which evidently had, for the Athenian audience, a comic character. The strophe ends with a long passage of trochees, relieved only by an occasional irrationality. The pace would naturally be fast: a slow *tempo* would kill the effect.

Of the humour of the rhythm there can be little doubt, and if one can for the moment imagine oneself in an Athenian theatre, with all the political excitement of the day in the air, one can almost feel this humour, especially where the triple measure enters. The English words, adapted from Mr Hickie's prose translation are, of course quite inadequate to do more than show what the chorus is about: moreover their sense has little interest to an English reader, especially when taken apart from the context.

In modern music quintuple rhythm has only hitherto been employed for emotional effects, and, with few exceptions, our composers have confined it to instrumental music. It has certainly not yet become sufficiently familiar to allow of its use in comic opera. Perhaps, who knows? in course of time this resource may be again added to the ordinary materials available to composers.

Let us now examine some ancient music in which quintuple measure is employed for religious purposes. We have, in discussing the foot, alluded to one of the two Delphic Hymns to Apollo. Both are published by M. Theodore Reinach in the *Bulletin de Correspondance*

Hellénique, 1893, Part II, and are therefore easy to compare. It is not necessary to quote more than we have already done in Ex. 13, page 47. It will be noticed that in those five bars no less than three different forms of the pæon are used, viz.

(*a*) | ♩ ♪ ♩ | (*b*) | ♫ ♩ | (*c*) | ♩ ♫ |

Another form, (*d*) ♫♫[1] frequently occurs in both hymns, and the four forms are intermingled in such a way that there is no feeling of monotony, no commonplace repetition.

In Ex. 13 form (*a*) occurs in two successive bars. This frequently happens also with (*b*) and (*c*), never with (*d*), for there was a prejudice against successions of primary times. Very rarely a single form occurs in more than two bars following one another. In one place, however, form (*b*) occurs in no less than five bars running. But in the first three of these five bars, the first two notes are slurred on a single syllable, producing the accentual effect of (*a*).

It will be seen then that the use of quintuple measure in comedy and religion was entirely different. In the one case a certain gaiety and vulgarity is obtained by constant repetition of a single form, and the application of irrationality: in the other a gravity and solemnity, by an equally constant interchange of various forms of diæresis in the successive feet. The *tempo* in the latter case would undoubtedly be grave, but the interchange of form in the feet would have at least as much to do with the difference of ethos as the *tempo*. Irrationality does not occur in either of the hymns: perhaps, like the modern pause, it was too dramatic or emotional to be much used in a canticle composed for the temple of a god.

In the first hymn the rhythm is pæonic throughout; in the second there is a coda in glyconics, a form of which we shall speak later.

How were these hymns performed? From internal evidence, and from a notice by Lucian, M. Reinach concludes that they were executed by a chorus of Dionysiac artists from Athens, one part of which sang the melody, while the other performed the dance which was always associated with choral music. There was also an accompaniment of flute and cithara. Gevaert thinks that the melody may have been sung by a solo voice, while the chorus danced. In either case the performance would be one that required special rehearsal beforehand, and one may perhaps find a modern analogy in a festival performance of one of the great hymns of the Latin Church, such as the "Te Deum," or "Stabat Mater," in which chorus, soloists and orchestra take part, while the congregation listens.

[1] See p. 44, for Aristoxenus' remarks on this form.

CHAPTER VII

Quintuple rhythm in Tragedy—The "Electra" of Sophocles and of Strauss—Glyconic rhythm—Music that is unfettered by rhythmical phrases—Aristides on the ethos of rhythm—The influence of the different forms of rhythm on mind and body, described by Aristides—Cleonides on the ethos of song—The ethos of Italian Opera—Dr Abert's *Lehre vom Ethos in der griechischen Musik*.

QUINTUPLE measure is used in tragedy as a means of expressing intensity of emotion. Ajax in his madness, Oedipus the King, in his mental agony, Creon, at the sight of his son's dead body, express themselves in pæons. But the method of employment differs from those we described in the last chapter, for the tumult of feeling is represented by a mixture of quintuple with triple rhythm, in the manner of the dochmiac, described on page 51.

And, since the Greeks were moderate in all things, the tumultuous dochmiacs, of Sophocles, at least, do not last long, but are invariably followed or intermingled with triple rhythm.

We quote, as an example of the tragic use of quintuple rhythm, a few words from Sophocles' "Electra." The passage is that in which Electra recognises her brother Orestes, whom she believes to have been murdered.

Ex. 49. Sophocles, "Electra," Duet between Electra and Orestes, *vv*. 1232 &c.

El.
'Ι - ὼ γο - ναί,

γο - ναὶ σω - μά - των ἐ - μοὶ φίλ - τά - των

ἐ - μόλετ' ἀρ - τί - ως

ἐ - φεύρετ', ἤλθετ', εἴ - δεθ' οὓς ἐ - χρῄ - ζε - τε.

Or. 6/8 ♪ ♩ ♪ ♩ ♪ ♩ ♪ ♩ ♪ ♩ ♪ ♩
πά - ρεσμεν· ἀλ - λὰ σῖγ' ἔ - χου - σα πρόσ - με - νε.

El. 3/8 ♪ ♩. | ♩ ♩ | &c.
τί δ' ἔσ - τιν;

Translation, from E. H. Plumptre's *Tragedies of Sophocles*, London, 1867.

El. "O offspring, offspring of a form most dear,
Ye came, ye came, at last,
Ye found us, yea ye came,
Ye saw whom ye desired.
Or. Yes, we are come. Yet wait, and hold thy peace.
El. What, now?"

The musical reader will, with a little effort, soon assimilate the time and accent of this example, and must, we imagine, feel the almost sobbing intensity of the rhythm in the first three lines, and the restraining influence of the two 6/8 time verses. The principle of construction shown here, in which quintuple and triple rhythm act in conjunction or contrast, is the same in all the other passages of the kind in Sophocles' tragedies.

Those who have heard the Hoffmansthal-Strauss version of the play will appreciate the difference of treatment between the ancient and modern works. In the latter the mind is kept on a continual stretch from beginning to end, by every modern device in music. This is in accordance with the strenuousness of modern life: the Greek, living at less pressure, and with the fear of Nemesis before him, exercised more restraint. When we have to express tragic emotion, we harrow the feelings to an extent that would have been repugnant to the calm mind of the Greek in classical times, who required that there should be dignity in all great art. We use the expression "classical times" advisedly: we refer to the period which produced the great dramatists, the poets, and the leader Pericles, under whose rule Athens was beautified with the temples whose ruins excite the admiration of mankind. For in later times it would appear that this masculine restraint in art gave way, probably in response to popular demand, to a more effeminate style, coinciding with the gradual decay of Greek power.

In thus comparing ancient and modern ideals of musical expression, we must be careful not to imagine that because Greek musicians used their effects sparingly, while our Wagners and

Strauss's and Debussys pour them out in an avalanche of passion, the one art is inferior to the other, or that modern art necessarily shows thereby any symptoms of deterioration. On the contrary, the difference is merely one of social conditions. A decay of national power and character is generally accompanied, as in the case of Greece, by a weakening of artistic strength; and we may infer from the ever growing strength and power of modern music that there are, as yet, no seeds of decay in the leading modern nations, in spite of some superficial signs that may seem at first sight to be pointing to this. Or, if we wish, we may put the matter in the reverse order. The strength of modern nations has not yet begun to decline, therefore we may safely say that the methods of modern musicians, however distasteful they may be to a generation nurtured on Beethoven and Bach, are not necessarily signs of deterioration, but may be due to increasing power.

On page 88 we referred to the glyconic rhythm. Authorities are not entirely agreed as to the manner in which this rhythm was sung, and in the Delphic Hymn, where the engraver might have given us an opportunity of settling the question, he has, unfortunately, omitted the rhythmical signs, probably because the matter was too familiar to his contemporaries for him to trouble about it[1].

The rhythm was said to have been invented by one Glycon, an unknown Alexandrine poet[2], and was much in favour with Horace and other Latin poets. The view generally accepted in Germany, and probably nearest to the mark, is, that the glyconic is a trochaic tetrapody, one of whose feet is a cyclical dactyl. There are supposed to be three forms of glyconic, numbered according to the position of the cyclical dactyl, as shown in Ex. 50.

Ex. 50.

First glyconic

Second „

Third „

We do not know that any special æsthetic effect is attributed to it. It has a dance-like and somewhat amorous lilt. The first subject of Grieg's Violin Sonata in F, op. 8, has a glyconic character, through such phrases as

[1] Reinach, in *Bulletin de Corr. Hell.*, 1893, Vol. II. p. 369.
[2] Gevaert, *La Mus. de l'Ant.* Vol. II. p. 138.

GLYCONIC RHYTHM

Ex. 51. Grieg, Violin Sonata in F, op. 8.

How charming this simple style of rhythm can be in vocal music is shown by Gluck, who unwittingly makes free use of glyconics in a nuptial chorus in *Alceste*. It is true that the ancients, probably owing to their dislike of a feminine ending, disallowed the cyclical dactyl in the final bar of the phrase, but the principle of the trochaic tetrapody in the form of a four-bar phrase broken by one cyclical dactyl, is employed, with few exceptions, throughout this chorus.

Ex. 52. Gluck, "Alceste," Chorus No. 5.

Bellermann's *Anonymus*, page 93, says, "Flowing songs and melodies are those which are symmetrical in time, and yet unfettered by it. The time of the whole cannot be measured, but the component parts are measured." On page 22 he indicates that the expression κεχυμένα "flowing" is applied to an ode which has melody alone, without rhythm: in other words, when its notes are equal, and it is not divided into rhythmical phrases or recognisable rhythmical figures. Aristides says on this point (Meibom. p. 32), "Melos must be considered as to whether it has formal construction or is in unbarred melodies (ἀτάκταις μελῳδίαις) called 'flowing songs' (κεχυμένων ἀσμάτων)."

No description of such songs is vouchsafed to us by either author; each refers to them as if the matter were familiar to his readers, and then passes on to discuss the elements of rhythm. Vincent, in his *Notices des Manuscripts*, p. 50 *note*, suggests that they were something equivalent to plainsong, and in this he is followed by Gevaert. Can it be that for special purposes the Greeks after all made use of something analogous to our recitative, and that the symmetrical written notes were allowed to be freely interpreted by the performer?

An important section in Aristides' treatise refers to the different effects on the mind that differences of rhythmical structure may produce. Like most of the more important parts of the theory, "ethos" or "character" of the different rhythms is very slightly alluded to, and makes us keenly feel the loss of further information. No doubt it was more fully discussed in works which are lost.

We quote the beginning of the passage in App. A, 13: the translation is as follows:

"Of rhythms, the more gentle (hesychastic), starting from the theses, are soothing to the mind. But those which bring the entrance of the voice from arses are agitated."

The exact sense of the latter sentence is somewhat doubtful. It may be read, "those which, starting from arses, bring an instrumental accompaniment to the voice, are agitated." But the general meaning is clear, namely, that the rhythm which commences with arsis has the opposite effect to that which commences with thesis, and this is sufficient for our purpose. By putting the matter to a practical test, it will be found that we shall generally make a more vigorous or a more tranquil effect, according to whether we treat the first foot, or first portion of a phrase as a thesis or an arsis.

The difference of effect is noticeable here. But we must guard against applying the rule too rigidly, for modern resources are beyond anything conceivable to the ancients, and the effect of rising or falling accentuation, as explained by means of Ex. 53, may often be rendered nugatory by some particular application of harmony. The theory is given us, and it is open to musicians to apply it or not, as each thinks best. It undoubtedly exhibits many passages of classical music in a new and interesting light, if applied to them.

Ex. 53. Beethoven, Sonata, op. 28.
Scherzo. *Allegro vivace.*

"And those (rhythms) which have all the feet in the periods complete are the more graceful."...That is, where the phrases are not curtailed by cutting off the final foot or part thereof, through catalexis. The manuscript is mutilated here. Meibomius suggests that the sentence probably concluded with "and those that are incomplete are the opposite."

We moderns do not observe this distinction further than to say that a poetic line is either catalectic (curtailed), or acatalectic (uncurtailed, complete). We attach no special significance to the graceful or otherwise effect between the two forms. With musical phrases our teachers are apt to consider any three-bar phrase as catalectic, and it often is, when it occurs in the midst of four-bar rhythms. But it is not catalectic when it forms the fundamental length of phrase in a period.

"And short (rhythms) that have rests are more simple and petty; long ones are more magnificent." Rests do not appear to have been allowed within a rhythm; they could only occur at the end. They could divide rhythms from one another. It is evident that Aristides and his contemporaries would not have approved theoretically of the short phrases divided by rests that are so frequently met with in modern music, *e.g.* many parts of the music of *Parsifal.* Yet from Ex. 49 it would appear that short broken phrases which the theorists would have considered petty, were used for strong dramatic expression, as they are with us.

"And those (rhythms) which are arranged in equal proportion are the more beautiful through their evenness: but those in uneven relation are the opposite."

That is, phrases divided into two equal portions were considered by the Aristoxenian school to be more beautiful than the other species, in which the phrase was divided unequally. This view was held even before the time of Aristoxenus, for Aristotle, in his eighth problem, says "that duple rhythms have a more tranquil character, uneven a more emotional: and amongst the latter, some produce more vulgar movements, others more noble[1]."

Aristides continues: "In the midst are those which have the relation 2 : 1, that is, uneven as to the feet, but even as to the phrase."

That is to say, a triple-time phrase, divided into two equal portions, as Ex. 25, p. 59. The rhythm here partakes, according to our author, of both even and uneven proportion: even, as to the complete rhythm, and uneven, as to the individual feet. Whether he considers the arrangement satisfactory or the reverse he does not say, but it must have been as common and as necessary in ancient music as in modern.

"Of (rhythms) in even proportion, those which consist of short notes alone are very rapid, hasty, and smooth; but a mixture (of long and short notes) is usual."

This is easily understood; a continuous flow of short even notes in even time, such as the Prelude in D major of the first book of the Wohltemperirtes Klavier, gives the impression of rapidity, of heat (energy) and a smooth steady flow; but rhythms are more usually composed of short and long notes intermingled.

"And if the feet consist of a combination of the longest times, the more will a calming of the mind be manifested. Hence we hear the short notes employed in the Pyrrhic Games, the mixed notes in ordinary dances, and the very long notes in the divine hymns (ἱεροῖς ὕμνοις) where they are used to the fullest extent."

Meibomius remarks on this, "It must be noted that all antiquity considered that hymns and sacred cantilenas should be sung very slowly and with gravity." Such music undoubtedly has a certain effect of mystery and awe on the mind.

"Those who make these hymns their one favourite study bring their mind to moderation, which is healthiness of the soul, through the equality and length of the notes. Wherefore those also whose pulses make their movements in this kind of time are exceedingly healthy."

The power of music in mental diseases has, we believe, long been recognised by the medical profession. That music is not used in

[1] Gevaert, *La Mus. de l'Ant.* Vol. II. p. 60, *note.*

relief of bodily ailments is probably because few moderns are sufficiently sensitive to it. The power it may have on the spirits of an ordinarily healthy mind and body is rarely alluded to, yet it is very real with those who have a musical organisation.

To such as these it may be exceedingly inspiring or intensely depressing. The Germans say, "I have been elevated by such and such a composition." Every musical person must have noticed the elevation of mind he experiences after hearing music which has satisfied his ideals; the depression that ensues from a bad performance, or even a competent performance of music that is intrinsically poor; the exhaustion after an emotional work, such as "Tannhäuser" or Bach's "Passion Music"; the delightful feeling of peace with himself and all the world after a beautiful musical service in a church, and the opposite effect of a bad one. Many of us feel these things, but we do not talk of them. They are undoubtedly healthy, or the reverse, to the body as well as the soul. The ancients not only appear to have felt them more keenly and generally than we do, but they took the trouble to write about them. They attributed them to the various species of rhythm and mode employed, but more especially to the rhythm. It is evident, however, that the writers of the treatises rarely if ever heard performances of the music they describe. We know from our experience, that an incompetent performance may ruin the finest efforts of a composer, and similarly, a good performer can infuse into bad music a sort of quasi-merit that makes it attractive. On this point there is no mention in any of our ancient authors. They appear to be analysing the written compositions of the great masters, and to arrive at conclusions from their own ideal of how things would actually sound, much as a modern musician might carefully study a score which he has no chance of hearing performed.

When Aristoxenus and his successors wrote, the zenith of Greek classical art had been passed: music was in its decline, and the efforts of the great theorists were directed to propping up the falling edifice by showing how this or that ethical effect was produced on the mind by those whom they referred to as "the ancients." Aristoxenus lived some two centuries after the Periclean period; he was therefore separated from it by about a century less than the time that separates us from the culmination of the polyphonic era under Palestrina.

But our music did not decay after Palestrina; on the contrary it threw out fresh branches. He was contemporary with the Reformation, and the new liberty obtained thereby did not tend to destruction or decay, but to the constructive work of the development of art and literature, untrammelled by ecclesiastical domination. Music henceforward gradually opened out new forms, new powers of expression; in course of time grew to its present wonderful development, and is still growing. This is entirely the opposite of what happened in Greece. With us there was a gain of liberty: with Greece liberty was lost through foreign conquest, and art declined with its loss.

"But rhythms in the relation of three to two are, as I have said, the more inspiring. Of these the epibatos $\left(\begin{smallmatrix}5\\4\end{smallmatrix}\ \overset{ar}{\quad}\ |\ \overset{th}{\quad}\ \right)$ moves us the more, disturbing the spirit with its two-fold thesis, and exciting the soul to the highest extent by the magnitude of its arsis."

The word we have translated by "more inspiring" is ἐνθουσιαστι-κωτέρους, literally, "more enthusiastic." The more we read, the more must we feel convinced that the ancients had an admiration for quintuple rhythm incomprehensible to the earlier investigators of their theory, and somewhat difficult for us to appreciate.

The occasional use of this species interests us from an intellectual point of view, as a bold experiment, but we can hardly say that it excites us and kindles enthusiasm, more than any other species.

Perhaps the taste for all music, great and trivial, classical and popular, vigorous and sentimental, is in reality an acquired product, only to be obtained through a certain amount of familiarity. The author of the Nineteenth Problem remarks that a familiar tune is more pleasant than a new one, and discusses the reasons. We may say that a familiar form of rhythm is more likely to interest us than one to which we are unaccustomed, and the quintuple species is not familiar to us.

"Of the proportion two to one, the simple trochees $\left(\begin{smallmatrix}3\\8\end{smallmatrix}\ \right)$ and iambuses $\left(\begin{smallmatrix}3\\8\end{smallmatrix}\ \right)$ display rapidity, and are warm, and suitable for the dance. And the orthioi $\left(\begin{smallmatrix}3\\2\end{smallmatrix}\ |\ \right)$ and semantoi $\left(\begin{smallmatrix}3\\2\end{smallmatrix}\ \right)$, through their abounding in the greatest sounds, lead to decision of character. And these are the simple forms of rhythm."

That the iambus and trochee and their kindred forms are suitable to the dance will at once be recognised. That the practice of singing the long notes of the orthios and semantos would have much effect in giving decision to the character of our youth may be open to doubt. With the ancients music took much the same place in education as the two dead languages at our public schools, and this is why so much stress is laid on the effect on the character supposed to be produced by this or that form of rhythm. Even we ourselves would consider that if a boy is to be taught music, the effort of acquiring an acquaintance with the severe music of the great masters would do his character more good than merely learning to play waltzes, or the sentimentalities of the drawing room.

"The compound feet are more impassioned, because for the most part they consist of simple feet whose ratio to one another is uneven, producing much disturbance."

Our author is evidently here thinking of the dochmiacs, prosodiacs, and enoplius, whose structure we have discussed in Chapter V. These irregular forms were much used in ancient times.

"Nor does even the order of feet remain the same, but sometimes the rhythm begins with a long and ends with a short, or *vice versa*, sometimes it begins with thesis, sometimes with arsis, and the periods are variously constructed. The greater the inequality, the more impressive are the compound rhythms. And if such rhythms excite dissimilar movements of the body" (*i.e.* in dancing), "they will bring about no small perturbation of the mind."

Tumultuous effects in modern music are not always produced by differences of construction in successive periods, as described here, but more often by disturbance of accent through syncopation, *sforzando*, the simultaneous use of triple and duple time, and impressive harmonic effects. Our exceptionally emotional effects are produced through rhythm quite as much as through harmony.

"Those rhythms that adhere to one species of time are less emotional; those which change to other species draw the soul in contrary directions by each change, constraining it to assimilate diversity."

We have a most impressive and beautiful instance of "change to other species" in the Trio of the Ninth Symphony, where the triple time, that has been impressed on us at enormous length in the Scherzo, changes to duple.

There follows a further discussion, in which the author asserts that those who make too violent changes are "dreadful and destructive," and he refers again to the moderation and strength of character induced by spondees $\left(\begin{smallmatrix}2\\4\end{smallmatrix} \; ♩ \; ♩\right)$, the warmth of trochees $\left(\begin{smallmatrix}3\\8\end{smallmatrix} \; ♩ \; ♪\right)$, and pæons $\left(\begin{smallmatrix}5\\8\end{smallmatrix} \; ♩ \; ♪ \; ♩\right)$. But the short equal notes of the pyrrhichius are mean and ignoble, while longs and shorts mixed without rhythmical proportion are altogether licentious. Those who make music without rhythm do not exalt the mind, but merely distract the observation.

Rhythms which are taken at a rapid pace are hasty. (The word means, literally, "warm.") Those which move slowly are relaxing and soothing. Some are intermediate, neither fast nor slow, but symmetrical in construction.

Then there are others which, being compact and voluble, are vehement and terse: these exhort to activity. And those rhythms which are put together with a superfluity of sounds[1], are flat and insipid.

Here ends the portion of Aristides' work that deals specially with the ethos of rhythm. There are, in all ages, those who, like him, look upon violent changes as destructive of art; but when the art is in an advancing stage, it may often happen that what are called the destructive tendencies of any particular age, are accepted without question by succeeding generations, as, for example, Monteverde's innovations, and Beethoven's defiance of the then orthodox rules. But the Aristoxenian school had justification for deploring changes, since its exponents lived in a period of decadence, and any change would be likely to be for the worse rather than the better.

It has been seen that the ancients were alive to the æsthetic differences between fast, slow, and moderate *tempo*, and it is interesting to observe that there were then, as now, composers of vapid music, who captured the unthinking by a "superfluity of notes."

Cleonides (Pseudo-Euclid) alludes to the ethos or character of various kinds of melody in the following passage (App. A, 14).

"There is change (metábolē, modulation) of melopœia (melodic construction) when the song passes from the diastaltic (exalted) character to the systaltic (narrow, contracted), or to the hesychastic (tranquil); or from the hesychastic to either of the others. The character of the melopœia is diastaltic when it tends to nobleness or masculine elevation of the soul, and to the heroic actions and passions which result from these feelings. The diastaltic style is specially used in tragedy and other (compositions) which bear the same kind of character.

"The systaltic ethos is that through which the soul is drawn to humility, or an effeminate disposition. It suits the passions of love and compassion, songs of lamentation and similar things.

"The ethos of the melody is hesychastic when it tends to a calming of the soul, to a free and peaceful condition of mind. Of this character

---

[1] *I.e.* without contrasts.

are hymns, pæans, laudatory odes, didactic songs, and everything of a similar kind."

Westphal considers that this passage is part of the direct teaching of Aristoxenus, or at any rate of his school[1]. We have already seen how the rhythmical construction affected the character of music; and the melodic construction contributed towards producing a suitable ethos. The diatonic genus, for instance, the genus in which tones predominated over semitones, gave a strong and dignified character to melody: the chromatic, in which semitonic successions prevailed, had a more complaining and pathetic character[2].

This kind of difference still holds good to-day to a limited extent; there is, for example, more virility in the diatonic music of a Bach or Beethoven, than in the somewhat cloying chromatic melodies of Spohr. But the emotion conveyed by the chromatic melos of Wagner is made virile by the intensely energetic rhythm.

To the various modes, the Dorian, Phrygian, Lydian, &c., were also attributed ethical characteristics, but in this the ancients were not agreed[3]. We moderns have discarded the ancient modes in favour of one major and three kinds of minor mode, the forms that have been found suitable to those combinations of sound which we call harmony. And we, like the ancients, are not entirely agreed as to the ethos of our modes. To take a single instance, most funeral marches are written in the minor mode, which is supposed to be more suitable than the major for the expression of grief; yet the "Dead March" by Handel, which, in England at least, takes precedence over all others, is not only in the major mode, but is purely diatonic throughout.

The conscious use of this or that means to give a particular character to music is legitimate enough so long as the composer is able to infuse sufficient of his own personality into the material to conceal artifice. But the labelling of compositions under the heading of diastaltic, hesychastic, systaltic, would be too artificial for modern ideas, too cramping to modern genius. Theory, like fire, is a good servant, but a very bad master; a little of it is necessary and beneficial; to be overpowered by it is disastrous.

In the eighteenth century the various portions of the Italian opera were categorised and labelled in a manner that has some analogy to the theory just described, though the list was not of the three-fold order so dear to the ancients. The number of classes was

---

[1] Westphal, *Aristoxenos*, p. 88. [2] Westphal, *Aristoxenos*, p. 242.
[3] See Chappell, *History of Music*, p. 99.

five; for a description of them we cannot do better than quote from the article by the late Mr W. S. Rockstro in *Grove's Dictionary*, under the word "Opera."

"The airs entrusted to these several performers were arranged in five unvarying classes, each distinguished by some well defined peculiarity of style, though not of general design; the same mechanical form, consisting of a first and second part, followed by the indispensable *Da Capo*, being common to all alike.

"1. The *Aria cantabile* was a quiet slow movement, characterised in the works of the best masters by a certain tender pathos...."

This would somewhat correspond to the systaltic ethos of the Greeks.

"2. The *Aria di portamento* was also a slow movement, and generally a very telling one. Its rhythm was more strongly marked than that of the *aria cantabile*, its style more measured....Flowing and graceful in design, its expression was rather sedate and dignified than passionate...."

We have here something akin to the hesychastic ethos.

"3. The *Aria di mezzo carattere* was open to great variety of treatment. As a general rule it was less pathetic than the *aria cantabile*, and less dignified than the *aria di portamento*, but capable of expressing greater depths of passion than either. Its pace was generally, though not necessarily, *andante*, the second part being sung a little faster than the first, with a return to the original time at the *Da capo*...."

This is diastaltic.

"4. The *Aria parlante* was of a more declamatory character, and therefore better adapted for the expression of deep passion, or violent emotion of any kind...."

This again would correspond, more or less, to the ancient idea of the diastaltic ethos.

"5. The *Aria di bravura*, or *d agilita*, was generally an *allegro*, filled with brilliant divisions, or passages of rapid *fioriture* calculated to display the utmost powers of the singer for whom the movement was intended."

This does not come under any of the three categories, for the Greek ideal does not seem to have encouraged, in great works of art at least, mere personal display. Such exhibitions of skill were not unknown in the public games, but they took no place in the theory of composition. For the chief object of the great masters of dramatic music was then, as in the latter half of the nineteenth and the present century, to move the soul of the listener by expression, rather than to excite his astonishment.

That composers like Handel, Buononcini and others could produce satisfactory works of art under such stringent conditions as those described above, is perhaps as strong an evidence of their genius as anything else that they did. That new generations of composers, such as Gluck in the eighteenth century, and Wagner in the nineteenth, should have rebelled against such a tyranny of convention is only natural. The tyranny seems to have been greater for our composers than for their ancient *confrères*. Rockstro does not speak of any change of style in the course of an aria, by which the dramatic situation could be enhanced, while Cleonides commences his description by referring to changes of ethos in the course of the song. Our old Italian opera was more artificial than Greek drama. Fortunately for us, reformers appeared, who were able to infuse new life into our dramatic music before it entirely sank under the weight of its own conventionality. Unfortunately for the Greeks, no new geniuses appeared, and their art died out.

Since writing this chapter our attention has been called to Dr Abert's *Die Lehre vom Ethos in der griechischen Musik* in which the subject of Ethos is more fully treated than elsewhere. Westphal in his *Allgemeine Theorie der musikalischen Rhythmik*, 1880, was, we believe, the first to suggest that the ethical theory of Aristoxenus might to some extent be applicable to the music of modern Europe, and his views have been accepted by others with useful results. Lussy, for example, in his *L'Anacrouse dans la Musique moderne*, 1903, shows how the presence or absence of the anacrusis may make a phrase diastaltic or hesychastic. Dr Abert gives quotations from the Greek writers bearing on the ethos of modes and genera, but for our subject the important part of his work is the third chapter, "Das Ethos in der Rhythmopoeie." After showing from Plato, Aristotle, Hermogenes and others, the ancient views as to the ethical force of rhythm, and quoting the passages in Aristides to which we have referred in this chapter, he describes "Rising and falling Rhythms[1]," quoting, in addition to Aristides, a passage in Quintilian, *Acres, quae ex brevibus ad longas insurgunt: leniores, quae a longis in brevibus descendunt:* "Vehement are those which rise from shorts to longs: more gentle those which descend from longs to shorts[2]."

---

[1] These are discussed in the present author's *Rhythm of Modern Music*, Macmillan, 1909.
[2] *E.g.* the iambus and anapæst are "rising," the trochee and dactyl are "falling" rhythms.

He discusses the beginnings and endings of verses in connection with ethos. The beginnings are connected with the anacrusis; of the endings he says, "Of far greater significance than the beginning is the ethos of the ending of the verse. Here, also, it is the long syllables which give the verse a fixed distinct character, while a short note at the end makes a halting, maimed impression and may weaken the whole verse. The catalexis also plays an important part in deciding the ethos." The short note at the end produces a feminine ending. Aristides[1] defines the catalectic metra as "those which withdraw a syllable from the final foot in order to obtain the gravity of the longer ending." This can easily be understood by musicians, who know that the final close of a phrase may occur on the third accent, while the note is sustained over the fourth: thus,

in which the first verse is complete, and the second catalectic: and Aristides would consider that the long note on the word "Gott" gives gravity to the phrase.

With regard to the three "styles" or "tropes," of rhythm, Dr Abert draws from the passages in Aristides that we have quoted the following general rules:

1. Feet in which the longs prevail belong to the hesychastic trope. Those in which the shorts predominate are of the systaltic, and those in which longs and shorts are mixed in about equal proportions, may be applied to all three tropes.

2. Feet which begin with the thesis have a more hesychastic character, while those which begin with arsis are more diastaltic or systaltic.

3. The larger the measured pauses that occur, the further removed is the composition from the systaltic and the nearer is it to the other two styles. (Surely by *emmetrische Pausen* the author means notes of relatively long value?)

[1] Meib. p. 50.

4. The rhythms of the even species have a hesychastic, those of the uneven a diastaltic or systaltic character. Three-time bars occupy a sort of middle place.

Together with these rules there is yet another, which is not of less importance in regard to the ethos, namely that regarding the *tempo*, the *agogē* of rhythm. Aristoxenus says[1], "While the proportion by which the genus is distinguished remains the same, the actual magnitude of the individual feet is decided by the *tempo* (*agogē*)."

That is to say, the actual space of time occupied by a given number of feet varies according to the *tempo* whether *allegro* or *adagio*, but the species of rhythm, whether even or uneven, remains the same. We have already quoted on page 78 Aristides' reference to *agogē*.

"It is clear," says Abert, "that one and the same rhythm performed in different *tempi* must produce differences of ethos, and that the *agogē* is of the greatest importance in studying the three styles of rhythm. This is most evident in rhythms of the triple species, the iambuses and trochees. Thus, the latter performed as semantoi[2], belong to the hesychastic style. If, on the contrary, they are taken *allegro moderato*, as, for example, in the Aeschylean chorus, they have a vigorous, energetic ethos, approaching the diastaltic. Finally, the trochees of comedy, which were performed *prestissimo*, have a wild extravagant character, on which is imprinted the systaltic style. In quite a general way it may be assumed that the hesychastic trope demands a slow *tempo*, the systaltic a quick, while the diastaltic is in the midst between the two extremes[3]."

So far as we are aware Dr Abert is the first to have opened new ground by suggesting that the ethos has to do with *tempo*, and with the endings of phrases as well as with the thetic and anacrusic forms to which previous theorists have for the most part confined their attention. To the musician it will seem so self-evident that the character of a piece is affected by its *tempo* that the only wonder is that no one should have noticed it before. But a new subject is like a newly discovered country: in neither case are all its possibilities revealed to the first pioneers.

Equal feet in the thetic form, namely, dactyls and spondees, were looked upon as the most dignified and elevated of rhythms, and the dactylic hexameter was called "heroic metre." The dactylic pentameter, on the other hand, was supposed to have a more tender ethos, suitable to elegies and lamentations. Yet Brahms uses dactylic

---

[1] Harmonics. Meib. 34.   [2] See p. 97.   [3] Abert, *Die Lehre vom Ethos*, p. 128.

pentameters as the basis of his very vigorous Rhapsody in E flat, in which the ethos is anything but tender and elegiac. The character of this composition is distinctly diastaltic, in spite of its five-bar rhythm: for the *tempo* is *allegro risoluto*, and it affords a good example in favour of Dr Abert's suggestion that ethos depends on *agogē* as much as on form. We shall have to refer to other modern pentameters in a later chapter.

Anapæstic rhythm, the anacrusic form of even time, has, as we have seen, an energetic character, owing to its "rising accentuation": yet when it takes the form of what G. Hermann calls "spondeic anapæsts," *i.e.* two equal long notes in the order arsis thesis, the ethos is mournful, and both in Greece and Rome it seems that this rhythm, with a slow *agogē*, accompanied the solemn steps of the funeral procession. Euripides often made use of it in connection with his heroines, and Aristophanes parodies the "lamentation anapæsts[1]." Of Beethoven's two Funeral Marches, the one in the Sonata, op. 26, is in slow anapæsts, not spondeic, while that in the Eroica Symphony is dactylic, with alternating anacrusic and thetic rhythms. Chopin's Funeral March is thetic for the most part, with, however, a beautiful "metabole of arsis and thesis" where the key temporarily changes to D flat.

The mournful ethos in all these examples is produced by the use of the minor mode and the slow *tempo*, rather than the special rhythmical forms.

Trochees, except in the slow form of the orthios and semantos (page 42, Nos. 8 and 9), chiefly belong to the diastaltic and systaltic style, but this again is influenced by the *tempo* in which they are performed. In contrast to the "dignity" (σεμνότης) of the dactylic, the trochees have "hastiness" (γοργότης[2]) though at a moderate pace they also have a certain amount of dignity. They accompanied the cordax, and scenes of combat. We have shown on page 84 how Bach could use the slow trochee for religious music.

The Iambic is more than any other the rhythm of forward, energetic movement[3]. It never falls to the expression of languid tenderness.

Ionic rhythm (page 50) was always considered as languid and soft and voluptuous. Aristides calls it vulgar[4], and some of the Roman poets allude to "lascivious ionic dances." The *ionicus a minore* (Ex. 16, p. 50) is considered more dignified than the *ionicus*

[1] Abert, *Lehre vom Ethos*, p. 134.
[2] *Lehre vom Ethos*, p. 139.
[3] *Lehre vom Ethos*, p. 140.
[4] Meib. p. 37.

a majore. The form was first used by Anacreon, and its ethos is systaltic.

Westphal endeavoured to show that ionic or six-time rhythm in modern music was distinguished from triple in that its phrases were dipodic instead of tetrapodic: but we doubt if this distinction can be upheld, or that there is really any difference between ionic and trochaic rhythm with us.

The Pæonic was originally a dance rhythm of a wild oriental character, and it entered Greece from the east in the earliest times. It was more especially connected with aulos music, and had an "enthusiastic" ethos[1]. We have shown in this and the previous chapter how it was used in classical and later times for tragedy, comedy, and hymnody, and how it is often mixed with other species. Dr Abert suggests that it may be closely related to the dochmius (Ex. 17, p. 51), concerning whose actual structure there is still uncertainty.

[1] *Lehre vom Ethos*, p. 149.

CHAPTER VIII

The Period—Eurhythmy or balance of periods in Greek music—The crousis in the Greek strophe—Its modern counterpart in the German Chorale, and in examples of the music of Schubert, R. Wagner, and Hubert Parry—The periodology of a Pindaric ode—The periodology of Bach's B minor Mass, and Christmas Oratorio, and of Handel's "Messiah."

IN Aristides Quintilianus and Martianus Capella[1], we meet with the technical term "Period." The somewhat chequered history of this word can be found in Westphal's *Allgemeine Theorie der Mus. Rhythmik*, pp. 22–24. For our present requirements the period must be understood as a combination of two or more rhythms, or musical phrases, in such a manner as to form a complete idea. The two or more rhythms can be conveniently referred to as "members," the English equivalent of the Greek technical name cola. The member may be divided into half-rhythms, the name then being semicolon, or less than a half rhythm may occur as a portion of the period; in this case it is a comma. The musical period therefore consists of a combination of cola, or colons, commas, and semicolons. Thrasymachus of Chalcedon adopted these terms for the divisions of rhetoric, and hence in course of time they came to be used for the signs marking the divisions in writing, *i.e.* the punctuation signs.

The period has been a fundamental principle in all ages, in prose, poetry and music. In its simplest form it has two members only, to which various names have been given. By grammarians they have been called Protasis and Apodosis; Antecedent and Consequent; by musicians, first phrase and second phrase; in German Vordersatz and Nachsatz; the first member or rhythm making, as it were, a statement, and the second confirming or completing it.

Thus, in Hebrew poetry:

Protasis
  Ponder my words, O Lord:
Apodosis
  Consider my meditation. } Period.

[1] Westphal, *Fragmente*, p. 54.

In Greek poetry:

Protasis

Οὐ - λυμ - πιον - ί - καν δέ - κευ

Apodosis

Χα - ρί - των ἕ - κα - τι τόν - δε κῶ - μον

} Period.

(PINDAR, *Olymp.* 4.)

In Prose:

Antecedent   *Consequent*
He went boldly to the door and knocked with an assured hand.
(R. L. STEVENSON.)

In modern Poetry:

Protasis
So is it now as it was then,
Apodosis
And as men have been, such are men.
} Period.

(SWINBURNE.)

In vocal music:

EX. 54. Wagner, "Meistersinger."

Jo - hannistag! Jo - hannistag! Blumen und Bänder so viel man mag!

In instrumental music:

EX. 55. Hubert Parry, "De Profundis."
Allegro energetico.

The Period of two members, being the simplest and most natural, figures very largely in both the popular and classical music of all ages. It is capable of great variety of treatment: the members may contain two, three, four or more feet, and they may be of equal or unequal length. But in modern music, classical and popular, the members, in the majority of cases, contain four feet each, the four feet being frequently divided into half-rhythms. In Example 55 we show a simple two-member period which is noticeable because its members are of three feet each, technically called tripodies. This form, comparatively rare in modern music, is used here with excellent effect. It is a ritornel in the chorus *Sustinuit anima mea in verbo*; it is immediately followed by a vocal period of three tripodies, and a lofty ethos arises from this rhythmical treatment, which raises the music above the commonplaces of everyday life, even though the simplest forms are used.

The two-member period alone by no means suffices for a highly developed stage of art. Sometimes a period contains many members; sometimes one of the members, or even a portion of one, is repeated, or anticipated. A half-rhythm or a single foot may be inserted between the two members, or added at the end, or placed at the beginning of the period. A familiar example of the addition of a half-rhythm or a single foot at the close of a period is the *Amen* at the end of a hymn; it is something external to the period, and yet intimately connected with it.

A period may contain only one member, or even only a portion of one, as in the thrice repeated "ich" at the opening of Bach's Cantata, *Ich hatte viel Bekümmerniss*. Theorists have catalogued many of the more obvious forms of period under special technical names, but we wish to spare burdening our readers with these as far as possible. Some will, however, be found in the glossary, at the end of the book, under the word " Period."

That the Greeks aimed at symmetry in the construction of their periods, and in the strophes which grew out of these, is natural, if we consider the formal nature of Greek Art. In this respect their music was like architecture: the form was not an end in itself, but a means to an end. Those who pay a passing visit to any of the Greek temples are at once struck with the grace and dignity of their general effect. Those who have leisure to study them in detail find that not only the temples themselves, but their component parts also are classified, and given technical names. So it is with the periods and the strophes of Greek poetry and music: they are classified and named, as a botanist names his specimens.

As an art becomes more democratic it loses extreme rigidity of form, or perhaps it is better to say, it relaxes its formality, to an extent that sometimes offends those who have been brought up in an older school. But it is scarcely possible that works of art can possess vital qualities unless there is some underlying element of formal construction present, even if it is not immediately recognisable to those who are unfamiliar with it. The traveller admires the Greek temples, though he may be ignorant of the principles of symmetry to which their grandeur of aspect is due.

The formal element in Greek poetry and music has been made the subject of remarkable investigations by J. H. H. Schmidt, Rossbach, and Westphal. The theory they propounded under the name of "Eurhythmy" may be briefly stated as follows:

Each strophe contains a certain number of periods, arranged in such a manner as to correspond with one another, to balance one another, in much the same way as the various features of an architectural design correspond and balance.

In modern poetry a somewhat analogous balance of parts is produced by means of rhyme: with the Greeks the correspondence was brought about entirely by rhythmical structure, to the appreciation of which it is believed that the melody contributed. Let us compare modern and ancient methods.

In Shakespeare's strophe,

> Take, oh take those lips away, } I
> That so sweetly were forsworn: }
>
> And those eyes, the break of day, } II
> Lights that do mislead the morn: }
>
> But my kisses bring again: } III
> Seals of love, but seal'd in vain. }

the first and second period are connected by interlacing rhymes, while the third period has its own rhyme. The Greek sense of form was more elaborate than this, and is in many cases beyond our rhythmical powers to appreciate, without some correspondence in melodic construction which would help us to grasp the rhythmical form[1]. We give a few examples of the rhythmical skeletons on which melodies were built: unfortunately we cannot, like the naturalists, reconstruct the complete work of art from the skeleton alone.

Ex. 56. "Antigone," Chorus No. 3, v. 582. Schmidt, p. cxv.
Strophe and antistrophe. (The double bar shows the end of a rhythm.)

In Ex. 56 the first period contains two hexapodies, *i.e.* rhythms of six feet each. The second period has four rhythms, of which the first and fourth are hexapodies, the second and third tetrapodies, or four-feet rhythms. Thus in the second period an eurhythmic correspondence is produced by the interlacing of tetrapodies and hexapodies, in a manner analogous to the rhymes of the Shakespeare strophe quoted above. The third period contains four tetrapodies,

---

[1] It may occur to the musical reader that Beethoven sometimes, in the course of a movement, utters a rhythmical figure *without* the melody that has previously clothed it, as, for instance, in the well-known drum passage towards the end of the Scherzo of the Fifth Symphony; or even makes use of a bare rhythmical figure by itself, as in the opening bar of the Violin Concerto. This device is possible with short figures occupying a very limited space of time. The correspondences known as Eurhythmy occupy spaces of time too large for the modern ear to appreciate, and it is perhaps for this reason that Westphal, after working at the theory with Rossbach for some years, eventually repudiated it.

of which the first two are exactly alike in internal structure, and the last two are alike, except for the *nuance* of giving a three-time note to the last foot but one.

The musician will notice that several of the rhythms end with a full bar, while their successors commence with the up beat. This would, of course, entail an ugly break in the rhythmical flow, if sung exactly as written here. But it was customary in the Greek strophe, as in the German Chorale, to introduce a *crousis*, or instrumental interlude, of a few bars, between most, if not all, of the rhythms. A beautiful modern example of exactly this treatment is found in Schubert's song "Der Leiermann." The pathos is greatly intensified by the instrumental interludes, which give the hearer full time to picture to himself each detail of the sufferings of the poor organ-grinder. So with the Greeks: their *crousis* served, by delaying the action, to impress each sentence, each musical phrase, on the audience. The *crousis* is made fun of by Aristophanes in "The Frogs" by introducing the words

phlat - to - thrat - o, phlat - to - thrat,

to imitate the kithara, between the rhythms of a ridiculous song, supposed to be sung by the shade of Euripides.

The musical period consisted, therefore, of a combination of members, divided from one another, and brought into relief, by short instrumental interludes. We moderns would scarcely tolerate such a constant checking of the action, though we occasionally make use of it for special effects. With us, as a rule, the strophe is sung without a break, the rhythms and periods being sufficiently marked by the closes and half closes of the music, while we generally place a ritornel between the strophes.

Richard Wagner, in the opening chorus of the "Meistersinger," adopting the style of the German Chorale, places interludes between the rhythms in a manner analogous to that of the Greeks, and utilises them for a highly imaginative introduction of some of the Leit-motives of the drama: while parts of Hans Sachs' monologue are made more impressive by the intervention of instrumental material between the vocal phrases. The chorus of pilgrims in "Tannhäuser," Act I, Scene 3, is also treated in the same way, each phrase being followed by a few bars of the shepherd's pipe. The construction of the soprano solo in Parry's "De Profundis" is very Greek-like in this respect; the words are divided thus,

A custodia matutina usque ad noctem: (*crousis*)
Usque ad noctem, speret Israel in Domino. (*crousis*)
Quia apud Dominum misericordia, (*crousis*)
Apud Dominum misericordia, apud Dominum misericordia,
(*crousis*)
Et copiosa apud eum redemptio. (*crousis*)

This construction is quite in accordance with Greek principles.

We must give a few more examples of eurhythmy in skeleton form. The eighth Pythian Ode was written for Aristomenes of Aigina, winner in a wrestling match. Aristomenes came of a family that had distinguished itself in wrestling at the Olympic and Isthmian games, and he himself had already won three prizes. The rhythms are Aeolian, that is, logaœdic. The ode contains five "triads," each consisting of strophe, antistrophe, and epode. The rhythms of each triad are alike: only the sentiments differ. The first triad addresses Hēsychia, the personification of peace or repose, and ends with praising the victor in the game. The second triad sings the fame of the heroes of Aigina and the family of the victor. The third deals with the worship of the hero Alkmaion. The fourth is in praise of Apollo, who gives victories in the games, and in the fifth the poet makes a contrast between the vanquished and victors, as an emblem of the uncertainty of human happiness. The logaœdic rhythm is suitable for dealing with the energetic character of a wrestler. Ex. 57 shows the rhythmical skeleton.

Ex. 57. Pindar, "Pythia," No. 8.
Strophe and antistrophe.

In the first period there is balance, in that the two rhythms are of four feet each, while contrast arises from the variation in position of the tribrach (three-note foot), the cyclical dactyl (dotted note foot) and the trochee (long-short).

In the second period, the first and third rhythms are of three feet each, and between them is a two-feet rhythm. Between the first and third rhythms there is a contrast of the same kind as in period I.

The third period contains two pairs of rhythms of respectively four and three feet, with a concluding rhythm of five feet. The tetrapodies appear to end with a feminine close, but this is not really the case, since in the majority of verses the fourth foot contains the end of one word and the beginning of another: hence the true phrasing would be indicated by the comma which we have placed in each fourth foot. Consequently the tripodic rhythms commence with the up-beat, and their preceding rhythms end with a long note, a feature we have referred to on page 103.

In the final rhythm, of five feet, neither the cyclical dactyl nor the tribrach appear. Let the reader imagine to himself for this rhythm a melody in the major mode, sung at a rapid pace, and he will see that the phrase might be made very trivial: but if he thinks of a melody at a slow pace in the Aeolian mode (our descending minor scale), ending with a drop from the tonic to the dominant, which seems to have been the orthodox form of final cadence, he will find that the effect may be very dignified.

The epode is analysed in Ex. 58.

Ex. 58. Pindar, "Pythia," No. 8.

Epode.

Here the first period consists of a group of $4+3+4+3$ rhythms, similar to that of the third period in the strophe, but without the concluding pentapodic phrase. But though similar in compass, there is a great difference in internal construction, as the reader will see.

The second period contains no less than six rhythms, in the order $4+4+6, +4+4+6$, of which no two are alike in anything except magnitude. So that here, as elsewhere, we get symmetry of outward form, combined with variety of detail.

We have probably by this time exhibited a sufficient number of dry skeletons to show the reader some, at least, of the principles of Greek periodology: it now remains to examine whether in the living art of to-day any similar principles are to be found, bearing in mind that form is not to be looked upon as an end in itself, but rather as serving some æsthetic purpose. That we shall find any modern composition exactly parallel in detail to any ancient Greek chorus is not to be expected; nor is it probable that any two Greek choruses are alike, in spite of the ancient ideas of balance and symmetry.

Adopting the simpler and more evident forms of dance music, modern Europe has agreed to accept the tetrapody as its normal rhythm for instrumental as well as vocal music, and hence its periods are for the most part formed by a combination of tetrapodies rather than of other magnitudes. We cannot therefore expect to find in it an extended use of eurhythmy in the sense of a well balanced arrangement of various magnitudes: eurhythmy there certainly is, but in the sense of beautiful and striking foot-schemes rather than period-schemes. That a certain feeling for eurhythmy of period influenced Mozart and Haydn is evident from some of their quartets, but it did not take so large a place with them as with Pindar and Simonides. As a rule they adhere to tetrapodic forms, varied by occasional dipodies and hexapodies.

At the same time, however, we shall find considerably more variety of magnitude in the rhythms in great choral works than in instrumental music: and in this matter our musicians approach Greek ideals, though without the exactitude of balance of the latter.

With our classical song-writers identity of magnitude in the rhythms is often avoided: sometimes they make their musical magnitudes depend entirely on the construction of the poetry, sometimes they give an added charm to the words by a delicate and suggestive change from the expected musical rhythm. In this matter their high sense of art causes them unconsciously to approach to something like Greek ideals.

To quote at any length from the enormous mass of modern music would be impossible, and we must content our readers as best we can with skeleton analyses, from well known or easily accessible compositions, leaving the reader, if he wishes, to make further investigations for himself.

In most choral music the phrasing is dependent on the musical material, rather than on the words, which are of secondary importance as far as the rhythm is concerned. The music expresses their ideas rather than their external form. Syllables are extended to a degree unknown to the ancients, and words are repeated, a device rarely employed by them. The words also occasionally overlap musical phrases, a feature which we seem to have in common with the ancients.

Ex. 59. Bach, B Minor Mass, Kyrie. (Fugue.)

Bach, B minor Mass. First Kyrie.

The signature is C, there are two feet in a bar, and the *tempo* is *adagio*.

The movement opens with an introductory period 2 + 2 + 4 feet. This is followed by a long ritornel, leading to the Fugue.

The final thesis of a rhythm frequently coincides with the first thesis of its successor, causing an overlap, as shown in Ex. 59. In working out the colotomy which underlies this fugue, we have considered that full closes in the tonic or nearly related keys constitute the ends of periods, and other kinds of cadence the ends of rhythmical members. As a rule cadences are more or less concealed by suspensions or other devices. (See page 70.)

Period I.   6 + 10 + 6 + 8 + 5 + 2 (37 feet).

This period ends with a full close in the relative major, coinciding with the ending of the word *eleison* in all the parts, but concealed in order that there shall be no break of continuity, by the following exquisite orchestral device.

Ex. 60. Bach, B minor Mass, Kyrie, Bars 43, 44.

Period II.   8 + 5 + 10 + 4 (27 feet).

It ends at bar 58 with a full close in the supertonic, again coinciding with the end of *eleison* in all the parts.

Period III.   2 + 7 + 6 + 6 + 4 + 5 (30 feet).

This ends with a full close in the dominant minor, and is succeeded by another lengthy ritornel. We may be permitted, perhaps, to look upon these three periods as being somewhat analogous to the strophe of the Greek chorus; but it will be observed that there is nothing of the balance of rhythms that corresponds to the so-called eurhythmy of the Greeks. On the other hand, our composer departs very far from the conventional "four-bar" phrasing of ordinary music, and in this respect he has the same feeling for variety of phrase-magnitude as had the Greeks.

After the ritornel the fugue recommences, and forms what we may look upon as the "antistrophe." Like the "strophe," this portion contains three periods, but its colotomy differs from that of its predecessor.

Period I. $6 + 10 + 6 + 6 + 4$ (32 feet).

This period comes to an end at bar 93, with a full close on the last syllable of *eleison*, in the tonic.

Period II. $4 + 7 + 2 + 6 + 2 + 6 + 4 + 3$ (34 feet).

Ending with a full close in the dominant minor at bar 110.

Period III. $2 + 2 + 3 + 6 + 5 + 5 + 5$ (28 feet).

Here the first movement of the Mass ends. Artistic symmetry of design is imparted by the general, not mathematically precise, balance of the periods. An ordinary period may have 8, 12, or 16 feet: the periods here are of tremendous proportions, befitting a gigantic work of art. The first period of the strophe contains no less than 37 feet, and the other two 27 and 30 respectively: and the periods of the "antistrophe" have much the same proportions. Can the human ear grasp such large dimensions of time? No, it certainly cannot, but the composer knew when to relieve the strain by coming to an end of his period and starting afresh: and he sees that the strain is about equally distributed throughout the two portions of the fugue. We are in the position of a near beholder of a great cathedral; he sees the details, but cannot take in the whole at once. If he goes to a distance he can see the symmetry of form that underlies the whole: and when the listener, by frequent hearing, has become familiar with this fugue, its grand proportions will make themselves felt in the satisfaction, the evergrowing interest, that increasing familiarity brings.

By these proportions, by the concealment of the phrases, by the imaginative orchestral work, the composer produces a sense of inconceivable grandeur, of continuity, of mystery, rising to the greatest heights of which music is capable. That this man, living an obscure life in a small German town, unconsciously made use of some of the rhythmical principles employed by the most artistic people the world has known, is a remarkable evidence of his profound knowledge of the deeper recesses of human nature.

In contrast to the contemplative character of the first *Kyrie*, the *Gloria in excelsis* has no concealment of its rhythms, which are brought out as clearly as possible; for here the ethos is that of praise, not mystery. After an opening ritornel, the chorus enters in a joyful trumpet-like motive, and carries out an introductory period of two pentapodies, which, by an overlap, make up nine bars, since each bar contains one foot. Then comes a ritornel, and the "strophe" begins. It is for the most part in overlapping five-feet rhythms (pentapodies), with occasional rhythms of four or seven feet (tetrapodies, or heptapodies).

The first period is divided from the second by a pentapodic ritornel, which overlaps the entrance of the voices for the second period. The latter is of two members only, a pentapody, and heptapody, the first overlapping the second. This period ends with a full close in the tonic at bar 78.

The third period is divided from the second by a crousis, and its first rhythm, a tripody, is also followed by a crousis. The period ends, at bar 100, with a change of time-signature (in Greek, "metabole of rhythm") to C, with two feet in the bar.

The diastaltic, trumpet-like material now gives way to one of those serenely flowing and exquisite movements with which Bach-lovers are familiar when tranquillity of mind has to be expressed in the music. The words at which the "metabole" takes place are *et in terra pax*. Here there is no mystery to be expressed, as in the *Kyrie*, no joyful exhilaration, as in the *Gloria*, but the repose and mental satisfaction of peace. And how does our composer treat it rhythmically? First there is a period of a single tripody, ending with a full close in the subdominant. The tripody announces the entrance of a new idea, and the accompaniment melts into a short crousis to give the audience time to assimilate it.

There follows a short "strophe" of one period only, containing tetrapodies and hexapodies. Neither the intermingling of rhythms of different "magnitudes," their mysterious concealment, nor the enthusiasm of the five-measure rhythms are suitable to the ethos implied by the words *pax hominibus*. Following the "strophe" is a ritornel, and, quite unexpectedly, the motive of *et in terra pax* enters as a sedate fugue subject, whose counter-subject is ornamented with somewhat conventional "divisions." The complete fugue contains three periods, as in that of the first *Kyrie*, but there is no "antistrophe," and there are other noticeable differences of treatment. The rhythms, instead of being concealed, are, for the most part, strongly punctuated by definite closes. Towards the end of the first period (the tonic full close in bar 145), the original tripody of bar 100 occurs three times over, isolated from its companion rhythms by the intervention of the crousis. The third period is divided from the second by a crousis, and thus the ethical treatment of the whole fugue differs entirely from that of the *Kyrie*, except in having three "periods," the form in which Bach usually constructs his fugues.

Bach was as fully master of the subtleties of rhythm as of all other technicalities of his art. If we open any volume of his works at haphazard we are pretty sure, before we have read many bars, to come upon some striking rhythmical device, some delicate *nuance*. Let us imagine that quite by chance we have opened the Christmas Oratorio, Part I, at the Aria, No. 4. The words "*Bereite dich, Zion, mit zärtlichen Trieben, Den Schönsten, den Liebsten, bald bei dir zu seh'n*" are set to a conventional two-membered period, in ordinary well-defined tetrapodies. But in the second period our attention is at once arrested by a beautiful device. The salient words of the poetic text are brought into prominence by the alternation of voice and instrument in single feet, while the tetrapodic construction is strictly adhered to, and made very evident by the harmony, thus:

Ex. 61. Bach, Christmas Oratorio, Part I, No. 4.

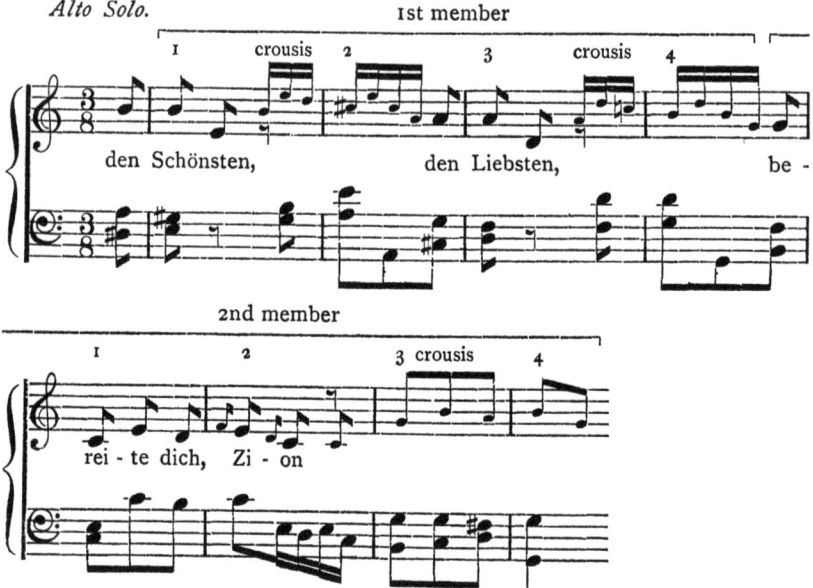

But this is not the only interesting feature of the aria. The movement is in the "*Da capo*" form, and the well-defined tetrapodic rhythms persist down to the word "*Fine*," while the contrasting section has the following colotomy:

Period I.   6 + 3 + 5.
Period II. 4 + 7.
Ritornel.
Period III. 2 + 4 + 5 + 4.

in which the contrast produced by variety of "magnitudes" is very Hellenic.

To enter fully into the inexhaustible rhythmical resources of this composer would require a volume to itself. We now pass on to the works of his great contemporary.

Handel approached his art from a different standpoint from that of Bach. He was in no sense a recluse working out his own high ideals with little reference to popularity, but a man of the world, anxious to appeal through his genius to the largest possible circles. His audiences, energetic in action, strong in political and personal character, were frivolous and contemptuous in their attitude towards music and musicians. Handel had therefore to frame his music in such a manner that it should force itself on the attention, that it should command respect by its sincerity, and hence there must be no misunderstanding about his rhythms and harmonies. His sturdy and practical character was eminently fitted for the task. The subtlety and mystery so often expressed by Bach could have little or no meaning to the British public of that day: and the predominance of the *prima donna*, the *primo uomo*, who, with their audiences, considered that vocal display was the chief end of music, made such an exalted ethos as that of Bach an impossibility in the country which Handel adopted as his own. To produce music as an effective vehicle for the display of vocal tone in the solo or in the choral body was absolutely essential.

"Messiah." Chorus, "Behold the Lamb of God that taketh away the sins of the world."

The signature is C, and there are two feet in the bar. The *tempo* is *largo*, the key G minor.

The first period ends at bar 15, with a full close in the key of F. The second concludes the chorus. The colotomy is as follows:

Ritornel.
Period I.   4 + 4 + 4 + 4 + 5 + 4 + 2 + 2 + 2.
Period II. 4 + 4 + 4 + 2 + 4 + 5 + 4.

There is no overlapping of rhythms, but the verbal text is more or less independent of them. Perhaps the musical rhythms would be more plain if we read them through without reference to the words, as if the composition were for instruments alone.

Ex. 62. Handel, "Messiah."

[Musical notation: Largo, SATB setting of "Behold the Lamb of God, that taketh away," with rhythm groupings marked as 1st rhythm, 2nd rhythm, and 3rd rhythm.]

This example shows the first two rhythms, and all the others proceed on similar lines. There can be no mistake about the tetrapodic construction, and nothing is left to the imagination. The individual accent of the feet is as strongly marked by the dotted notes as in a march or *maestoso* movement, while the chords consist, for the most part, of an alternation of tonic and dominant harmonies, generally in their fundamental position. It will be noticed that the rhythms commence with the second half of the bar and end with the first beat. The pentapody of bars 10–12 serves to reverse this order, and make the rhythms end on the third beat. Period II therefore commences with the first half of the bar, and its rhythms end on the second half until near the end, when another pentapody occurs, in order to bring the final close on the first beat of a bar, in the orthodox manner.

Aria, "He was despised and rejected."

The composition of this number is said to have moved Handel very deeply, and we may therefore expect to find some expression of his emotion in its rhythmical structure. In this we are not disappointed, and one is forced to admire the genius which knew exactly how far it might venture in an imaginative direction, without going too much above the heads of its audience.

The movement is in the *Da capo* form, the key being E flat, with the contrasting section in C minor. The *tempo* is *largo*, the signature C, and there are four feet in the bar. There is only one departure from the conventional tetrapodic structure[1], where the intensity of emotion overflows in a single phrase of ten feet. The majority of rhythms, including the last mentioned, are "catalectic," *i.e.* their last thesis is expressed by a silence, which is here used with peculiar fitness. There is a Greek-like treatment in the employment of the crousis, not only to give opportunity for contemplation, but also to enable the composer to change the position of the principal accent in the phrase.

The colotomy is as follows, the primary time being the quaver:

Aria.

Period I (preceded by ritornel). 4 (crousis) + 4 (crousis).

Period II.   4 (crousis) + 4 (crousis) + 4 + 4 + 4 + 8, ending at bar 21.

Period III. 4 (crousis) + 4 (crousis) + 8 + 10 + 8.

Period IV. 4 (crousis) + 4 (crousis) + 4 + 4 + 4.

C minor section.

The single period consists of tetrapodies, broken by rests and separated by the crousis.

Ex. 63. Handel, "Messiah."

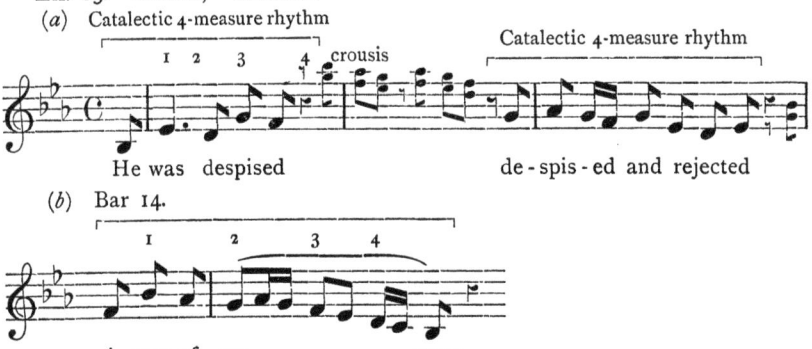

[1] Under tetrapodic we include eight-feet and two-feet rhythms, these being merely parts or multiples of four.

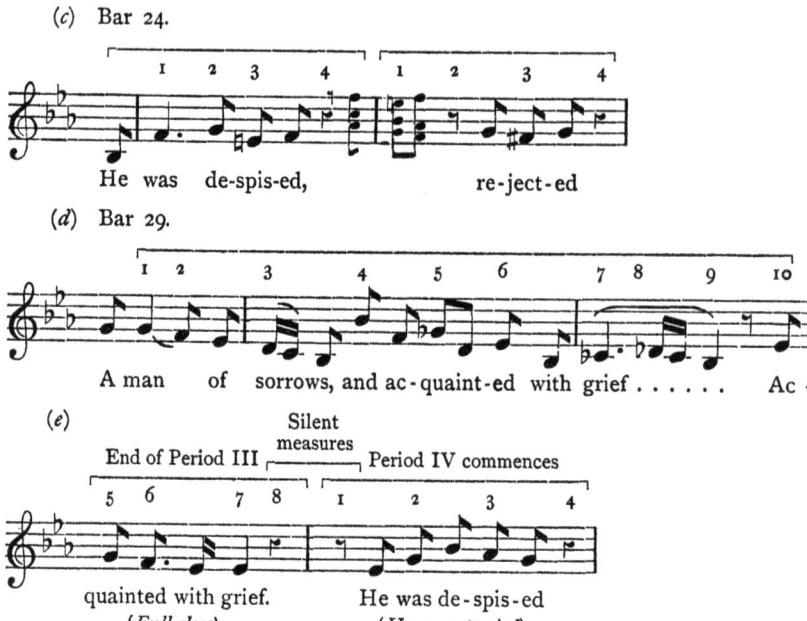

Ex. 63 (*a*) shows the first two rhythms, with their intervening crousis. The chief accent in each case is on the first thesis, and the reader should notice the effect of the momentary silence in the "catalexis," or cutting off of the final thesis.

In (*b*) the order of accentuation is changed, the strongest accent falling on the principal word, "sorrows." Handel could have maintained the previous order if he had wished, by placing the bar-line between the F and B flat: but the change of order has an important æsthetic signification.

In (*c*) the second phrase is curtailed, both at the beginning and end; the device of thus bringing a single word into prominence is similar to that of Bach, described on page 120, and the æsthetic result is the same.

In (*d*) we have the phrase of ten feet already referred to. Like the others, it is catalectic, and it is combined with a harmonic effect of peculiar pathos.

In (*e*) a new period begins with a silent thesis, and the voice enters entirely alone; the contemplation of the idea in the text has become too tense for instruments. This, at least, is how Handel wrote it, and seems to be how he felt it. In an edition we have before us, purporting to embody Mozart's additional accompaniments, there is an unfortunate filling up of what we call the "silent measures" by a somewhat commonplace repetition of the tonic triad, which quite destroys the imaginative effect of the rests.

One word more. The 8 + 10 + 8 rhythms of period III are, unlike the other rhythms, accompanied by sustained chords. Handel well knew what he was doing when he altered both the "magnitudes" and the style of accompaniment at the same time. This treatment causes an increase of solemnity, and at the same time prevents any monotony that might, perhaps, arise from the too frequent repetition of tetrapodic rhythms with the accompaniment moving always in quavers.

This great aria shows how imaginative a rhythm can be evolved by a highly gifted composer while adhering to the orthodox phrase of four feet with conventional harmonies.

"And with his stripes we are healed."

If we take the music of this fugue apart from the words, we shall find that it has more or less the feeling of being in tetrapodic rhythm, though this is not very clearly defined. The entries of the subject almost invariably occur where we should expect a new rhythm to commence. See Ex. 64.

Ex. 64. Handel, "Messiah."

Handel originally wrote this chorus with eight minims in a bar, which may perhaps imply that he felt the phrases as falling into eight-minim lengths, the minim being the primary time; giving a single bar to each rhythm would have the effect of placing a chief accent on one of the feet in the phrase, as we have seen in the aria, "He was despised[1]." There is no division into periods.

The movement is continuous throughout, and in this respect, as well as in the indefiniteness of its rhythmical divisions, it is somewhat akin to the polyphonic style, examples of which Handel's public would occasionally hear sung in the cathedrals.

[1] Or it may have been merely that the subject of the fugue was common property in ecclesiastical circles, and that church musicians usually made the minim (as they do now) their primary time, instead of the crotchet or quaver. In Bach's "Forty-eight" the same subject, not intended for ecclesiastical purposes, is written with the crotchet as the primary time.

CHAPTER IX

The colotomy and periodology of Gluck's "Orpheus," Haydn's "Creation," Mozart's "Don Giovanni" and Requiem, and Beethoven's Ninth Symphony.

Gluck, "Orpheus."

The first chorus consists of four periods, whose rhythms are fundamentally tetrapodic. The occasional entrance of the solo voice (Orpheus) in the single word "Eurydice" as an anacrusis has a beautiful effect, the choral rhythms being, with one unimportant exception, thetic, since they commence with the first beat of the bar. The bar is here equivalent to the foot.

The Aria, No. 7, "Cerco il mio ben così," has the following interesting construction:

Ritornel, or crousis, of one bar.
Period I. $3 + 3 + 3 + 4$, ending with a full close in the dominant.
Crousis of two bars.
Period II. $3 + 3 + 3 + 2 + 3$, ending in the tonic.
Crousis of one bar.
Period III.
Repetition of the final phrase of period II, extended to four measures, and further lengthened by a pause on the penultimate thesis.

The movement is fundamentally tripodic, with occasional variations for the sake of contrast. There is no special dramatic signification in the form here, the æsthetic effect being due to the charm of comparative rarity.

The first section of Eurydice's Aria, "Che il fiero momento," is also tripodic: but its periods conclude with a pentapodic rhythm, by which the interest is enhanced.

The best known number of this opera, "Che faro senza Eurydice," is for the most part in conventional form as to its rhythms and periods, but the second period (in G major), in which Orpheus calls to Eurydice, has dipodies, in which the silent second thesis seems to imply that the caller is listening for a response.

An example of absolutely simple tetrapodic form, as innocent of all *nuance* or device of any kind as an ordinary hymn tune, is found in the Finale, where Orpheus, Eurydice, Amor and the chorus, sing a whole movement in two-member periods. The scheme is as follows:

Period I. $4 + 4$ Full close,
Period II. $4 + 4$ Half close,
Period III. $4 + 4$ Full close,
Period IV. $(2 + 2 = 4) + 4$ Full close,

and so on to the end. Such simplicity is delightful in the eighteenth century atmosphere of the whole work. When it occurs, as it very frequently does in present-day music, in connection with commonplace melody, and ideas intended only to catch the ear of the vulgar, it is intolerable to the cultivated musician. Compositions founded on this scheme sooner or later become wearisome even to those for whom they are intended, and then they disappear, or "go out of fashion[1]."

Haydn, "Creation."

The opening words of the chorus, "And the Spirit of God," allotted to a single period, move in slow, long-drawn pentapodies, the crotchet being the primary time[2]. The first rhythm is anacrusic and catalectic, thus,

anacrusis   1   2   3   4
And the | Spirit of | God moved up- | on the face of the | waters;

5
catalexis, the rhythm being completed by a chord.

---

[1] A class of popular music that endures from generation to generation is the national anthem. The patriotic words of such a composition give it an important element of permanence: but the tune must also have some special rhythmical element, or we should find complaints that such and such a nation has not a satisfactory national anthem. We venture to suggest that no tune as simple in rhythmical construction as the above Chorus of Gluck would have a chance of permanently engaging the affections of a people to the extent that would raise it to the dignity of a national anthem. Rhythmical device of some kind must be present.

In "God save the King," there are two unequal periods, whose rhythms are all dipodies, not tetrapodies. The first period has three members, the second four. The unusual form has been a subject of discussion, but we believe that it is just this "irregularity" that causes the tune to retain its perennial popularity, while fault is often found with the words.

In "La Marseillaise" the anacrusis, catalexis, and anticipation of the close of a phrase help to raise the tune above the commonplace. It was composed by an enthusiastic amateur, and its rhythmical devices are an unconscious expression of his feeling.

In "Die Wacht am Rhein," which is entirely tetrapodic, there is plenty of variety within the feet: change of "scheme" in the Aristoxenian sense.

The Austrian National Hymn has no exceptional construction, and is probably almost the only instance in which a simple melody alone has been able to conquer the permanent affections of the populace without the aid of special rhythmical devices.

[2] It will be remembered that dactylic pentapodies were associated in the Greek mind with elegies and lamentations. This is by no means the case with us.

The composer, through his rhythmical scheme, brings before us so vivid a picture of the idea conveyed by the words, that we almost seem to have the action of the drama before our eyes.

The second pentapody of the period is made dramatic by rests, and by the extension through a whole foot of the final major triad, *fortissimo*, thus,

anac.   1   2   3
And God | said (*crousis*), | Let there be | light (silence):
                     4   5
           and there was | light.
                (*fortissimo*)

The sudden *fortissimo* is very fine from a purely musical point of view, but it has always struck us as being somewhat near the indefinite line between "word-painting" and the expression through music of the dramatic idea, rather than of the individual words. But this must always be a matter of opinion; we imagine that there can scarcely be two opinions about the beauty and dramatic significance of the above period as a whole.

The Aria "With verdure clad" is tetrapodic, and has two feet in the bar. Its first period has three members, the third of which is a repetition of the first, with the difference that the melody is here divided between the orchestra and the voice, instead of being given to the voice alone. This is a device used by classical composers of all epochs. In the present instance it has no æsthetic significance beyond its freshness of effect.

The second period, ending with the full close in the tonic, has the form 4+6, the latter rhythm being catalectic in the voice, complete in the instruments.

In the next period the word "plant" is extended by "divisions" over several rhythms, which are separated by rests. Dividing a single syllable into two or more portions was a common practice with the composers of the eighteenth century: it originated in Italy, where the voices had a natural flexibility and agility for which material was demanded on which these qualities could be exercised. Custom, early associations, and education have a strong influence on the appreciation of music, and the northern nations, having been taught that all good things musical came from Italy, learned to accept and assimilate everything offered by Italian singers. Such passages as the one to which we are alluding, though contrary to dramatic propriety, and making nonsense of the text, not only cause us no aversion when we are accustomed to them, but, on the contrary, are really delightful in the hands of a great artist. We admire the flexibility of the voice, we are charmed by its tone-quality, and the personality of the singer, which is necessarily brought into prominence, attracts us, so that we lose sight of the fact that such passages of *fioritura* are dramatically superfluous and meaningless. By a fortunate arrangement of our nature, we do not always seek the strictly logical in art; if we did we should live in a very dull world.

The words "Here shoots the healing plant" are now repeated in a three-membered period, broken by pauses and crousis.

The middle section of the song consists of a period of three hexapodies, all of which are catalectic. The repetition of the opening section calls for no comment. There is here no rhythmical device, no appeal to the deeper feelings: all is as clear and bright as the air of a sunny day. The composer places in the forefront the pleasure that is derived from hearing a beautiful voice, and a complete command of vocal technique. As a rule, songs like this were composed with special reference to the capacities of some individual singer; but in the present instance this does not appear to have been the case. Formality of harmony and melody blends with periods which have just enough unconventionality to escape being commonplace.

To those brought up on Bach, and the great composers of the last fifty years, this music seems formal and conventional: yet it has its charm for those who can temporarily place themselves, in imagination, in the musical atmosphere of the year 1797[1].

Mozart, "Don Giovanni."

Leporello's opening solo "*Notte e giorno faticar*" ("Night and day I work so hard") is set to a rollicking melody in tetrapodies, there being two feet in the bar. It is preceded by the usual ritornel. The first period, which ends with a full close in the tonic in bar 32, consists of seven members, but by the repetition of two of these, the actual period is extended to nine.

Its scheme is:

Period I. $4 + 4 + 4 + 6$ (pause) $+ 5$ (crousis) $+ 5a + 6 + 6a$.

---

[1] A considerable amount of pleasure may be derived from many kinds of music of the past if we can obtain a more or less vivid idea of the circumstances under which it was first heard: to enjoy it thoroughly we must make the necessary effort of imagination to place ourselves *en rapport* with the circumstances, just as we do when we witness a play dealing with historical or legendary material. The effort with music is greater, since in many cases there is no scenery or action to assist. Thus, much of the harpsichord music of the past is formal in itself, but if we imagine the courtly gallants of Queen Elizabeth's day, for example, dancing to it, and listening to it, it appears in a new light to us. We can, in fact, "acquire a taste" for music of past generations, and this taste gives so much pleasure that it is well worth the effort.

Rhythm 5 a is a repetition of 5 and 6 a of 6, the latter being extended to 8 by two additional feet.

The repetition of 5 emphasises the semi-humorous assertion "*voglio far il gentiluomo*" ("I will be a gentleman") by adding "*e non voglio più servir*" ("and no longer will I serve") to the same melody, and the latter sentence is repeated twice over in the two concluding rhythms. It is very true to life: the uneducated man emphasises his assertions by repeating them over and over again.

In the second period, in which Leporello mockingly addresses his absent master, there is a similar repetition: and in the third he again repeats the words we have quoted, to their own melody.

In the fourth period the words "*ma mi par che venga gente*" ("but I think that some one comes"), "*non mi voglio far sentir*" ("I don't wish that they should hear"), are set to a kind of patter on one note, ending, however, with a repetition of the melody of "*e non voglio più servir.*" Mozart has happily contrived to utilise his rhythms and melodies to burlesque the natural expressions of a discontented servant.

A ritornel now brings Donna Anna and Don Giovanni on the scene. She, in her anxiety, utters a single period of 4 + 4 feet, and, after a *crousis*, is answered by Don Giovanni in a mocking repetition of the same period, slightly altered to suit the bass voice. Here again the composer utilises the conventional repetition of a musical period for a dramatic object: Donna Anna is excited, and Don Giovanni, in the same melody, tells her that her excitement is in vain.

In the next period, while the two are shouting at one another, Leporello adds a bass part in long notes, commenting thus, "*Che tumulto! o ciel! che gridi! Il padron in nuovi guai!*" ("What a noise, oh heavens, what shouts! master's in another mess!"). The trio is carried on in regular periods, for the most part in tetrapodies, and the dramatic element is brought out by the contrapuntal arrangement of the parts, so that our composer here, again, is able to subordinate the conventional forms to the dramatic situation.

Towards the end, while Leporello, in another "patter," is debating whether he ought to interfere, the Commandante appears, and, in excited broken phrases, an altercation ensues between him and Don Giovanni, the musical material, however, adhering to orthodox tetrapodic construction. During a ritornel they fight, and the Commandante falls, mortally wounded. He utters a dying speech, which gradually becomes more broken up as he gets weaker, while

Don Giovanni mocks him, and the chattering Leporello expresses his fright in rapid dotted notes.

The art exhibited in this movement has much in common with that of the Greeks. The repetitions and patter of the serving man may be compared with Aristophanes' burlesque imitation of the rhythms common to the populace of his day. (See page 85.) The clever adherence to conventional musical form in general, combined with details suitable to the situation, reminds us of the methods of the old Greek dramatic poets: and throughout there is an intensely human expression, as there is with them.

In the duet "*Là, ci darem la mano*[1]," by a delicate rhythmical *nuance*, the same melodic phrases are made to express the masterful persuasion of Don Giovanni and the fluttered excitement of Zerlina,

Ex. 65. Mozart, "Don Giovanni."

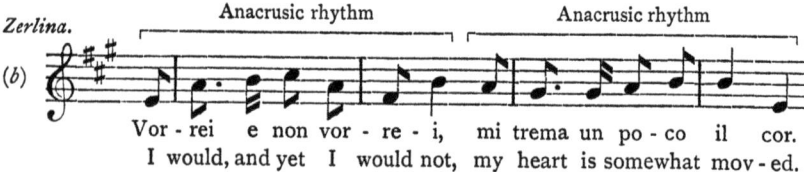

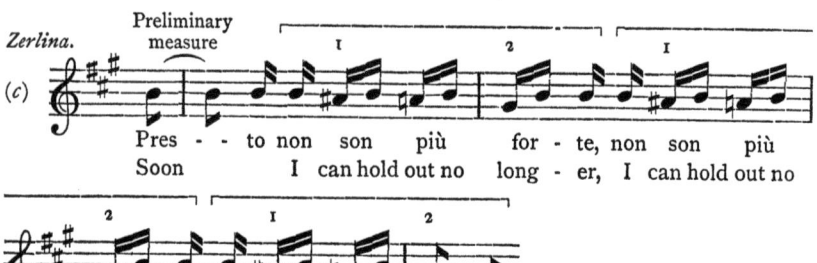

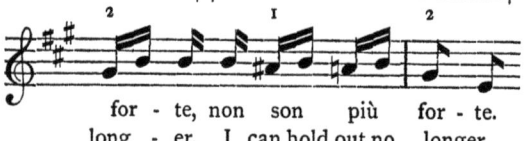

[1] To fully appreciate the delicacy of Mozart's rhythmical treatment here, it is necessary to have a more exact idea of the meaning of the Italian text than can be conveyed by any translation that has to be fitted to the music. For example, *Dar la mano* does not mean to "give the hand," in the lover's sense, but to "shake hands on it," to conclude a bargain, or make a promise. Don Giovanni is not a lover who falls on his knees before his mistress, but one who carries things through by force, and Mozart was fully aware of this characteristic.

as she gradually gives way to him: thus the orthodox musical form is preserved, and yet dramatic requirements are fulfilled. Don Giovanni, in whose utterances there is no hesitation, no beating about the bush, calmly attacks his rhythms on the down beat, while the undecided answers of Zerlina are returned in the same melody with the anacrusis. It will be remembered from Aristides that anacrusic forms are "more agitated," thetic more calm.

This alteration of a single note is a stroke of genius, by which the same music is made to express two different characters; it is continued down to the double bar, where, Zerlina having given way, the joy of the lovers is expressed in a series of dance-like iambic rhythms.

The "colotomy" calls for no comment. The periods are all in orthodox pairs of tetrapodies, except where Zerlina feels her fortitude giving way, which she expresses in the agitated dipodies of Ex. 65 c.

Though from the point of view of purely musical form the repetition of phrases is satisfactory and pleasing to the audience, it undoubtedly sometimes delays the action, in spite of Mozart's genius. Thus, in the first section of Zerlina's song, "*Vedrai, carino, se sei buonino, che bel remedio ti voglio dar*" ("You shall see, dear, if you are good, what a fine remedy I can give you"), the rhythms and periods repeat one another with justification, for they are discussing a single subject, viz. the remedy. In the second section, however, in which the remedy is applied, by Masetto, at her suggestion, laying his hand on her heart to feel how it beats, the many repetitions of "*sentilo battere*" ("feel how it beats"), written merely in order to make this section balance the first from a musical point of view, cause the action to drag. And in the Finale, again, the repetition of words to make the musical form complete and orthodox, is dramatically unnecessary.

A noticeable feature in the opera is the frequency with which an aria begins in even and ends in uneven rhythm. Mozart often contrives to make this convention fall in with some dramatic purpose, as in the dance-like duet between Don Giovanni and Zerlina. But throughout the set pieces of the opera, the lyrical element is more in evidence than the dramatic in the rhythmical structure. This was in keeping with the ideas of the day, and it is an evidence of Mozart's genius that he was able to amalgamate the two elements as frequently as he did.

Mozart, "Requiem."

The words "*Requiem æternam dona eis Domine*" seem, at first sight, to be set without periodic form, somewhat in the manner of Palestrina. But this is not really the case, for there is an underlying tetrapodic construction which makes the first seven bars take the following Greek-like balance:

Period I.   4+4+2+4+2.

Mystery is produced by the "procatalexis," that is, the omission of the opening thesis, from each voice part as it enters. The construction will be understood from the analysis in Ex. 66.

Ex. 66. Mozart, "Requiem."

End of Period.

The succeeding period, to the words "*et lux perpetua luceat eis,*" has a dipodic catalectic, and a complete dipodic and tripodic rhythm.

The soprano solo "*Te decet hymnus,*" &c. has a period of two pentapodies and is followed by a choral period of the same kind.

The words *Kyrie eleison, Christe eleison, Kyrie eleison,* are set to a double fugue, which is not divided into distinct periods as in the Bach example described in Chapter VIII. There is an underlying feeling of tetrapodic rhythms, not concealed by harmonic devices as with Bach; but continuity of effect is produced by the overlapping of musical motives and words. Such continuity is a salient feature in much of the best ecclesiastical music, and in fugal work: the rhythms are not always separated clearly, as in lyrical music. In Bach's *Kyrie*-Fugue the periods are distinct, in Mozart's they are not.

A composition of this kind is not occupied with a continuous narrative or dramatic action, or with lyrical music. On the contrary, the interest is concentrated on giving musical expression to the single idea, enunciated in a very few words. The words themselves are, as a rule, scarcely distinguishable, except at the entrances of the theme: the audience well knows the idea that is being musically treated, and hence it is unnecessary that the words should be always heard. Rhythmical form is obtained by the harmonic basis, while the continuity, that is essential if the work is not to have a halting, cut-up effect, is produced by the constant overlapping of words and of musical motives.

The vocal fugue, though rhythmically following general principles like those of the ancients, is the musical form that is furthest removed from Greek ideals in the matter of the words. It will be remembered that at the Council of Trent it was proposed to banish polyphonic music from the Church, because the words were undistinguishable in the network of counterpoint. To the calm logical mind, holding views similar to those of Philodemus of Gadara, to whom allusion has been made in the Introduction, nothing can be more senseless than to sing in such a manner that the meaning of what is sung cannot be understood: and in this Aristotle and everyone else in Greece would have agreed with Philodemus. But there is this great difference between Eastern and modern European music, that in the former poetry is the predominant partner, and in the latter pure music has attained such a development as frequently to overshadow the claims of its verbal partner[1]. Hence it comes that in a fugue the

---

[1] Westphal uses the definitions "Christian Music" for that of modern Europe, and "Non-Christian" for the more or less unison music of all other civilisations, whether past or still existing.

voices are used as instruments to convey musical expression, rather than the precise meaning of the words each time these are uttered.

One can hardly conceive what a loss it would have been to mankind in exalted pleasure and refinement, had the logical party prevailed at the Council of Trent.

Beethoven.

Under Beethoven instrumental music arrived at a point of development that raised it from the position of a servitor to that of the equal partner, or even, to some extent, the rival of vocal music. The symphony became as important a composition as the oratorio or mass: the overture, formerly a light fugue followed by a dance, from being merely a cover for conversation, was now beginning to take the form of an epitome of the chief musical themes of the opera about to be performed, and was intended to be seriously listened to.

Beethoven is far better known by his nine symphonies than by his choral music: the massive sound of the orchestra, with its immense variety of "colours," was now able to appeal to mankind at least as powerfully as the choral body. It did not displace the chorus in the musical world: it merely asserted a power over the emotions equal to that of its elder sister, and was no longer only a subordinate. In the Ninth Symphony, a product of Beethoven's ripest development, we have a work of art in which instrumental and vocal music take an absolutely equal share, and this work is therefore suitable to examine in order to see in what direction "periodology" and "colotomy" were now tending.

We consider that the first period of the opening movement ends with the tonic full close, as shown in Ex. 67. There is a preliminary half-rhythm in the accompaniment, analogous to the preliminary *crousis* of a Greek chorus. Like the two bars that introduce the Eroica symphony, these two feet give no clue to the species of rhythm that is about to follow: the sustained chord on the horns eliminates any accent that might be heard in the strings, and we are purposely left in the dark. The melody enters with the shortest possible anacrusis, and merely strikes the root and fifth of a triad: we are as much in the dark as to the tonality as we are with regard to the rhythm. Then, if we hope to get light through the end of the first melodic rhythm, we are disappointed: the first and the second rhythms are catalectic: their final thesis is cut off, and thus the attention is still kept in suspense. The third rhythm is complete at the end, but incomplete at the beginning, its first thesis being omitted: mystery is piled on mystery. The fourth member of the period is incomplete at its beginning, is a half-rhythm, and there is a

Ex. 67. Beethoven, Ninth Symphony.

End of Period I and commencement of Period II.

change of harmony, not on a thesis, as might be expected, but on a weak note. All this time a *crescendo* has been going on, starting from *pianissimo*. There has been no harmony beyond a bare fifth: the mode is kept a secret. The number of notes increases in each successive rhythm, the interest becomes more intense, the mystery is maintained. Finally, on the last member of the period, the full orchestra enters, *fortissimo*, and thunders out the tonic triad and dominant seventh in melody, while at the same time it makes the rhythm clear, and drives both rhythm and tonality home, as with the blows of a cyclopean hammer.

"What does it all mean?" the critics of the day might well have said. Such mystery, such ambiguity of key, mode, and rhythm, must have seemed madness to the lovers of the clear-cut periods of Mozart's and Haydn's symphonies, and of Beethoven's own early works. "Give us something like your septet," said some one to the composer, during the second or third "period" of his creative career. But Beethoven was working out the destiny of music, and that destiny is to appeal to mankind not always through simplicity and charm, but through the sense of mystery that is inherent in man, and that finds its expression in music more than in the other arts.

It will be noticed that the rhythms are all tetrapodies except the last. Musicians seem to have tacitly agreed about this time to give up using the occasional tripodies of Mozart and Haydn, and to accept the tetrapodic magnitude as normal for all instrumental music, dividing it into half-rhythms at will, or adding half-rhythms to it, while considering other magnitudes as more or less abnormal. When a pentapody is introduced, it generally is made, as in the present instance, to overlap the succeeding rhythm, so that the tetrapodic balance of the period is not disturbed. This

Ex. 67 *a*. Beethoven, Ninth Symphony.

careful balancing of periods owes its origin to the same feeling that produced the eurhythm of the Greeks; the difference is one of degree only. We balance tetrapody against tetrapody, they balanced groups of magnitudes against other groups of magnitudes.

Period II begins with the overlap. Its first member is divided into half-rhythms. Its second is a half-rhythm only, and its third is divided like the first. Its fourth member is a pentapody, and catalectic. Each new rhythm in this period contains new material, and the accents are well marked and decisive, in contrast to those of the first period. The haze has cleared away; everything now stands out in detail. The effect is entrancing[1].

Period III is a return to Period I, but in tonic instead of dominant harmony. As we have now obtained a firm hold on the rhythm and tonality, the mind is free to contemplate and enjoy the material by which it was at first mystified.

The fourth period, Ex. 68, begins with dipodies, not only separated

Ex. 68. Beethoven, Ninth Symphony.

by silences, but broken by internal rests, the "empty times which complete the rhythm" of the Greek theorists. The material is taken from the decisive part of Period I. The accentuation is strongly marked by a *sforzando* on each thesis. The motive itself is

---

[1] In analysing these two periods the writer was reminded of an experience he once had when approaching the island of Alderney in a sailing yacht. The sun was just rising, the sea was calm, the island, though near, was shrouded in mystery by a bright early morning haze on the surface of the water. The compass was the only guide, while the mind was alert with a pleasant expectancy as to when and how the landfall would be made. Suddenly the haze lifted, and every detail of the island shone out in the morning sun with a beauty that seemed magical. In the passages quoted in Exs. 67 and 68, Beethoven has given artistic expression to much the same kind of elevation of soul, of mystery and expectation, as was aroused by the intense beauty of nature on that memorable morning off Alderney.

monopodic, and this fact is impressed by giving it alternately to strings and wind, while our attention is chained by the alternation of powerful *sforzando* chords on the full orchestra with complete silence. Having thus excited us, the composer increases the rhythmical interest by uttering the motive in a more concentrated form. There follows a motive from Period II, in which frequent *sforzandos* impress a sense of vigorous determination, and then comes the fifth period, Ex. 69.

Ex. 69. Beethoven, Ninth Symphony.

Here the gently uttered anapæsts have a feeling of strength in repose, after the excitements of the *sforzandos* and rests. This period consists of $3 + 3 + 3$ rhythms, each overlapping its successor, and thus producing the equivalent of $2 + 2 + 2$.

Period VI begins with overlapping rhythms, and a fresh scheme

Ex. 70. Beethoven, Ninth Symphony.

of foot, in which the melody is sustained, while there is an underlying agitation in the accompaniment. In the second part of the period the theses are omitted in the melody, and at the same time the accompaniment becomes more agitated: two elements tending to increase of interest.

Period VII also commences with overlapping tripodies.

Ex. 70 *a*.   Beethoven, Ninth Symphony.

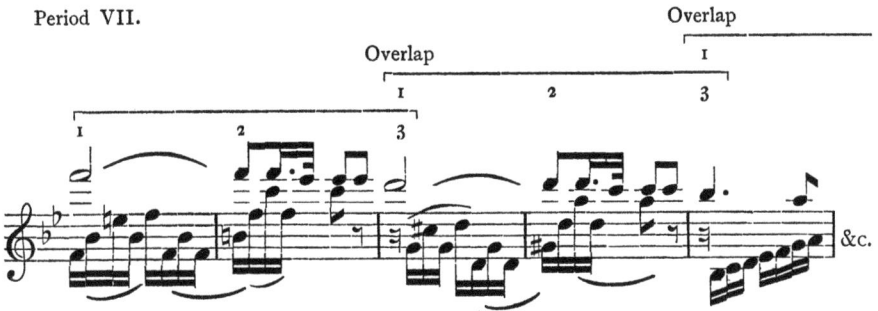

The sustained character of melody continues, the accompanying movement being softened by *legato* instead of *staccato* notes. This tranquil period rouses itself out of its repose, and leads to a climax, in which the full orchestra thunders out a martial rhythm, as if to say, "a truce to these soft delights: let us have action." But the

Ex. 70 *b*.   Beethoven, Ninth Symphony.

tranquil ethos conquers, and in Period IX we have an example of that delightful Beethovenian effect where a sustained melody is accompanied by a rhythmical figure that has been previously announced as a leading motive. In the present instance what we have called the "martial" figure is heard *pianissimo* beneath the melody, as if conquered, and kept in restraint by it.

In Period X the bass instruments, which have hitherto played a

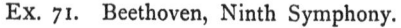
Ex. 71. Beethoven, Ninth Symphony.

more or less subordinate part, begin to assert themselves in gigantic intervals, with powerful syncopations, the latter being driven well home by a hammer-like quaver on the drums and trumpets. The whole orchestra takes part in this strenuous effort, except the upper strings, which accompany it in a florid passage, like sea birds hovering over the wake of some great ship.

Period XI opens with a melodious passage on the oboes and flutes marked *espressivo*; but the "martial" figure occasionally breaks in, and, in Period XII, completely conquers. With this period we arrive at the point, where, in the ordinary course, there would be a double bar and repetition sign.

We do not propose to analyse the movement beyond this point. We have explained sufficient to show how in the modern European civilisation it has been found possible to appeal to the soul through the agency of instruments alone, which cannot express any concrete ideas. And the "aisthēsis" thus set in motion has much in common with the feelings inspired by certain aspects of nature. The motive force is the application of rhythmopœia to an entirely modern rhythmizomenon, namely, the mass of sound produced by the orchestra. A great symphony is a tone-poem, a drama without words. The Greeks theoretically considered instrumental music as meaningless: only words, they said, could give sense to musical sounds. Yet they knew that the trumpet could inspire the warrior, the aulos could give life to the march, the lyre was associated with poetic ideas. There was an elementary knowledge that instruments alone had some kind of effect on the "aisthēsis," but, like their elementary knowledge of the effects of electricity, they did not bring it to practical purposes. Our composers have travelled an immense distance beyond them, and have created a great art out of a rhythmizomenon that was only known in its embryo condition to this imaginative and artistic nation.

Scherzo.

If all the repetitions indicated by the composer were played, this movement would contain no less than 1316 bars, founded on a pair of tribrachs, and a pair of cyclical dactyls. The tribrachs give light-hearted gaiety, the cyclical dactyls are more weighty in character. The contrast produced by the four-time trio (which is not included in the 1316 bars) is self-evident.

How can an audience tolerate a repetition of two simple rhythmical schemes carried to such an extreme length? Moreover, the periods, of two members each, are of the simplest and most elementary kind possible: they have the form found in the most ordinary hymn tune or popular song. The genius of Beethoven, at the culmination of his career, could make use of such a simple and apparently elementary appeal to the mind, to produce a monumental work of art that will certainly endure as long as our system of music continues to have any message for man. Let us examine his methods.

The movement commences with an introductory period of two tetrapodies. Like all the rest of the rhythms, these give the impression of being in *syzygies* or pairs of feet, one of which is more important than the other; in other words, one is a thesis-foot, the other an arsis-foot, as explained in Chapter V. Whether a conductor is conscious or not of this feeling, we doubt if it is possible to perform the movement without giving some effect to it, however slight.

The introductory period is broken by silences on the arsis-feet: its construction is imaginative in the extreme. The feet of the first

Ex. 72. Beethoven, Ninth Symphony.
Introductory Period.

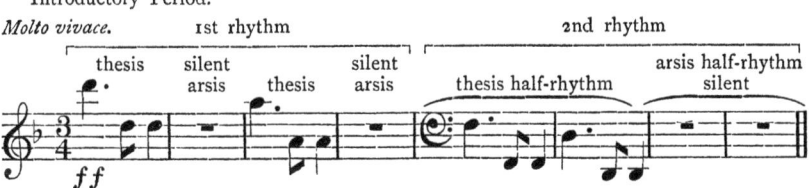

rhythm are in syzygies, those of the second are in pairs of syzygies. Could anything be more calculated to excite alertness in the hearer?

There follows a succession of unbroken and scarcely separated periods, each being of two members, each member being tetrapodic, while the first foot of each tetrapody is a thesis-foot.

Ex. 73. Beethoven, Ninth Symphony, Scherzo.

In the eighth period there is a change: the syzygies become anacrusic, that is, the alternation is arsis, thesis, instead of thesis, arsis. This contrast of ethos is brought about by the introduction of a pentapody as the second rhythm of Period No. VII and is im-

Ex. 74. Beethoven, Ninth Symphony, Scherzo.

pressed on us by the discords, which naturally suggest a thesis, while they resolve on an arsis.

Period No. X is surely anacrusic, although in the edition before us the phrasing of the wind parts indicates the reverse.

We venture to think that a conductor trying the two readings shown in Ex. 75 would prefer the greater vigour of the first, although it may not be the one indicated in his score.

In Period No. XIII a return is made to the thetic ethos by means of an overlap. This period contains a beautiful melody, beneath

Ex. 75. Beethoven, Ninth Symphony, Scherzo.

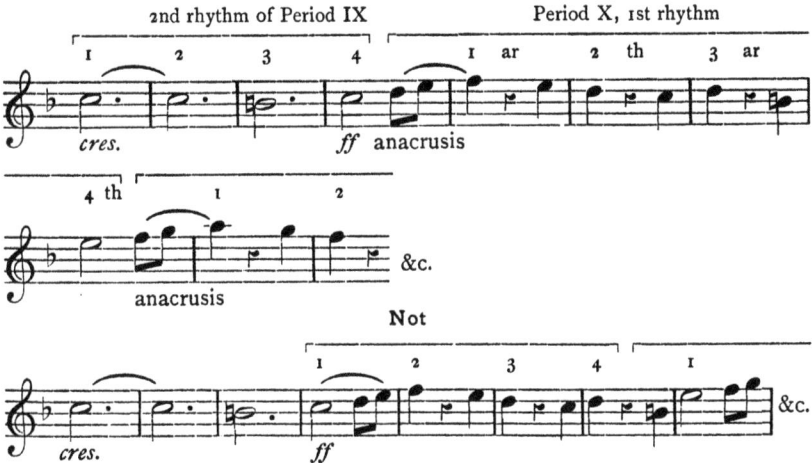

which the ever busy tribrachs are heard, though no longer in *staccato* but *legato* notes.

Ex. 76. Beethoven, Ninth Symphony, Scherzo.
Period XIII.

The final period before the double bar is significant, its second rhythm being catalectic to the extent of no less than three silent feet;

Ex. 77. Beethoven, Ninth Symphony, Scherzo.
Period XV.

a bold and striking appeal to the intelligence of the audience. But the tremendous rhythmical life that has been previously impressed on us, together with the rapidity of the *tempo*, enables us mentally to carry on the rhythm of the catalexis without effort.

The rest of the movement must be left to the reader for analysis. In it occur the well known changes from "rhythm of four bars" to "rhythm of three bars," *i.e.* from tetrapodic to tripodic rhythms. The trio, with its gentle character, yet overflowing with strong and healthy life, must also be left to the reader.

Adagio molto e cantabile.

The tetrapodic form of rhythm is strictly observed throughout. Overlaps are rare, but occasionally a fine effect is obtained by repetition of the final half-rhythm of a period on a new combination of instruments. There is an introductory single-member period, ending with an overlap, and the first period proper begins with the entrance of the first violins in bar 3. There are two feet in the bar. The periods of the first section, in the key of B flat, show some likeness to the eurhythmic balance of the Greeks. Their form is,

Period I. $4+4+2$
Period II. $4+4+2$
Period III. $4+2+6+2$
Period IV. $2+4+4$.

The dipody is in every case a repetition of the two preceding feet. The architectural[1] structure, if we may so express it, is very Greek in its design.

The fourth period modulates to D major, and there is a change of rhythm-species from duple to triple. The feet are now slow iambuses, syncopated into one another. This fundamental rhythm is heard in the bass, while the violins perform an ornamentation above it, reminding one of a finely wrought frieze over the simple Doric columns of a Greek temple.

EX. 78. Beethoven, Ninth Symphony, Adagio.

The periods in this section all contain two tetrapodic members. A modulating period, consisting of a single tetrapody only, leads to a variation on the first section, in the original key of B flat.

[1] Or, to use a newly coined word, the "architectonal."

The fourth section is a variation on the second. In its latter half the motion is augmented by the substitution of quavers for crotchets in the bass.

The fifth section is a return to the first, with modifications, and transposed to the key of E flat.

The sixth section is in the original key of B flat, and is a variation on the first, but there is an important change of rhythm-species and construction. The signature is 12/8; the quaver is the primary time, the species is trochaic, and each tetrapodic phrase occupies the compass of a single bar. The last mentioned feature is found in some other places amongst Beethoven's latest works.

The underlying rhythmical forms must be sought in the harmonic construction: the rhythms are often welded into one another by the ornamental passages of the first violin. About the middle of this long flowing section the movement is suddenly interrupted by a trumpet call, and we are reminded of the opening motive by two major spondees, which make a complete break, recalling us from the even tranquillity of the continual tribrachs in the bass to the languishing melancholy of the opening bars.

Then the tribrachs are resumed, together with the ornamental passages of the first violin; again they are interrupted by the trumpet call, and again resumed, to continue to the end. This long section may be compared with the settled orderly course of life of the average man, which is occasionally broken by some unusual event, and then resumed in the ordinary course again.

Presto.

After the long tranquillity comes turmoil. The Presto, starting on the anacrusis with a tremendous discord, made all the more impressive by the syncopation, opens with a catalectic octopody, or rhythm of eight feet. Of periodic symmetry there is no thought; rhythms of unsymmetrical length follow one another, a single foot even standing by itself here and there. Portions of the previous movement are heard, intermingled with a masterful recitative on the bass strings. The whole forms a dramatic tumult. Then follows the melody to which, later on, Schiller's "Ode to Joy" is to be allied. This melody is in such regular rhythms and periods that it requires no analysis. Variations on it are heard, and the tumult endeavours to begin again. But it is interrupted by a vocal recitative, in which the performers are called upon to tune themselves more pleasantly, more joyfully.

The concluding portion of the work consists practically of vocal and instrumental variations on the "Joy" melody. The colotomy and periodology are simple in the extreme. The "semantic trochee" (page 42) is used with overpowering effect to the words "*Seid umschlungen Millionen*," and is accompanied by dactylic figures in the orchestra. It leads to a resumption of the "Joy" melody, which now appears in trochaic rhythm, with an ornamental accompaniment on the strings. Various changes of *tempo* and rhythm-species occur, but the periods are for the most part normal, and the rhythms are generally in well-defined tetrapodic form.

CHAPTER X

The colotomy of Schubert's "Erlking"—Mendelssohn and Schumann—Richard Wagner's adaptation of Greek rhythmical principles to the music drama—The colotomy of Brahms' songs—The colotomy of Hugo Wolf—Conclusion.

Schubert.

The genius of this composer was peculiarly sensitive to rhythmical expression, and features analogous to those of Greek music are not uncommon with him. In the first subject of the great posthumous D minor quartet, we undoubtedly have two examples of *crousis*, in the single foot which occurs twice over in bars 19 and 25, the bars in which the first violin and violoncello utter four crotchets on the note A. And what a deliciously fresh effect these isolated and apparently interpolated bars give, though to the superficial observer they seem to occur at random in the midst of four-bar phrases. Again, in the opening bars of the C major symphony, the unison passage for the horns is in two distinct tripodies, followed by a sort of sigh on the final dipody of the Greek-like period 3+3+2. In the *Andante con moto* of the Unfinished Symphony, after the introductory two feet, the melody enters on the violins with a 5+5+3 period, in the midst of which the two introductory bars are repeated as a *crousis*: could anything be more Greek in its symmetry, its grace, and its avoidance of the commonplace?

In his songs Schubert instinctively uses a colotomy that seems exactly to suit the matter in hand. Conventionality is thrown to the winds, while form is preeminently in evidence as a means of expression. We shall analyse the whole of the "Erlking," and the reader will be able to find many other instances for himself that give proof of Schubert's wonderful instinct for expression through his colotomy.

We must look on the "Erlking" as a drama in miniature, in which four persons take part, viz. a Narrator, a Father, a Son, and the Erlking himself. The accompaniment is in extremely rapid triplets throughout, expressive of the haste and anxiety of the father, who urges his horse to its utmost speed. The terror of the son seems to be expressed by a *leit-motiv* of two feet, Ex. 79.

Ex. 79. Schubert, "Erlkönig."

The important ritornel, after a preliminary foot, contains two periods, each being of three members, with the colotomy $2 + 2 + 3$. The unusual form of these two periods undoubtedly contributes something towards the weird and unearthly ethos of the ritornel.

Ex. 80. Schubert, "Erlkönig."
The Primary time has the value of the crotchet.

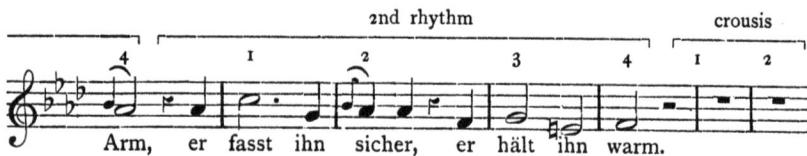

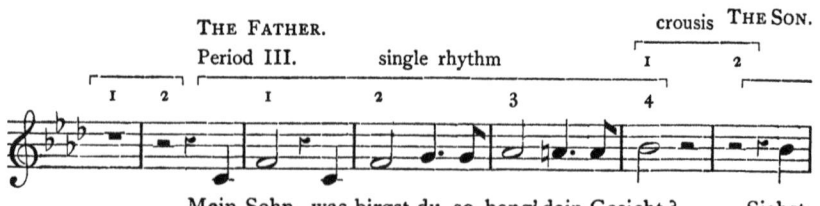

SCHUBERT'S ERLKING 151

SCHUBERT'S ERLKING

er-reicht den Hof mit Müh' und Noth; *catalexis* in seinen Armen das Kind war todt.

The voice enters with an overlap. Its periods are of two members each, and the members always contain four feet, except where this balance is altered in accordance with dramatic requirements.

In the first member of Period I the narrator asks himself a question, and a crousis gives time for reflection before he answers it in the second member. Period II continues the answer, and there is no occasion for crousis here. A pause ensues, filled in by a crousis, during which, what we may call the "terror-motive" is heard. The father continues, unchecked, his headlong ride: the situation is weird and uncanny.

In Period III the father, in a single rhythm, asks his son why he hides his face. Again a crousis intervenes between the question and answer. In Period IV the son replies by another question: Does not his father see the Erlking? Each successive question is now followed by a dramatic pause, in which the crousis continues to utter the "terror-motive."

In Period V the father answers laconically, again in a single rhythm, shortened by catalexis, that it is merely a delusion caused by the fog.

A new form of crousis introduces the Erlking in person, and here the ethos of the music changes as if by magic. The "terror-motive" disappears: the octaves and chords, whose insistent repetition has such a weird effect, give way to gentleness and charm, though the triplet movement never ceases: the horse always continues to gallop.

The key is now major: the rhythm takes the scheme ; harmony and melody are simple in the extreme. The Erlking, in suave and seductive tones, endeavours to tempt the son, by offering childish games and flowers and fine clothes. But the child is not to be thus tempted. In his terror he screams to his father

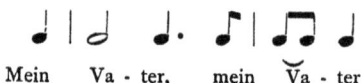

Mein Va - ter, mein Va - ter

The repetition of the words is in quicker notes than the first utterance; the rhythmopœia of these two bars follows a natural impulse to hasten the rapidity of utterance, in a time of intense excitement. The breathless agony of the son is further indicated by the crotchet rest, dividing the rhythm into half-rhythms.

In a catalectic tetrapody the son asks his father if he does not hear what the tempter is promising: agitation is expressed by the irregularity with which the poetic feet are set to the musical feet, there being sometimes two feet in a bar and sometimes one only.

A crousis allows the father time to answer. In another laconic period, 2 + 3 feet, broken by rests, he says that the wind is blowing in the dry leaves. Then a crousis brings the Erlking again on the scene. A new change of ethos occurs. The tempter will try flattery. In place of the long seductive notes of the sixth period, the primary time is now changed from the crotchet to the quaver, so that, without any alteration of *tempo*, the rhythms take exactly half the time they formerly occupied. It is a remarkable stroke of genius: the horse continues its gallop, the fiend whispers his flattering appeal in rapid words. No crousis intervenes; all is haste and hurry: will the boy give way to him? More alarmed than ever, the son repeats his appeal of Period VIII in a higher key; the father tries to soothe him, and explains that it is only the gray old willows that are frightening him.

The "terror-motive" reappears. In Period XIV the fiend begins with the rapid notes of Period X, but ends by a return to the longer, more impressive notes, in a threat to use force.

For the third time, and without an intervening crousis, the boy screams to his father, in a still higher key than before: this time he feels himself actually in the grip of the fiend. The "terror-motive" continues: the father shudders: he urges his horse to hasten the pace: he reaches the castle at last. The narration is carried on in short broken phrases. The climax of the tragedy, " In his arms the child lay dead," can no longer be expressed in rhythmical form: broken recitative takes its place, and the song ends with an intensity of pathos that is almost overpowering.

The rhythmopœia, or formal element, is used, as in the Mozart examples already quoted, for expressional purposes, the dramatic feeling being brought out by the varied rhythmical details. Though not cast in the form of strophe, antistrophe, and epode, in every other respect the song has all the rhythmical variety and expression of a Greek chorus, and is another instance of the similarity of means employed by ancient and modern artists in making their appeal to human nature through rhythm.

Schumann and Mendelssohn.

Variety of "magnitude" in the members of periods is only one amongst the many means of rhythmical expression available to the composer, and Schumann and Mendelssohn, while making use of every other known rhythmical device, rarely employ this particular one. In their scores we find, as a rule, page after page of music falling into well defined groups of 4 or 2 feet, a feature which is perhaps more marked in Mendelssohn than in Schumann, for Mendelssohn makes no effort to conceal it.

Schumann on the other hand often disguises regularity of design in various ways, and this probably militated against the immediate acceptance of his music at a time when an easily grasped form was considered all important. Amongst his favourite effects is that of introducing an unexpected harmony, or a new phrase, on the final foot of a period, in such a way that the tetrapodic or dipodic succession is apparently, but not really interrupted, as in the slow movement of his first symphony.

EX. 81. Schumann, Symphony No. 1.

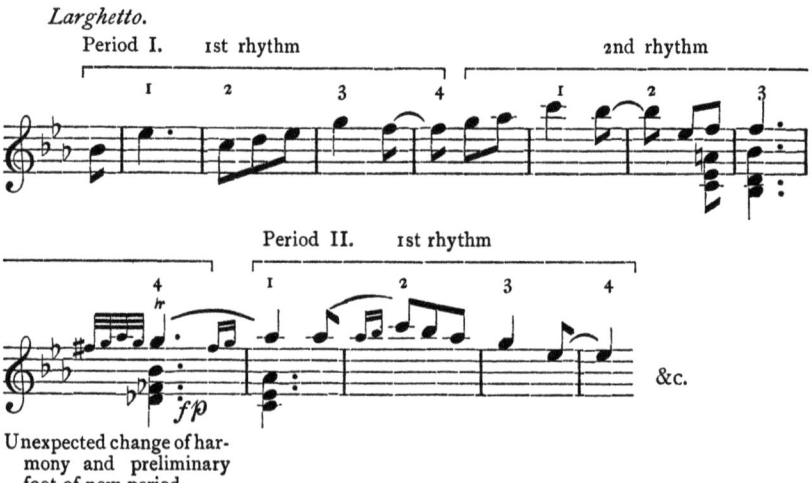

Unexpected change of harmony and preliminary foot of new period.

The simplest way to make the passage immediately understood by an audience would have been to continue the dominant harmony through the final foot of Period I: to have made the "gravity of the longer ending," alluded to by Aristides. (See page 103.) But Schumann brings in the element of surprise by the introduction of an unexpected harmony on this "longer ending," and at the same time anticipates the commencement of Period II by a preliminary foot, while retaining the four-bar grouping intact.

In his fifth Novellette he produces a festive gaiety through variation of accentuation in the different members of the period, and, by a comparatively rare exception, he makes a period of $2 + 2 + 3 + 2$, instead of an equal balance in all the members. The accentuation is

Ex. 82. Schumann, Novelletten, No. 5.

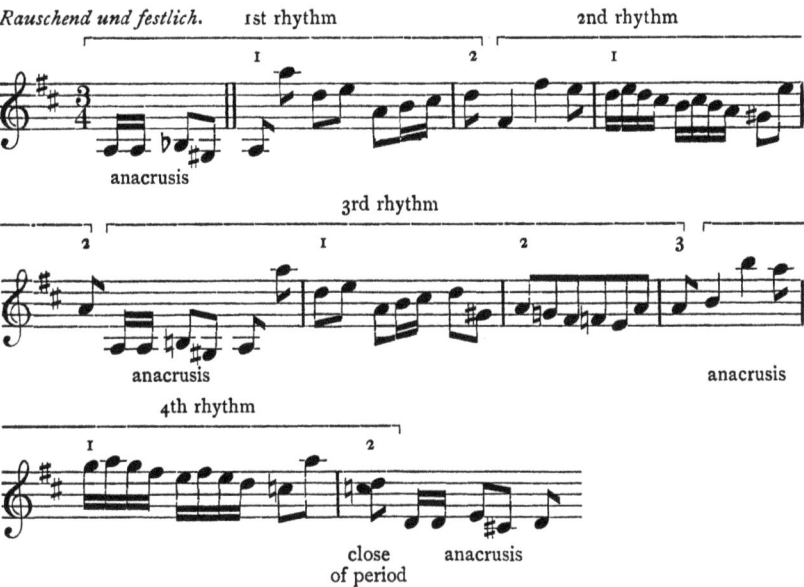

very clever. The first rhythm has an anacrusis of the value of three quavers, which brings the accent on the low A of the melody. The third rhythm has an anacrusis of five quavers, bringing the accent on D of the same melody. The third rhythm is extended to three feet, and thus admits of the bass imitating the melody, and at the same time introduces a break in the dipodic succession, suggestive of festal relaxation.

In his songs, Schumann, while generally retaining the tetrapodic form, makes exquisite use of rhythmical devices for expression, as, for instance, in Liederkreis, op. 39, No. 5, "Mondnacht," the feminine closes followed by a catalexis: in Dichterliebe No. 13, "Ich hab' im Traum geweinet," the crousis is used in a way that would have delighted Aristoxenus: in the same cyclus No. 7, the words "Ich grolle nicht, und wenn das Herz auch bricht," are expressed in a tripodic rhythm, while the rest of the song is tetrapodic.

Mendelssohn makes little effort to conceal the formal element, and this, probably, is one reason for his music being immediately accepted throughout the civilised world, and retaining its extreme popularity with the general public in the English-speaking and Italian races, who like instrumental music that is easily understood at first hearing, and not too remote or imaginative[1].

Mendelssohn rarely disguises the ends of his periods and rhythms: they are all as clear cut as crystal, and when he occasionally departs for a few bars from the tetrapodic form, there is no doubt about what he means. Thus, the opening subject of his Rondo brillante, op. 29, begins with hexapodies (the arpeggios are preliminary feet), and this artifice is evident at first hearing.

The precise definition of the formal element, the want of rhythmical appeal to the mind, has caused a certain reaction in the popularity of Mendelssohn's music amongst those who have learned to appreciate the more imaginative methods of which Bach was the first great exponent. The same cause may be at the root of the dislike that many musical persons now have for Handel.

Chopin.

Chopin, while generally adhering to the tetrapodic construction, sometimes departs from it with very expressive results. In his Nocturne in G minor, op. 15, No. 3, the *tempo* being *lento* and the expression *languido e rubato*, variety of "magnitude" plays no small part in the general effect.

Ex. 83. Chopin, Nocturne, op. 15, No. 3.

---

[1] But the British public learns to assimilate more imaginative music, as is proved by the enthusiasm with which the greatest works of art, many of which at first met with coldness and hostility, are now received. The master-pieces of Bach, the Fifth and Ninth Symphonies of Beethoven, the music-dramas of Wagner, now draw audiences as large as the more easily assimilated works of Mendelssohn. Enthusiastic and self-sacrificing conductors and executants, backed by optimistic concert agents, working at a loss for many years, have created a public demand for elevating music where there was no spontaneous desire for it.

The conclusion of the first rhythm is held in suspense by the addition of three extra feet beyond the expected four, making a seven-feet member or heptapody: the second rhythm has one unexpected additional foot, and the two members together make a period of the unusual construction $7 + 5$. This irregularity of magnitude undoubtedly contributes in no small degree to the yearning character of the opening subject. In its latter part the movement settles down to the normal tetrapodic form.

Richard Wagner.

Music-drama is distinguished from Opera by features so important that it is necessary to explain its details at some length in order to get a clear idea of its rhythmical structure.

It is a revival of the principles of the old Greek ideal of drama, in which the triad of poetry, melody, and the bodily movements and gestures classed together as the dance, are combined to produce a complete work of dramatic art. Each member of the triad has its own special office. The words convey to the audience the sense of the drama; melody gives expression and feeling to the sense of the words, while the dance, by which rhythm was anciently made evident to the eye throughout the drama, is now represented by the rhythmical movement of the orchestra.

The words of the actor are never to be spoken but always sung. They must be allied to what Wagner calls "verse-melody," that is, melody which arises from them, as opposed to melody which can exist for itself alone, and therefore is equally intelligible whether sung or played on an instrument. The latter he calls "absolute melody"; it is the melody of the operatic aria, based on harmony and tonality, and constructed in the rhythms and periods demanded by absolute music. According to Wagner, absolute melody cannot give dramatic expression to the significance of the words, since it exists chiefly for itself, the words being of secondary importance. Thus the same absolute melody can be sung to different words, as when, for example, a second stanza is added to the first, and sung to the same melody. The significance of the words of the second stanza must necessarily differ from that of the first, and if the melody expresses the one it cannot properly express the other. In such a case, as Wagner explains it, the poet varies his words but not his melody. The melody dominates the verse, whereas in drama the contrary should be the case.

Verse-melody requires to be varied to suit each verbal phrase, and this kind of music can be most satisfactorily produced when the poet and composer are one and the same person, so that verse and melody come into being simultaneously, as was the case with the Greek drama.

The object of verse-melody is expression: it exactly expresses the words, both in accent and feeling. Thus, in Isolde's first utterance, "Wer wagt mich zu höhnen?" the melody rises to a high note on "höhnen," the chief word of the phrase. The next phrase, in which she calls to Brangäne, "Brangäne, Du, wo sind wir?" is broken by rests, which vividly express her excitement. Brangäne's conciliatory answer, "Blaue Streifen steigen im Westen auf: Sanft und schnell segelt das Schiff an ruhiger See. Vor Abend erreichen wir sicher das Land," is in calm tetrapodies, unbroken by rests, and in quiet melodic intervals, suitable to the soothing character of the words.

Such melody is entirely subservient to the poetry. Played on an instrument it would be meaningless, for it does not follow the canons of musical form.

The object aimed at is a return to the ancient idea, in which melody is to give expression to words and the words are not to be a mere vehicle for the performance of absolute melody by the human voice. This explains Aristotle's remark that melody without words, played on an instrument, is meaningless. He evidently alluded to dramatic melody, or what Wagner calls verse-melody.

Rhythm is the most important element of expression in music-drama, and Wagner seems to have made a study of rhythm as exhaustive as that of Aristoxenus, though he has not dedicated any special treatise to it. "Oper und Drama," in which his views on rhythm are expressed, was written long before the publication of the works of Schmidt, Westphal, and others on Greek rhythm.

"Whatever number of accents," he says[1], "we have to allot to a phrase or portion of a phrase, in accordance with the mood that has to be expressed, they will never be of entirely equal strength. The sense of a speech does not allow of equal strength in its accents.... The feeling, also, does not allow of an equal strength in the accents, because it can only be excited by easily perceptible, sharply defined differences in the agent of expression....We will examine the influence which the unequal strength of accents has on the rhythm of the phrase. When we wish to give effect to the difference between weaker and stronger accents without the assistance of a conglomeration of secondary words, we can only do it in a way that corresponds

---

[1] *Oper und Drama. Gesammelte Schriften*, 2nd Edition, Vol. IV. p. 122. We have paraphrased freely where the sense is involved by long parenthetical sentences.

to the thesis and arsis of a musical bar, or, what is the same in principle, the thesis and arsis bars of a musical period. The thesis and arsis bars or half-bars only make themselves felt by standing in a relation to one another similar to that by which the intervening fractions of the bars are made evident.

"Accented and unaccented half-bars, when they stand naked alongside one another, as in the church choral-melody, can only be perceived as a rising and falling of accents through the introduction of rhythmical life in the portions lying between the two halves of the bar."

Wagner is here thinking of the so-called "figurierte Choral" in which the long drawn minims of the melody are enlivened by more rapid rhythmical motives in the accompaniment. We English have nothing equivalent to "figurierte Choral," since we sing our church hymns at a *tempo* that gives effect to the "arsis and thesis of the half-bars" without need of external assistance. It is interesting to notice that Wagner, without having studied Aristoxenus, arrives at the same conclusion with regard to the necessity of rhythm being easily perceptible, and that he proposes to give effect to slow melody by the addition of what Aristoxenus would call "rhythmopœia of the chronoi podikoi." (See pp. 49, 55, and Ex. 56.)

"The verbal-phrase demands the same accentual relations as the musical phrase. The unaccented words or syllables which we place in the arsis, rise, in ordinary speech, by increase of sound, to the chief accent, and fall again, by decrease of sound....The number of preparatory or succeeding syllables depends on the sense of the poetic speech, which should be expressed as tersely as possible. The more necessary, however, it appears to be to the poet to increase the number of these syllables, the more characteristically can he thereby enliven the rhythm, and give special significance to the accent....His resources in this respect are infinite, but he can only be cognisant of them when he transforms accented speech-rhythm to musical rhythm, through the endless variety of dance movement. Pure musical measure offers to the poet possibilities of expression by speech that are denied to merely spoken verse."

It will be remembered that Aristoxenus makes the dance an agent of rhythm. Wagner uses his music in "an endless variety of dance movement."

"Melody itself[1] was originally a necessary expression of feeling, and developed itself, in combination with word and gesture, to the

---

[1] *Oper und Drama. Gesammelte Schriften*, 2nd Edition, Vol. IV. p 143.

fulness which we can still observe in true folk-melodies. Poets, whose works are the outcome of reflection and intelligence, could not model their melody according to the expression of their words; still less was it possible for them to obtain new melodies from their methods of expression, because the progress of general development was from feeling to intelligence, and the growing intelligence felt itself only hindered if it gave itself to the expression of feeling that was far from it.

"Hence, so long as the lyric form was recognised and demanded by the public, the poet, who was incapable of inventing melodies, varied the poem, and not the melody. Melody now gave only an outward form to the poetic thought, and text-variations were placed under an unchanged melody. The enormous wealth of form in the Greek lyric poetry, particularly in the tragic choruses, cannot be explained as arising out of the meaning of these poems. The didactic and philosophic sense of the songs is usually in such strong contradiction to the sensuous and ever-changing rhythm of the verse, that we can only understand the variety of utterance as determined by the melody, not by the poetic intention."

The author goes on to say that he considers that the Greek poets made use of ancient and well-known melodies for the drama: but later discoveries seem to indicate that this was not always the case, and that melody was connected with words by a certain, apparently artificial, rule. (See page 73.) But our knowledge on this point is as yet too scanty to enable us to form a theory with any degree of certainty.

With the Greeks the bodily movements and gestures of the chorus, called the Dance, not only conveyed rhythm in visible form, but were expressive of the meaning of the words. In place of the Greek dance Wagner uses the modern orchestra.

"The orchestra[1] undeniably possesses a language, and the creations of our modern instrumental music have discovered this to us....We have now to show that the language of the orchestra is the means of giving effect to what is inexpressible in words (*Unaussprechlich*)."

"Let us now look[2] at the *Unaussprechlich*, which the orchestra can express with the greatest certainty, and this in combination with another *Unaussprechlich*, that of gesture. Gesture, while it gives visibility to the inner feelings through the movements of limbs and face, is so far *unaussprechlich* that only speech can indicate the feeling which gives rise to this or that gesture. Anything that

---

[1] *Ges. Schr.* Vol. IV. p. 173.   [2] *Ibid.* p. 174.

speech can completely express does not require to be accompanied or strengthened by gesture: indeed, unnecessary gesture may even be disturbing. But in such a case the receptive organ of hearing serves as a mediator only, not as a means of exciting feeling. The communication of a circumstance about which speech cannot bring full conviction and excite feeling, requires strengthening through an accompanying gesture. We see therefore that when the hearing has to be excited to greater sympathy, the performer will involuntarily appeal also to the eye: ear and eye must work together to make appeal to the feelings with full conviction."

"That which is inexpressible by words[1], but expressible by gesture, can now be imparted to the hearing by the language of the orchestra."

"The orchestra obtained this faculty from accompanying the most perceptible of gestures, namely, those of the dance: and the dance required to be thus accompanied, for its full comprehension. Orchestral melody is related to the movements of the dance in much the same way as song-melody is related to the words of poetry. Gesture and orchestra-melody make a comprehensible whole. Both dance-gesture and orchestral music make themselves felt through rhythm....The downward movement of the foot is to the eye exactly what the accented beat of the bar is to the ear...."

"Orchestra-melody[2] therefore completely supplies the place of gesture."

"The chorus of Greek tragedy[3] has left behind it the modern orchestra as the representative of the feeling necessary to drama, in order that feeling can freely develop itself through this agency to countless varieties of manifestation. But the tangible, individual, human representative is removed from the orchestra to the stage, where, as an actual partaker of the drama itself, it unfolds the germ of human individuality which lay in the Greek chorus, to the highest independent bloom."

When Wagner speaks of the orchestra as moving in dance rhythms, he does not mean to imply the style of the society dance, or the ballet, with sharply defined regularity of phrasing, framed according to the rules of absolute music. Struck, as we have seen, with the endless variety of rhythmical expression as exhibited in the Greek drama, he makes use of a similar variety in his orchestra-melody; and the figures of the mimetic dance are replaced by the melodic and rhythmical figures to which Hans von Wolzogen has

---

[1] *Ges. Schr.* Vol. IV. p. 176.   [2] *Ibid.* p. 177.   [3] *Ibid.* p. 190.

given the name of "Leitmotiven." "The life-giving centre of dramatic expression," says Wagner[1], "is the verse-melody of the actor. The preparatory absolute orchestra-melody[2] anticipates it: the 'idea' (Gedanke) of the instrumental motive proceeds (leitet sich) from it."

The whole thing is one of the most daring experiments in the history of art, and, fortunately for us, it has been justified by its success. Genius, learning, and courage, have combined to resuscitate the spirit which inspired the highest efforts of ancient drama, and to clothe it in a modern dress, for the elevation and benefit of the civilised world of to-day.

The orchestra-melody is carried out in striking and constantly changing rhythmical figures, expressive of every change of emotion, and the general atmosphere of what is about to be performed is foreshadowed in the prelude. Thus, the long-drawn notes of the opening bars of the "Tristan" Introduction, with their hexapodic phrasing, intermingled with silences (Ex. 36), form what Wagner would call the "gesture" of the sufferings of Tristan, torn between his insatiable longing and his sense of duty. The theme is in two portions, consisting, respectively, of a rising and a falling chromatic passage. It is succeeded by a theme which, commencing with the arsis foot, and containing a striking alternation of relatively longer and shorter notes played *crescendo*, intimately expresses the rapture of sudden passion which seizes the lovers when their eyes meet.

"The poet[3] has to determine the rhythm-species entirely by what he intends to express. He must himself bring his material to a recognisable measure, not let it compel him to this or that. He determines it as recognisable when he distributes the accents according to their character, whether stronger or weaker, in such a manner that they form a breathing-section, or phrase, which must correspond to a succeeding section; and the latter must appear as a necessary complement to the former, for an important point of expression only makes itself felt by an indispensable repetition, which strengthens or tranquillises as the case may be. The arrangement of the stronger and weaker accents, therefore, determines the rhythm-species and the rhythmical construction of the period."

The extract in Ex. 84 shows Wagner's use of rhythm. The love-philtre administered by Brangäne, in place of the cup of poison demanded by Isolde, has changed the latter's anger and hatred into

---

[1] *Ges. Schr.* Vol. IV. p. 190.
[2] *I.e.* in the *Vorspiele* which precede the several acts.
[3] *Ges. Schr.* Vol. IV. p. 125.

violent love, and rendered Tristan's emotion absolutely uncontrollable. He thinks of his duty to King Mark, but can no longer resist; his honour is lost. The pair gaze into each other's eyes, and utter each other's names; their rapture is expressed in the orchestra-melody of Period I, with its passionate and voluptuous rhythm. As they embrace, the "gesture" of Tristan's suffering is represented by a tumultuous intermingling of the two elements (p. 164) of the opening

Ex. 84. R. Wagner, "Tristan und Isolde," Act I, Scene 5.

motive of the Introduction, its rhythm being changed from long slow notes to rapid syncopation, expressive of intense agitation. It is repeated in an ascending *crescendo* sequence, and forms Period II.

In Period III the lovers are so entirely lost to everything that they do not hear the sailors and trumpeters proclaiming the approach of King Mark. The syncopation of the orchestra-melody becomes more violent than before, indicative of the increasing intensity of their passion.

In Period IV the rhythm suddenly changes to an explosion of rapid descending passages, expressive of the despair of Brangäne when she discovers the effect of her deception. The "quick death" demanded by Isolde has been changed to "endless misery."

It will be noticed that the orchestra-melody carries on the action here, as it does throughout each act, without a break; the closes and half-closes of "absolute music" are entirely absent. Yet the fundamental element of rhythmical period and member underlies the whole as regularly as with Mozart or the Greek dramatists, while the accentuation of both verse-melody and orchestra-melody is carefully adapted to express the dramatic meaning of the situation.

The quotation is short, but we hope it will serve to show what Wagner means when he says that the rhythm of the orchestra-melody replaces the mimetic dance and gesture of Greek tragedy. Hence the large place rhythm occupies as an expressive element in his music-drama. If the Greeks had known any kind of music comparable in magnificence to that of the modern orchestra, may we not assume that they would have utilised it, in addition to the dance of their chorus?

When, in the course of a drama, occasion arises for lyric treatment of the text, Wagner uses the tetrapodic phrases of "absolute music" and marks them as definitely as does any other composer. An exception occurs in the "Preislied," for in the days of the Meistersingers the tetrapody had not yet become the orthodox basis of all music. And how attractive is the old-world phrasing of this song!

Brahms.

While the tetrapodic is naturally the prevailing phrase with Brahms, he is fully alive to the charm of variety, and makes frequent use of other "magnitudes." This is by no means the result of chance, but of a knowledge derived from an intimate study of the effect of rhythmical variety on the mind. In his instrumental music he constantly uses the pentapody or tripody as the basis of his colotomy, and in his songs he sometimes approaches Greek variety of period. "Wie bist du, meine Königin?" is a fine example of this.

Ex. 85. Brahms, "Wie bist du, meine Königin," Op. 32, No. 9.

This passage is repeated and followed by a middle section in a new key.

The verse is tetrapodic, each verse being complete:

Period I. "Wie bist du, meine Königin,
           Durch sanfte Güte wonnevoll!
Period II. Du lächle nur—Lenzdüfte weh'n
           Durch mein Gemüthe wonnevoll!"

Here there is no question of drama; the idea does not lend itself to, or require, the forcible accentuation, the strongly marked rhythm of "verse-melody." The rhythmical form of the words would suggest some such musical rhythm as

But Brahms, while causing the accents of his melody to coincide with those of the words, departs from conventional tetrapodic form, and produces "absolute music" with a most attractive variety of period.

The first period contains two tripodies: the second has two tetrapodies separated from one another by a crousis of one foot, while the second rhythm contains a cæsura dividing it into two half-rhythms.

The same melody is repeated for the second stanza. The third stanza, which we have called the "middle section" has the same rhythmopœia of its feet as the first, allied to a new melody in a new key. By a delicate *nuance* the composer, while retaining the rhythmical figures of the feet, makes the second period of this section contain two pentapodies instead of two tetrapodies, and adheres to this construction for the second period of the final stanza, in which he returns to the original melody and key.

Could anything be more delicate and Greek-like than this departure from the tetrapodic form? The song presupposes a high degree of culture on the part of both singer and audience; no performer accustomed only to conventional rhythms could do it justice, and it could never "hit the popular taste" in the sense of being whistled in the street or played on barrel organs, for its feeling is too intimately bound up with its unconventional rhythmical scheme.

With one more composer we must finish our short comparison of Aristoxenian colotomy and periodology with that of modern music. Amongst the greatest of our song writers is the late Hugo Wolf, whose "music does not merely fit the words carefully, though Wolf does make it do that more carefully than any other composer has done or tried to do; his method is more fundamental than that. He makes one feel that he has composed the poetry as well as the music—that the poetry and music are the simultaneous product of one brain[1]."

He, in fact, did for lyric music what Wagner did for dramatic, and both acted on the ancient principle that the poet and musician must be, or appear to be, the same person. Wolf so thoroughly identified himself with the poetry that he appears to have written it.

Ex. 86. H. Wolf, "Im Frühling," Mörike-Lieder No. 13.

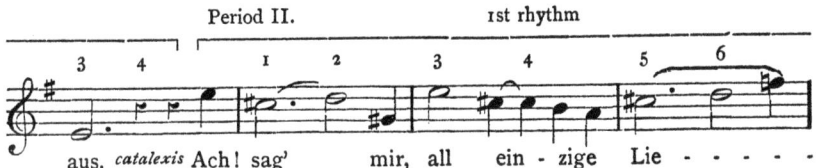

The poet is lying half asleep on a bank, indulging in vague day-dreams. Wolf gives expression to the wandering, half unconscious, meditation, by a diversity of "magnitudes," of which the scheme is,

Period I.   6+4+4
Period II. 7+2+4.

That is to say, the colotomy is derived, not from the requirements of regular musical form, but from the ethos of the poetic text. The melody is beautiful in itself, without the aid of harmony, and seems

[1] Grove's *Dictionary of Music*, New Ed. Vol. v. p. 558.

to express exactly the sense of the words. It will be noticed that in Period I it lies more or less in a low register, and in Period II, where a "*Steigerung*" takes place at the thought of love, the melody expresses it by a higher range of notes. This method of expression was well known to Greek theorists, who look upon a change of *tasis*, or pitch, in a new period, as almost tantamount to a change of key or mode. Instances occur, probably for expressional purposes, in the Delphic "Hymn to Apollo."

The above example is typical of Wolf's method of combining melody with poetry. But he adds an equally expressive pianoforte part, in which some marked rhythmical figure recurs again and again, as a kind of Leitmotive, having an intimate connection with the feeling to be expressed: he uses the piano as Wagner uses the orchestra, not for a subordinate accompaniment, but as taking an equal share in the expression of feeling. In "Auf eine Wanderung" (Mörike-Lieder No. 15), the curiosity and lightheartedness of the traveller, as he enters a small unknown town, are shown by an alternation of *staccato* cyclical dactyls and tribrachs, "*leicht bewegt*"; but when his heart is touched by a beautiful voice which he hears at a window, the light cyclical dactyls give way to more sedate trochees, and the style becomes *legato*.

The most dramatic of the Mörike songs is "Der Feuerreiter" (No. 44). The piano part, beginning low down on the instrument *pianissimo*, with the figure ♩♩♩ ♩♩♩ ♩♩♩ ♩♩♩ played very rapidly, announces that something is wrong. It works up the scale, increases in strength to *fortissimo*, a crowd gathers, and the mystery is solved by the words "Horch! das Feuerglöcklein gellt!" Then suddenly the rhythm makes a dramatic change from triplets to duplets, *fff*, at the wild shout "Hinterm Berg, hinterm Berg, brennt es in der Mühle!" With a new change of rhythmical figure the "Feuerreiter" frantically gallops to the scene and is swallowed up by the flames. In such songs as these Wolf's periodology is what the Greeks would call "Irregular" and specially adapted for dramatic purposes. See App. B, page 182.

But he makes use of perfectly regular periods when the material suits them, as in "Nixe Binsefuss" (Mörike-Lieder No. 45), or in "Storchen-Botschaft" (No. 48). In the latter the signature, by the way, is 12/8, and each rhythm occupies the space of a single bar. In the humorous song "Abschied," No. 53 of the same set, the music, by a regular waltz, expresses the delight of the poet at having kicked an interviewer down stairs.

In giving the idea conveyed by the words of a song its rightful place, in not subordinating the claims of poetry to those of music, Wolf was simply carrying to its logical conclusion a feeling that occasionally found expression, as we have seen, in many of the great composers. We have shown how Bach, Handel, Mozart, Schubert, sometimes utilised the forms of music to convey the sense of the words, rather than make use of the words merely as a vehicle for music. But with them music was always really paramount; it would never have occurred to them to put musical form entirely aside, and the words had always, more or less, to bend themselves to the music, however carefully the fact was concealed by the art of the musician. The *Da capo* aria is a case in point. A certain percentage, generally the larger portion, of the words, has here to be repeated, and very delightful it is to hear the same melody sung twice over by a famous vocalist. But the adoption of this form was, as a rule, entirely due to the imperious demands of musical convention, not to the ideas conveyed by the poem.

We might indefinitely continue the comparison between Aristoxenian theory and modern practice, but we have probably by this time exhibited sufficient material to explain how much they coincide. Rhythm is a part of human nature, and was probably developed before melody. At the Paris Exhibition of 1889 we heard some South Sea Islanders performing on an instrument consisting of a number of pieces of bamboo, cut to certain lengths and tied loosely together in groups, each group representing a musical note. The notes were sounded by a group being pulled against a wooden bar, and the want of a resonating chamber was made up for by the number of bamboos which were tuned in unison for each note, so that a fairly powerful sound resulted. The scale was most elementary, consisting only of a keynote, its fourth and fifth, and the melody was an alternation of these three notes. But it was played with a lively and perfectly regular rhythm, which evidently gave great delight to the performers and the native listeners. Every now and then there would be a change of rhythmical figure, or of time-species from duple to triple, and the reverse; and the energy expressed by the rhythm was most satisfactory to the European musician, elementary though the schemes were. Out of such elements as these the Greeks evolved the lofty rhythmical system of the Periclean age: and out of the simple rhythm of the folksong and dance our musicians have been engaged for several centuries in evolving a rhythmical art that not only approaches that of the Athenians in grandeur, but is so nearly parallel in many of its features as to be capable of illumination through their theory.

The demand for musical rhythm is as much a part of human nature as that for melody. The rhythmical sense, like the melodic, varies with individuals, and is probably entirely wanting in a few cases, which, if they exist, must be as rare as those of want of the sense of relative pitch, generally alluded to as "want of musical ear." Where the rhythmical sense exists, in however slight a degree, it is capable of more or less development by cultivation. In this respect it is the same as any other faculty, and it will atrophy if entirely neglected, or will grow in a wrong direction if not carefully guided. If music is to be something more than a mere social distraction, if it is to penetrate into our nature, it must be made to express itself through a carefully conceived and carefully executed rhythmopœia. The ethos may be tranquil, languid, melancholy, or energetic, exciting, impressive. In the first case it will be expressed through time-divisions that have little variety, and a smooth accentuation. In the second case the rhythmopœia will contain strong contrasts of time-divisions, enforced by bold accentuation. In either case, if the performer fails to feel the ethos, or if his time-sense is deficient, he may play or sing the melody quite correctly, but the music will have no "character" in his hands, and can therefore never have the elevating effect on the mind that is the proper function of all music, great and small, humorous and serious, sacred and secular.

We have an advantage over the ancients in our power of combining several different rhythmical schemes simultaneously. But in its main principles the art of rhythm is developing along similar lines to those of old, and it may continue to do so. We have by no means arrived at the end of the rhythmical resources of modern music, and the searchlight of Aristoxenian Theory seems to suggest that the power of sound over the "aisthesis" may well increase in the future to an extent that we cannot conceive of at present. And such a development of pure music would be nothing but beneficial to the human race.

APPENDIX A

The majority of the following quotations are taken from "Die Fragmente und Lehrsätze der griechischen Rhythmiker" by Rudolf Westphal, referred to, for the sake of brevity, as "Fragmente."

1. Ῥυθμὸς δὲ τί ἐστι;—(a) Χρόνου καταμέτρησις μετὰ κινήσεως γινομένη ποιᾶς τινος. (b) κατὰ δὲ Φαῖδρον ῥυθμός ἐστι συλλαβῶν κειμένων πως πρὸς ἀλλήλας ἔμμετρος θέσις. (c) κατὰ δὲ Ἀριστόξενον χρόνος διῃρημένος ἐφ' ἑκάστῳ τῶν ῥυθμίζεσθαι δυναμένων. (d) κατὰ δὲ Νικόμαχον χρόνων εὔτακτος κίνησις. (e) κατὰ δὲ Λεόφαντον χρόνων σύνθεσις κατὰ ἀναλογίαν τε καὶ συμμετρίαν πρὸς ἑαυτοὺς θεωρουμένων. (f) κατὰ δὲ Δίδυμον φωνῆς ποιᾶς σχηματισμός—ἡ μὲν οὖν φωνὴ ποίως σχηματισθεῖσα ῥυθμὸν ἀποτελεῖ, γίνεται δὲ οὗτος ἢ περὶ λέξιν ἢ περὶ μέλος ἢ περὶ σωματικὴν κίνησιν.
BACCHEIOS SENIOR, in Jan, *Scriptores*, p. 313.

2. Itaque rythmici temporibus syllabas, metrici tempora syllabis finiunt.
SERVIUS, *De accentu*, quoted by Westphal in *Fragmente*, p. 43.

3. Νοητέον δὲ δύο τινὰς φύσεις ταύτας, τήν τε τοῦ ῥυθμοῦ καὶ τὴν τοῦ ῥυθμιζομένου, παραπλησίως ἐχούσας πρὸς ἀλλήλας ὥσπερ ἔχει τὸ σχῆμα καὶ τὸ σχηματιζόμενον πρὸς αὐτά.
ARISTOXENUS, *Stoicheia*, Book 2, *Fragmente*, p. 28, line 13.

4. Ὁ αὐτὸς δὲ λόγος κατὰ τοῦ μέλους, καὶ εἴ τι ἄλλο πέφυκε ῥυθμίζεσθαι τῷ τοιούτῳ ῥυθμῷ, ὅς ἐστιν ἐκ χρόνων συνεστηκώς.
ARISTOXENUS, *Stoicheia*, *Fragmente*, p. 28, line 23.

5. Ἄρσιν ποίαν λέγομεν εἶναι; Ὅταν μετέωρος ᾖ ὁ πούς, ἡνίκα ἂν μέλλωμεν ἐμβαίνειν. Θέσιν δὲ ποίαν; Ὅταν κείμενος.
BACCHEIOS THE ELDER, in *Fragmente*, p. 67, line 10.

6. Πρῶτος μὲν οὖν ἐστι χρόνος ἄτομος καὶ ἐλάχιστος, ὃς καὶ σημεῖον καλεῖται. ἐλάχιστον δὲ καλῶ τὸν ὡς πρὸς ἡμᾶς, ὅς ἐστι πρῶτος καταληπτὸς αἰσθήσει.
ARISTIDES QUINTILIANUS, *Fragmente*, p. 49, line 3.

Aristoxenus himself says
Καλείσθω δὲ πρῶτος μὲν τῶν χρόνων ὁ ὑπὸ μηδενὸς τῶν ῥυθμιζομένων δυνατὸς ὢν διαιρεθῆναι, κ.τ.λ.
Stoicheia, Fragmente, p. 31, line 5.

7. Ὧι δὲ σημαινόμεθα τὸν ῥυθμὸν καὶ γνώριμον ποιοῦμεν τῇ αἰσθήσει, πούς ἐστιν εἷς ἢ πλείους ἑνός. τῶν δὲ ποδῶν οἱ μὲν ἐκ δύο χρόνων σύγκεινται τοῦ τε ἄνω καὶ τοῦ κάτω, οἱ δὲ ἐκ τριῶν, δύο μὲν τῶν ἄνω, ἑνὸς δὲ τοῦ κάτω ἢ ἐξ ἑνὸς μὲν τοῦ ἄνω, δύο δὲ τῶν κάτω, οἱ δὲ ἐκ τεττάρων, δύο μὲν τῶν ἄνω, δύο δὲ τῶν κάτω. Ὅτι μὲν οὖν ἐξ ἑνὸς χρόνου ποὺς οὐκ ἂν εἴη φανερόν, ἐπειδήπερ ἓν σημεῖον οὐ ποιεῖ διαίρεσιν χρόνου· ἄνευ γὰρ διαιρέσεως χρόνου ποὺς οὐ δοκεῖ γίνεσθαι.

ARISTOXENUS, *Stoicheia*, *Fragmente*, p. 33, line 1.

8. Προκελευσματικὸς δέ, ὁ καὶ πυρρίχιος, ἀπὸ τοῦ κἂν ταῖς πυρρίχαις κἂν τοῖς ἀγῶσιν αὐτοῖς χρῆσθαι.

ARISTIDES QUINTILIANUS, *Fragmente*, p. 56, line 1.

Pyrrhichius vero, i.e. proceleusmaticus, quia hic assiduus vel in certamine vel in ludo quodam puerili.

MARTIANUS CAPELLA, in *Fragmente*, p. 56.

9. Ὥρισται δὲ τῶν ποδῶν ἕκαστος ἤτοι λόγῳ τινὶ ἢ ἀλογίᾳ τοιαύτῃ, ἥτις δύο λόγων γνωρίμων τῇ αἰσθήσει ἀνὰ μέσον ἔσται· Γένοιτο δὲ τὸ εἰρημένον ἂν ὧδε καταφανές, εἰ ληφθείησαν δύο πόδες, ὁ μὲν ἴσον τὸ ἄνω τῷ κάτω ἔχων καὶ δίσημον ἑκάτερον, ὁ δὲ τὸ μὲν κάτω δίσημον, τὸ δὲ ἄνω ἥμισυ, τρίτος δέ τις ληφθείη ποὺς παρὰ τούτους, τὴν μὲν βάσιν ἴσην αὐτοῖς ἀμφοτέροις ἔχων, τὴν δὲ ἄρσιν μέσον μέγεθος ἔχουσαν τῶν ἄρσεων. Ὁ γὰρ τοιοῦτος ποὺς ἄλογον μὲν ἕξει τὸ ἄνω πρὸς τὸ κάτω· ἔσται δ' ἡ ἀλογία μεταξὺ δύο λόγων γνωρίμων τῇ αἰσθήσει, τοῦ τε ἴσου καὶ τοῦ διπλασίου. Καλεῖται δ' οὗτος χορεῖος ἄλογος.

ARISTOXENUS, *Stoicheia*, *Fragmente*, p. 34, line 6.

10. Ὁ δὲ ἀπὸ μακρᾶς ἀρχόμενος, λήγων δὲ ἐς τὰς βραχείας δάκτυλος μὲν καλεῖται......Οἱ μέντοι ῥυθμικοὶ τούτου τοῦ ποδὸς τὴν μακρὰν βραχυτέραν εἶναί φασι τῆς τελείας, οὐκ ἔχοντες δὲ εἰπεῖν πόσῳ, καλοῦσιν αὐτὴν ἄλογον. Ἕτερον δὲ ἀντίστροφόν τινα τούτῳ ῥυθμὸν ὃς ἀπὸ τῶν βραχειῶν ἀρξάμενος ἐπὶ τὴν ἄλογον τοῦτον τελευτᾷ, χωρίσαντες ἀπὸ τῶν ἀναπαίστων, κύκλον καλοῦσι, παράδειγμα αὐτοῦ φέροντες τοιόνδε

κέχυται πόλις ὑψίπυλος κατὰ γᾶν.

περὶ ὧν ἂν ἕτερος εἴη λόγος.

......ἐγκαταμέμικται τῷ στίχῳ πλὴν ἐπὶ τῆς τελευτῆς, οἱ δὲ ἄλλοι πάντες εἰσὶ δάκτυλοι, καὶ οὗτοί γε παραδεδιωγμένας ἔχοντες τὰς ἀλόγους ὥστε μὴ πολὺ διαφέρειν ἐνίους τῶν τροχαίων.

DIONYSIUS OF HALICARNASSUS, *De Comp. Verb.*, *Fragmente*, p. 42.

11. Τῇ γὰρ περὶ τὰς ῥυθμοποιίας ποικιλίᾳ οὔσῃ ποικιλωτέρᾳ ἐχρήσαντο οἱ παλαιοί· ἐτίμων γοῦν τὴν ῥυθμικὴν ποικιλίαν καὶ τὰ περὶ τὰς κρουματικὰς δὲ διαλέκτους τότε ποικιλώτερα ἦν.

PLUTARCH, Westphal's ed., p. 15, line 28.

12. Τὸ μὲν οὖν ἴσον ἄρχεται μὲν ἀπὸ δισήμου, πληροῦται δὲ ἕως ἑκκαιδεκασήμου διὰ τὸ ἐξασθενεῖν ἡμᾶς τοὺς μείζους τοῦ τοιούτου γένους διαγινώσκειν ῥυθμούς.

Τὸ δὲ διπλάσιον ἄρχεται μὲν ἀπὸ τρισήμου, περαιοῦται δὲ ἕως ὀκτωκαιδεκασήμου, οὐκέτι γὰρ τῆς τοῦ τοιούτου ῥυθμοῦ φύσεως ἀντιλαμβανόμεθα.

Τὸ δὲ ἡμιόλιον ἄρχεται μὲν ἀπὸ πεντασήμου, πληροῦται δὲ ἕως πεντεκαιεικοσασήμου· μέχρι γὰρ τοσούτου τὸν τοιοῦτον ῥυθμὸν τὸ αἰσθητήριον καταλαμβάνει.

Τὸ δὲ ἐπίτριτον ἄρχεται μὲν ἀπὸ ἑπτασήμου, γίνεται δὲ ἕως τεσσαρεσκαιδεκασήμου. σπάνιος δὲ ἡ χρῆσις αὐτοῦ.

ARISTIDES QUINTILIANUS, *Fragmente*, p. 52.

13. Τῶν δὲ ῥυθμῶν ἡσυχαίτεροι μὲν οἱ ἀπὸ θέσεων προκαταστέλλοντες τὴν διάνοιαν· οἱ δὲ ἀπὸ ἄρσεων τῇ φωνῇ τὴν κροῦσιν ἐπιφέροντες, τεταραγμένοι.

Καὶ οἱ μὲν ὁλοκλήρους τοὺς πόδας ἐν ταῖς περιόδοις ἔχοντες εὐφυέστεροι καὶ...... οἱ δὲ βραχεῖς τοὺς κενοὺς ἔχοντες, ἀφελέστεροι καὶ μικροπρεπεῖς, οἱ δὲ ἐπιμήκεις μεγαλοπρεπέστεροι.

ARISTIDES QUINTILIANUS, *Fragmente*, p. 63.

14. Κατὰ δὲ μελοποιίαν γίνεται μεταβολή, ὅταν ἐκ διασταλτικοῦ ἤθους εἰς συσταλτικὸν ἢ ἡσυχαστικόν, ἢ ἐξ ἡσυχαστικοῦ εἴς τι τῶν λοιπῶν ἡ μεταβολὴ γένηται. ἔστι δὲ διασταλτικὸν μὲν ἦθος μελοποιΐας, δι' οὗ σημαίνεται μεγαλοπρέπεια καὶ δίαρμα ψυχῆς ἀνδρῶδες καὶ πράξεις ἡρωϊκαὶ καὶ πάθη τούτοις οἰκεῖα. χρῆται δὲ τούτοις μάλιστα μὲν ἡ τραγῳδία καὶ τῶν λοιπῶν δὲ ὅσα τούτου ἔχεται τοῦ χαρακτῆρος. συσταλτικὸν δέ, δι' οὗ συνάγεται ἡ ψυχὴ εἰς ταπεινότητα καὶ ἄνανδρον διάθεσιν. ἁρμόσει δὲ τὸ τοιοῦτον κατάστημα τοῖς ἐρωτικοῖς πάθεσι καὶ θρήνοις καὶ οἴκτοις καὶ τοῖς παραπλησίοις. ἡσυχαστικὸν δὲ ἦθός ἐστι μελοποιΐας, ᾧ παρέπεται ἠρεμότης ψυχῆς καὶ κατάστημα ἐλευθέριόν τε καὶ εἰρηνικόν. ἁρμόσουσι δὲ αὐτῷ ὕμνοι παιᾶνες ἐγκώμια συμβουλαὶ καὶ τὰ τούτοις ὅμοια.

CLEONIDES, in Jan, *Musici scriptores graeci*, p. 206.

APPENDIX B

GLOSSARY OF TECHNICAL TERMS

ACATALECTIC. Applied to a rhythm that has its full complement of arses and theses.

AGŌGĒ. Latin *ductus*, the motion of music, whether fast or slow. Agoge is equivalent to our *tempo*, as in *tempo moderato* &c.

AISTHĒSIS. The mental feeling, as opposed to physical sensation. Hence our word æsthetic.

ANACRUSIS. The unaccented note, or group of notes, that precedes and leads up to the first accented note of a rhythm. An anacrusic foot or phrase is one that commences with anacrusis.

ANAPÆST. An even-time foot whose figure is

$\frac{2}{4}$ ♫ | ♩

But any even rhythm whose feet for the most part commence with the arsis is classed as anapæstic rhythm, as the so-called "spondaic anapæst"  associated in ancient times with funeral marches.

ANTISTROPHE. See STROPHE.

APODOSIS. The concluding member of a period. In German *Nachsatz*.

ARRHYTHMICAL. Unrhythmical, or faulty in rhythm.

ARSIS. The unaccented portion of a foot. In German *Senkung, Schlechter Tacttheil, Aufschlag*. An arsis-foot is the unaccented foot of a syzygy or pair of feet. See page 50.

AULOS. A kind of oboe, the most important of the Greek wind instruments.

BRACHYCATALECTIC. A rhythm of which the whole of the final foot is represented by a rest. See CATALECTIC.

CÆSURA. The place where a rhythm, or a portion thereof, is divided from what follows. The place to take breath in singing.

CATALECTIC. A rhythm is catalectic when the final arsis is represented by a rest, and the first foot begins on a thesis. In other words, a rhythm whose arses number one less than its theses. But in this work we have applied the term in the sense of brachycatalectic, *q.v.*

CATALEXIS. The omitted portion of a catalectic or brachycatalectic rhythm.

CHOREE. See TROCHEE.

CHOREIC DACTYL. A triple measure in the form $\frac{3}{8}$ | ♩ ♫ |.

CHOROS. Latin *chorus*, the band of dancers.

CHRONOS ALOGOS. Irrational, or unproportional time, that is, a note whose value bears no simple relation to the primary time.

CHRONOS PODIKOS. The time occupied by the thesis or arsis of a foot.
CHRONOS PROTOS. Primary time, for an explanation of which see page 28.
CHRONOS RHYTHMOPŒIAS IDIOS. The time occupied by a group of feet forming the thesis or arsis of a complete phrase.
COLON. A member of a period, hence, a rhythm. In German *Rhythmisches Glied, Satz.*
COLOTOMY. The arrangement of music in recognisable phrase-magnitudes.
COMEDY. A jovial and popular festivity, originally connected with the vintage thanksgiving to Bacchus.
COMMA. A portion of a colon separated by a cæsura. In German *Rhythmisches Einschnitt.*
CORYPHÆUS. The leader of the chorus.
CRETIC or PÆON. A five-time foot.
CROUSIS. In a vocal composition, those portions that are allotted to the instruments alone, without the voice, to separate the rhythms and periods where required. The crousis fulfils two functions, being both an aid to expression, and a means of giving rest to the voice.
CYCLICAL DACTYL. A triple foot in the form $\frac{3}{8}\ |\ \text{♩.♩♩}\ |$.
DACTYL. The rhythmical figure $|\ \text{♩}\ \text{♩♩}\ |$. But all even rhythm is classed as dactylic rhythm.
DACTYLO-EPITRITIC. A rhythmical form formerly supposed to combine dactyls with trochees and spondees, thus $\frac{2}{4}\ |\ \text{♩}\ \text{♩♩}\ |\ \frac{3}{8}\ \text{♩}\ \text{♪}\ |\ \frac{2}{4}\ \text{♩}\ \text{♩}\ |$. But it is now thought that the second foot contained a three-time long, thus $\frac{2}{4}\ \text{♩}\ \text{♩♩}\ |\ \text{♩.}\ \text{♪}\ |\ \text{♩}\ \text{♩}$ and that the whole rhythm was of even species.
DIÆRESIS. The arrangement and disposition of the component parts of a rhythm or foot. In German *Tactabtheilung.*
DIASTALTIC ETHOS. The energetic character supposed to be produced by commencing a rhythm with the arsis.
DIATONIC. Moving by tones. The principal diatonic tetrachord is represented by the intervals E, F, G, A.
DICHRONOS, DISEMOS. See TIME.
DIPODY. A rhythm of two feet in length.
DISEMOS, DICHRONOS. See TIME.
DITHYRAMB. A choral song performed round the altar of Bacchus during the annual vintage thanksgiving.
DITONE. The major third, consisting of two tones.
DOCHMIAC. A compound foot combining the three simple species.
ELEGY. A poem, on any subject, composed in hexameters and pentameters. Later it came to be applied to funeral lamentations.
ENHARMONIC GENUS. The scale whose two tetrachords rise by the intervals quartertone, quartertone, major third.
ENOPLIUS. A compound foot suitable for war-songs.
EPIBATOS. Slow quintuple rhythm.
EPINIKION. A song of victory.
EPITRITOS. A rhythmical form which was formerly supposed to combine trochees with spondees, but is now thought to consist of even feet only.

EPODE. See STROPHE.

ERRHYTHMICAL, or ENRHYTHMICAL. Correct as to rhythm.

ETHOS. Character. Three kinds of Character were expressed in rhythm, the Hesychastic, or tranquil, suitable for religion and calmness, the Diastaltic, or energetic and dignified, and the Systaltic, or sentimental, suitable for lamentations or erotic compositions.

EURHYTHMICAL. Having beautiful, well balanced, or effective rhythm.

FOOT. The smallest combination of arsis and thesis by which rhythm is made perceptible.

GLYCONIC. A compound foot, in triple time. See page 91.

HEGEMON. (1) The leader of a chorus or semichorus. (2) The name given by Baccheios to the pyrrhic foot, *q.v.*

HESYCHASTIC ETHOS. The reposeful or tranquil character supposed to be produced by a rhythm that commences with the thesis.

HEXAMETER. A verse consisting of six feet.

HEXAPODY. A rhythm of six feet.

HYPORCHEMA. A choral hymn to Apollo, generally in quintuple rhythm, of a lively character, accompanied by dancing and mimetic action.

IAMBUS. A triple-time foot having a short arsis and long thesis. $\frac{3}{8}$ ♪ ♩

Triple measure in general is called iambic rhythm.

ICTUS. See STIGMA.

IONICUS. A compound foot, consisting of a spondee and a pyrrhic.

Ionicus a majore $\frac{3}{4}$ Spond. Pyr. ♩ ♩ ♫

Ionicus a minore $\frac{3}{4}$ Pyr. Spond. ♫ ♩ ♩

IRRATIONAL TIME. See CHRONOS ALOGOS.

KITHARA. A powerful form of lyre, used in the theatre.

LOGAŒDIC. A rhythm which was formerly supposed to combine trochees with dactyls, but is now thought to consist of triple measure only. See page 80.

MAGNITUDE, in Greek MEGETHOS. The relative space of time occupied by any kind of rhythmical combination.

MEASURE. The foot in Greek music. In modern music the measure sometimes, though not always, coincides with the bar. But it may commence with either the arsis or thesis, and two or more measures may occupy the same space of time as a bar.

In America the word Measure is applied to that which in England is called the Bar.

MELOS. The melodic side of music, as opposed to rhythmos, the rhythmical side.

MOLOSSUS. A foot containing three two-time notes.

MONOPODY. A rhythmical section consisting of a single foot.

NOMOS. Musical form generally. Equivalent to the word "form" as used by us in "Sonata-form," "Rondo-form" &c.

ORCHĒSIS. The act of dancing.

ORCHĒSTĒS. A dancer.

ORCHĒSTIC COMPOSITIONS. Choral songs performed with dancing.

ORCHĒSTIKOS. Suitable for dancing.

APPENDIX B

ORCHESTRA. The circular dancing place in the theatre, in front of the stage or proscenium.

ORTHIOS. An iambic foot in very slow tempo.

OVERLAPPING occurs where the final thesis of a member coincides with the first thesis of the succeeding member. In German *Tacterstickung, Tactverkettung*.

PÆAN. A choral song of thanksgiving addressed to Apollo.

PÆON. A foot of the value of five primary times, in the form $\frac{5}{8}\ |\ ♩\ ♪\ ♩\ |$
It is also called CRETIC.

PÆONIC SPECIES. Quintuple rhythm.

PENTAMETER. A verse of five feet.

PENTAPODY. A rhythm of five feet.

PERIOD. A musical sentence, containing one, two, or more members or rhythms.

A *simple stichic* period has two consecutive members of the same magnitude.

A *repeated stichic* period has three or more equal members.

The *stichic* was the form most favoured during the decadent Graeco-Roman period, and was used in the early Christian hymns to enable them to be easily caught up by the populace.

A *palinodic* period comprises two or more symmetrical groups of members, as Period 1 in the Epode of Pindar's 8th Pythian Ode, Ex. 58, page 114.

A *repeated palinodic* period is the most common of modern types, and is usually in the form of a long series of dipodic or tetrapodic members, as in our dance music. But it can easily be confounded with the stichic period. As a rule the melody decides, but sometimes it is undecided. A good example of repeated palinodic is found in the opening number of the "Blue Danube" Waltzes, in which the melodic figure of the first rhythm is repeated several times in different positions.

The *antithetic* period, only occasionally found in modern music, and equivalent to the Italian *rime abbracciate*, consists of a group of two members of different magnitudes, repeated in their inverse order, as 4+3+3+4. More complex arrangements are almost unknown in modern music, but something equivalent to the *mesodic* period is used throughout Hugo Wolf's song "Agnes," No. 14 of the Mörike-Lieder. It consists of a period whose members are divided by the insertion between them of a third member, of a different magnitude.

Ex. 87. H. Wolf, "Agnes," Mörike-Lieder No. 14.

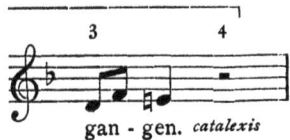

The *pro-odic* period is one whose ordinary members are preceded by an extra member, as in Bach's "Ich hatte viel Bekümmerniss" (page 109), or the opening bars of Beethoven's Fifth Symphony.

The *epodic* period is the reverse of the *pro-odic*, since it is succeeded by an extra member, as in the Amen of a hymn.

Other forms are recognised into which it is not necessary to enter here.

Irregular periods are those which have no strict symmetry. They were anciently used in the songs on the stage, to follow the dramatic action.

POUS. A foot, or measure.

PRIMARY TIME. See CHRONOS PROTOS.

PROCATALEXIS. The omission of a foot at the beginning of a rhythm.

PROCELEUSMATICUS. A foot containing two primary times. See PYRRHIC.

PROLEPSIS. A preliminary or introductory foot, heard before the regular rhythmical form commences.

PROSODIAC. A compound foot containing different forms of simple foot.

PROSODY. A poem sung to an instrument. The Greek accents, which were originally musical signs. Later, the laws of verse.

PROTASIS. The first member of a period. If there are more than two members, all the members are Protases except the last, which is called APODOSIS. In German *Vordersatz*.

PYRRHIC. A foot containing two primary times only. Also called PROCELEUSMATICUS and HEGEMON.

RHYTHM. Measure, proportion, symmetry, measured motion, measured time. The word was anciently applied to prose, architecture, and sculpture, as well as to poetry, music, and dancing. It was also used for the common objects of daily life, such as a well-fitting pair of boots. A RHYTHM is a member of a period, or even a single foot. The arrangement of the relative time-values of the individual notes is also called rhythm.

RHYTHMIZOMENON. The material, whether poetry, music, or the dance, which is subjected to rhythm.

RHYTHMOEIDES. Proper to the rhythm.

RHYTHMOPŒIA. The rhythmical arrangement of a given rhythmizomenon, *q.v.* The art or act of arranging rhythm.

SEMICOLON. Half a rhythm; but the word COMMA is more frequently used for any portion of a rhythm less than the whole.

SPONDEE. A duple foot containing two long notes, the first of which is the thesis. Music containing a preponderance of spondees is said to be in SPONDAIC rhythm.

STEIGERUNG. (German.) An increase of energy, interest, feeling, &c. leading to a climax.

STIGMA. A dot placed over a note to indicate accent. Its function is performed in modern music by the bar-line, which immediately precedes the accented note of a foot, or the principal accent of a dipody, tripody or tetrapody. In Latin ICTUS.

STROPHE. A combination of periods. It is generally followed by an ANTISTROPHE, exactly similar in construction, and the latter is often succeeded by the EPODE, of a different structure from the strophe and antistrophe.

"It is not permitted to composers to change the melody of strophes and antistrophes; whether their songs are in the enharmonic, chromatic, or diatonic genus, it is necessary that in all the strophes and antistrophes the same melodic design must be preserved. The rhythms also must not be modified; they must be invariable." (Dion. Halic. *De comp. verb.* XIX. quoted by Gevaert, Vol. II. p. 163.)

SYZYGY. A pair of feet, one of which is an arsis-foot, the other a thesis-foot.

TETRACHORD. A scale series of four notes. For example our major scale consists of the two tetrachords C, D, E, F, and G, A, B, C. Greek scales were similarly made up of a pair of tetrachords, which varied according to mode and genus.

TETRAMETER. A verse of four feet, or four pairs of feet.

TETRAPODY. A rhythm of four feet. The term TETRAPODIC rhythm may be applied to what is known as "Four-bar rhythm," whether the phrases are divided into half-rhythms or not.

THESIS. The accented portion of a foot. In German *Hebung, Guter Tacttheil.* The accented foot of a syzygy, or pair of feet. A rhythm is THETIC when its feet commence with the thesis.

TIME. Generally, the space of time occupied by a rhythm. But a rhythm is made up of "times" of various magnitudes, the smallest of which is the chronos protos, or primary time. A note of the value of two primary times is a chronos disemos, or dichronos, *i.e.* a "two-time note." Similarly higher values are called trisemos, or trichronos, "three-time," tetrasemos, or tetrachronos, "four-time," pentasemos, or pentachronos, "five-time," and so on. See also CHRONOS PODIKOS and CHRONOS RHYTHMOPŒIAS IDIOS.

TŎNĒ. The extension of a syllable to preserve the rhythmical balance.

TRAGEDY. Originally the goat-song: afterwards a serious drama.

TRIBRACH. A triple-time foot containing three short notes.

TRICHRONOS, or TRISEMOS. See TIME.

TRILOGY. A series of consecutive plays, performed on three successive days. By the addition of a preludial play the series became a TETRALOGY.

TRIMETER. A verse containing three feet, or three pairs of feet.

TRIPODY. A rhythm of three feet.

TRISEMOS, TRICHRONOS. See TIME.

TROCHEE, or CHOREE. A triple foot having its thesis long and its arsis short, the thesis preceding the arsis. TROCHAIC rhythm is triple rhythm whose feet commence with the thesis.

APPENDIX C

DACTYLO-EPITRITIC, LOGAŒDIC, AND DOCHMIAC RHYTHMS, AND RHYTHMICAL MODULATION. M. LOUIS LALOY'S VIEWS

ONE of the fundamental principles of modern music is that in any given period the accents should occur at equal distances of time: in other words, that the bars should be of equal length.

But modern composers are beginning to discover that an occasional violation of this principle may produce new rhythmical effects. Hence we meet here and there with transitory changes of rhythmical species within the period. This is the ancient metabolē or "modulation" of rhythm.

Thus, Debussy, in his "Hommage à Rameau" introduces, several times, an interchange of duple and triple rhythm, as shown below:

Debussy, "Hommage à Rameau."

This kind of mixture of species was not unknown to our Elizabethan musicians. In a madrigal recently edited by Mr Barclay Squire, the following passage occurs more than once:

John Farmer, "Fair Phyllis I saw sitting all alone" (1599).

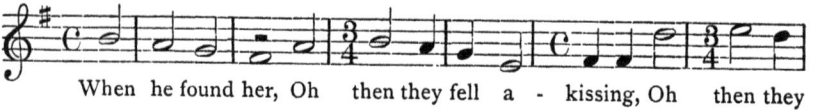

When he found her, Oh   then they fell a - kissing, Oh   then they

It will be noticed that these examples are not of the nature of the modern triplet, in which the component parts of the measure change from duple to triple, while the measures themselves remain of equal duration. Here the values of the measures are temporarily changed, and there is a sort of rocking to and fro between groups of two units and groups of three units.

M. Louis Laloy, in his "Aristoxène de Tarent" (Paris, 1904), suggests that, in the investigations of the last fifty years, too much effort has been expended on an endeavour to bring Greek metres under the law of what he calls "l'équidistance des temps forts." He contends that logaœdic rhythm, for example, was really of the nature of the alternations shown in the above examples: that "these rhythms expressed sweetness and tenderness through their changing nuances," and that "Sophocles and Euripides, attracted by these delicate alternations of rhythm, extended their use, so that with these poets the logaœdic became the universal rhythm, appropriate to all situations."

M. Laloy would abolish the cyclical dactyl, and make very sparing use of the three-time long. He would apply to the dactylo-epitritic, logaœdic, and dochmiac rhythms the rule given by Aristoxenus himself in his *Elements*, that the "long is equal to two shorts." That this rule is, however, not invariable in Greek music, he shows by reference to the Seikilos hymn, in which the three-time long is distinctly indicated by the notation.

He remarks that Aristoxenus is only treating of the first elements of rhythm, not of its application to the higher branches of composition, in which he would probably have modified some of the rules intended for beginners.

By the application of the rule of one long to two shorts the dactylo-epitritic rhythm of Pindar's first Pythian Ode, shown in our Ex. 42, p. 74, would work out somewhat as follows:

Pindar, First Pythian Ode. Dactylo-epitritic rhythm.

Χρυ - σέ - α φόρ - μιγξ, 'Α - πόλ - λω - νος καὶ ἰ - ο - πλοκά - μων

And the logaœdic rhythm of Sophocles, Ex. 45, p. 81, thus:

Sophocles, "Antigone." Logaœdic rhythm.

Εὐ - δαί - μο - νες οἴ - σι κα - κῶν ἄ - γευστος αἰ - ών

The dochmiacs would be as we give them in Ex. 17 *a* and *b*, but M. Laloy suggests that the second dochmiac may be a fiction of some rhythmicist.

He draws a comparison between the rise and development of modern harmonic modulation, and that of ancient rhythm. Our early composers, having discovered the importance of tonality, took pains to impress their key upon the listener. In the second stage they modulated sparingly, to immediately related keys, and in the third they discovered the charm of wider and more frequent modulation, until by the use of chromatic harmony there arose an amount of modulation that frequently obscured the fundamental tonality.

He suggests that the Greek rhythmicists at first confined themselves to groups of simple iambuses or dactyls, and their equivalents, in which each foot in a given period was of equal value: then they introduced a few "modulations" of rhythm, corresponding to the early changes of tonality in our music, and finally, in the epitritos, logaœdic, and dochmius, they used constant modulation, analogous to what he calls the chromatism of the present day.

Aristoxenus does not treat of modulation in the fragments that have survived: but M. Laloy considers that he must have done so in a later chapter, since it had so important a place in practice.

But even in this elementary work of Aristoxenus the equidistance of accented times is not preserved, for it is disturbed by irrationality, which renders its strict observance impossible. M. Laloy brings powerful arguments to show that the Greeks deliberately broke the rule of equidistance, and that they found a delight in the piquant rhythms that resulted from their modulations. Some, at least, of our modern rhythmical developments are in favour of M. Laloy's view, and, incidentally, of the view expressed on page 174 of the present work, that in its main principles the art of rhythm seems likely to develop along similar lines to those of old. But modern musicians have not yet arrived at a degree of perception that would enable a conductor to keep an orchestra or chorus together in such "modulations" as we quote from Pindar and Sophocles: and even if he succeeded in doing so, would a modern audience be capable of accepting them? The power to assimilate effects so subtle is not with us yet: may we not, however, indulge in the thought that it may come to us at some future time?

Examples of rhythmical modulation, similar in principle to the quotations we give from Debussy and John Farmer, are met with in the works of other composers, for instance in those of M. Vincent D'Indy, but they are very exceptional: may it not happen that, as our rhythmical powers develop, what is the exception now, will become a leading feature in certain forms of music at some future time, as M. Laloy contends was the case with the music of Sophocles and Euripides?

The power of musical perception is capable of development in several directions. Some years ago it fell to the lot of the present writer to give some lectures on Greek music, in which he endeavoured to bring before his audience practical examples of the methods of tuning the scale described by Aristoxenus. He was ably supported by the late Mr A. J. Hipkins, himself an enthusiastic student of Greek music. Mr Hipkins had four pianos specially tuned to represent Aristoxenian scale-intervals, and both he and the writer spent some time in practising little melodies based upon these scales. In the end, both performers found that they were rapidly assimilating, and really beginning to enjoy the unfamiliar intervals: but when it came to performing them at the lectures, the audience were entirely taken aback, and simply looked upon them as something very much out of tune.

If two musicians, entirely brought up on modern classical music, could so quickly assimilate and begin to enjoy the melodic intervals of Aristoxenus, it does not seem impossible that a conscious or unconscious revival of the rhythmical modulations of the Greeks might become acceptable to musicians and audiences of the future. If this were so, what a greatly enlarged field for expression would be available to future composers!

INDEX

Abert, Hermann, *Die Lehre vom Ethos in der gr. Musik*, 22, 23, 102
Accent, 25, 27
Aeschylus, 16; conquered by Simonides, 19
Æsthetic effects, desire for in religious ceremonies, 16 *note*
Agoge should be moderate, 78 *note*; Aristoxenus on, 104
Aisthēsis, rhythm appeals to the, 1, 2; aided by τονή, 44; affected by fine music as by beauty of nature, 142
Alcman, 15
Alypius, 30
Amen at end of a hymn, 109
Anacrusic feet, 28; anacrusic and thetic rhythms used alternately to portray different characters in "Don Giovanni," 133
Anacrusis, 2; Abert's view, 103
Anapæst, suitable for marches, 27; cyclical, 42; character of, 43
Anapæstic Cola, 83; an. rhythm has rising accentuation, 105
Ancient and modern dramatic methods compared, 90
Anonymus, Bellermann's, 6; allows extension of syllables for rhythmical purposes, 7; time signs in, 30; ictus, 33
Antecedent and Consequent, 107
Apodosis, 107
Apollo, 9; Festival of, 10
Archaic periods of music, 10
Archytas, 12
Arion, 15
Aristides, 7; objects to innovations, 99
Aristophanes, 18; "Knights," 85; "Peace," 86
Aristotle, 6; Nineteenth Problem supposed not to be by him, 6; reference to instrumental accompaniment, 10; his views opposed, 22; duple and triple rhythms, 95
Aristoxenian fragments discovered at Venice, 2; their interest for musicians, 6; list of feet, 57 *et seq.*; theory of magnitudes compared with melos of Wagner and Bach, 70, 71
Aristoxenus, Biography, 3; publication of works of, 3, 4; opposed to Pythagoras, 5; definition of rhythm, 24; rhythmical terms, 26; fragment of — recently discovered, 44; use of word *chronos*, 49; objects to two-time foot, 56; broken portion of his theory restored by Westphal, 60
Arithmetical nomenclature of notes, common to Germans, Americans and Ancient Greeks, 35 *note*

Arrhythm, 34, 48
Arsis and thesis, the movements of foot or hand, 27; ancient and modern views of compared, 50; the two portions of the foot, 55; ar. and th. of phrase explained by passages from modern composers, 58 *et seq.*; further discussed, 71-73. See also Thesis
Athena, nomos to, 11
Augustine, Saint, 5
Auletic and aulodic nomoi, 11

Baccheios the Elder, 5; definitions of rhythm, 24; describes the enoplius, 53
Baccheios, a quintuple foot, 50
Bacchic pæon, 43
Bacchus, 15
Bach, uses Aristoxenus' seventh "difference" in Matthew-Passion, 62; conceals his rhythmical divisions, 65; Motet, "Ich lasse dich nicht," 84; Prelude in D, 95; "Ich hatte viel Bekümmerniss," 109; — and diatonic music, 100; B minor Mass, 116-119; Christmas Oratorio, 120
Bar, thesis and arsis foot distinguished by the use of compound rather than simple bars, 77, 78
Basis, Aristoxenus' term for thesis, 25 *note*
Bassus, C., 4
Beethoven, dactyls, iambuses and anapæsts in his music, 38, 39; sonata op. 28, 94; change of rhythm-species in ninth symphony, 98; funeral marches, 105; uses rhythm without melody, 111 *note*; ninth symphony, 136 *et seq.*; adheres to tetrapodic balance while using pentapodies, 138; dipodies in ninth symphony, 139; syzygies in the same, 143, 144; eurhythmy in ninth symphony, 146; semantic trochee in the same work, 148
Bellermann, F., 2; his *Anonymus*, 4
Boeckh, investigates metre and rhythm, 2
Brahms, variations on Hungarian theme, 58; Rhapsody op. 67, 104, 105, 119; uses various magnitudes, 168; song, "Wie bist du, meine Königin," 169
Brittany, traces of Ancient Greek music in folk-songs, 9
Burney, comments on Greek rhythm, 2, 40
Byzantine music, 9

Capella, 6
Catalectic and acatalectic rhythms, 94
Catalectic metre, Aristides on, 103
Catalexis and ethos, 103
Charisius, 5
Choerilus, 16

INDEX

Chopin, example of various feet combined, 48; funeral march, 105; Nocturne in G minor, 158
Choral music was in unison or octaves, 12
Chorees, irrational, 41; a dance measure, 42
Choreic dactyl, 29, 42
Choros, 12
Chromatic tetrachord, 12
Chronoi podikoi, 49, 50
Chronos, used in various senses, 49
Chronos protos, 28; theory of survives to the commencement of mensural music, 29
Chronos rhythmopœias idios, 49, 50
Cimon, 16
Cleonides on ethos of melody, 99
Colon, 107
Combination of species, 48
Comedy, origin of, 15; aims of, 18; logaœdic rhythm in, 84 *et seq.*; rhythm of, 84 *et seq.*; *tempo* in, 87; dipodies in, 87
Comma, 107
Complexity of ancient rhythm, 53
Compound times, 35; — rhythms perturb the mind, 98
Cretic, 12, 43
Crousis between rhythms exemplified in Schubert's "Leiermann," Aristophanes' "Frogs," Wagner's "Meistersinger" and "Tannhäuser," Parry's "De Profundis," 112; Schubert's D minor quartet and unfinished symphony, 149; "Erlking," 154, 155
Cyclical dactyl, 2, 4, 40, 42, 44; in tragedy, 82, 83; in "Come lasses and lads" and Beethoven's ninth symphony, 83; — anapæst, 42, 44

Dactyl, derivation of word, 38; dignity of the, 105
Dactylic species, 37; catalogue of its feet, 42; dactylic pentameter has a tender ethos, 104
Dactylo-epitritic rhythm, 75, 185
Decline of Greek music, 96
Delphi, 2
Delphic Hymn to Apollo, in pæonic rhythm, 39; contains a form objected to by Aristoxenus, 44; example from, 47; further discussion of, 87, 88
Deus ex machina used by Euripides, 17
Diæresis, 37; æsthetic effects due to, 51
Diatonic, chromatic, enharmonic with their various tunings available for melody, 14
Dichronos, 35
Didymus, 13; definition of rhythm, 24, 26
Diomedes, 5
Dionysius of Halicarnassus, 4
Dionysius of Thebes, 21
Dionysus, worship of, 15
Disemos, 35
Dithyramb, 15
Dithyrambic chorus, Simonides gains a prize with, 19
Divisions (vocal), 129

Dochmiac, description of, 51, 185; use in tragedy, 89; character of, 98
Dorian mode, 11; — rhythm, 79
Dowland, "Awake, sweet Love," difficulty of sustaining long notes relieved by application of Aristoxenian theory, 55
Drama begun, 15; sung throughout, 18

Eighteen-time rhythm, 65; in "Antigone" and "Tristan," 66; used by Schubert, 67
Elatio, 27
"Electra," of Sophocles, 89; of Strauss, 90
Elegy, 11; perfected by Simonides, 19
Eleusinian mysteries imitated by Aeschylus, 16
Empty times, or rests, 30
Enoplius, 53, 54; character of, 98
Epibatos, 38, 43; disturbs the spirit, 97
Epigram, perfected by Simonides, 19
Epitritic rhythm in Handel's "Judas Maccabaeus," 78, 79
Epitritic-dactylic rhythms, 79, 185
Epitritos, 75
Equal proportion, Aristides' view of, 94
Eratosthenes, 13
Errhythm, 34
Ethical character of modes, 100
Ethical rules, Abert's, 103
Ethos, or character, 35; discussion of, 93-105
Eurhythm, Eurhythmy, 34, 35, 48; found in balance of periods, 107-115
Euripides, 17
Extension of syllables, 25; called τονή, *peripleo, rhythmoeides*, 44

Flowing song, 92
Foot, or measure, description of, 27; Aristoxenian definition of the, 35; differences of, 36, 37; simple and compound, 54
Fortunatianus, Atilius, 5
Fugal vocal music, its rhythmical characteristics, 135

Genera, Romans could not appreciate, 22
Gevaert, 3
Gluck, uses glyconics in "Alceste," 92; "Orpheus," 127, 128
Glyconic rhythm in Delphic hymns, 88; description of glyconic rhythm, 91
Greek melodic ornaments passed into the neumes of the Church, 71
Greek music, a branch of musical system of Babylon and Assyria, 9; decline of, 20, 21
Greek Poetry, period in, 108
Grieg, violin sonata op. 8, 92
Gymnopaidæa, 12

Half-rhythm, 109
Handel, his use of cadences compared to that of Bach, 71; — and Pindar exercise restraint, 79; Dead March, 100; his aims compared with those of Bach, 121; "Messiah," 121-126
Hastiness of trochees, 105
Haydn's "Creation," 128-130

Hebrew Poetry, period in, 107
Hebung, 27
Hegemon, or leader of the chorus, his difficulties, 27
Hegemon, the two-time foot, 41
Heliodorus, 5
Hephaestion, 5
Heptachord, Terpandrian, 11
Hermann, 2
Heroic metre, 104
Hesychastic rhythms, 93
Hexameter, 10, 11
Hexapody, 111
Hymnody, quintuple rhythm in, 87; long notes in, 95
Hyporchemata, 12

Iambic species, 37; catalogue of its feet, 41
Iambus, derivation of word, 38; various forms of, 41; produced by musical phrasing, 45, 46, 50; suitable for the dance, 97
Ictus, 31–33
Instans, the mediæval *chronos protos*, 29
Instrumental accompaniment, 10; complex, 19; above the melody, 20
Instrumental music, development of, 136
Ionic rhythm, languid and voluptuous, 105; first used by Anacreon, 106; Westphal's views of, 106
Ionicus, 50
Irrationality, Aristoxenus' description of, 39; again coming into use, 40, 41; in Pythia No. 1, 78; in comedy, 85–87
Italian opera, 18; classified analogously to Greek music, 100; ethos of, compared with Greek ethical rules, 102

Karneia, 10
Kircher, discovers a Pindaric melody, 73
Kitharody, 10
Krexos, a decadent, 20

Lamentation anapæsts, 105
Lamentations, 11
Lampros, 21
Largo, ancient method of expressing, 45
Lasos, of Hermione, master of Pindar, 19; writes a book on melos, 20
Leophantus, definition of rhythm, 24, 26
Levatio, 27
Ligature, origin of, 46
Limitation of phrase-magnitude, Aristides on, 65
Logacœdic rhythm, 80–86, 184; employed by Bach, 83, 84; in comedy, 84; suitable to the character of a wrestler, 113
Long notes calm the mind, 95; at end of phrase, 103
Longinus, 5
Lussy, *L'Anacrouse dans la musique moderne*, 102
Lydian mode, 11
Lyric Poetry, 19

Mallius, Theodorus, 4

Marathon, elegy for those slain at, 19
Marius, T., 5
Measure, used for Bar in America, 35 *note*
Meibomius, 3 *note*
Melody does not demand intervals so definite as harmony, 13; meaningless without rhythm, 26
Members of period, 107
Mendelssohn's rhythm, 156, 158; Rondo brillante op. 29, 158
Mental effect of music, 95, 96
Metabole, 76
Metre and rhythm, difference between described by Servius, 25
Mixed rhythms, 51
Modern modes and ethos, 100
Molossus, 42; in Chopin's waltz op. 42, 48; in Schumann's third symphony, 58
Monro, D. B., "Modes of Ancient Greek Music," 32, 73 *note*
Morelli, librarian of St Mark's, 6
Motion, implied in technical term sonata-*movement*, 25
Movement, essential to rhythm, 24
Mozart, "Don Giovanni," 130–133; Requiem, 133–135
Music, mysterious power of, 9
Music drama differs from opera, 18
Musica fracta, 55 *note*

National Anthems, note on construction of, 128
Nibelungen Ring, form of, suggested by Greek drama, 16
Nicomachus, definition of rhythm, 24, 26
Nineteenth Problem, doubt as to its authorship, 6; notices the difference between our appreciation of a familiar and a new tune, 97
Nineteen-time rhythm, 67
Nomoi, 10; *orthioi*, 12
Notation constructed, 12
Note, used in various senses, 49

Octave-species, 11; seven in number, 13
Olympos, 10, 11
Orchēsis, Orchēstra, Orchēstes, Orchēstikos, 12
Orestes, fragment of music of, 17, 51
Orpheus, 9
Orthios, 10; a solemn triple-measure composition, 11; description of the foot, 42; leads to decision of character, 97
Oxyrhynchus Papyri, quotation from, 44

Pæan, 11, 12
Pæon, not to be confused with pæan, 11; construction, 38; various forms of, 43; Aristoxenus on the, 44; in Delphic hymns, 88; epibatos, 12, 38, 39, 43, 45; diaguios, 38, 39
Pæonic species, 37; suited to hymns, 39; catalogue of its feet, 43; originally a wild dance, 106
Pæstum, referred to by Aristoxenus, 20
Palestrina-music, 11 *note*

INDEX

Peisistratides, 15
Pentameter, 11
Pentapodies in Brahms' Rhapsody op. 119, 67; in Pythia No. 1, 67
Periclean and Palestrina epochs compared, 96, 97
Period, 107–115
Phaedrus, definition of rhythm, 24, 25
Philodemus of Gadara, an opponent of music, 22
Philoxenus, an Alexandrian grammarian, 5
Philoxenus, a contemporary of Aristoxenus, 20, 21
Phrase divisions, 50; necessity for limitation of, 54; not so keenly felt by moderns as by Greeks, 65
Phrygian mode, 11; in tragedy, 15
Pindar, chief exponent of lyric poetry, 19; referred to by Plutarch, 21; example of rhythm in Olympia No. 3, 29; origin of Pindar's odes, 73; a supposed Pindaric melody, 73–77; Olympia No. 10, 80; rhythmical analysis of Pythia No. 8, 113, 114
Plainsong, origin of the ligatures in, 45
Plato, calls Lydian and Phrygian modes barbaric, 11; his views opposed, 22; objects to polyphonic accompaniment, 53
Plotius Sacerdos, 5
Plutarch, 8; refers to instrumental accompaniment, 10; Plutarch's account of second Spartan institution, 11
Poetry, ancient, based on quantity, modern on accent, 28; period in, 108
Polymnastos, 11, 12
Pompeian frescoes exhibit two men playing a duet, 20
Positio, 27
Pous, used in various senses, 50
Pratinas, 21
Preludes, 10
Primary time, 29
Priscianus, 6
Procatalexis, use of in Mozart's Requiem, 134
Proceleusmaticus, 41; double, 42
Prose, period in, 108
Prosodiacs, 51–54; not to be confounded with prosody, 53, 54; effect of, 98
Protasis and Apodosis, 107
Psellus, 6
Punctuation signs, origin of, 107
Pyrrhic games, short notes in, 95
Pyrrhiché, a war-song, 37
Pyrrhichius, a two-time foot, 37; called hegemon, 41; used in the pæon, 44; considered ignoble, 98
Pythagoras, 5
Pythic contests, 11
Pytho, nomos to, 11

Quartertones introduced, 12
Quintilianus, Aristides, 4
Quintilianus, Fabius, 4

Quintuple rhythm, much employed, 9; the cretic, 12; again coming into use, 39; in Tschaïkowsky's Pathetic symphony, Paderewski's "Chants des Voyageurs," D'Indy's sonata, Chopin's sonata, 68; in ancient comedy, 86 *et seq.*; in hymnody, 87; in tragedy, 89; is inspiring, 97

Rapid *tempo*, 99
Religious dance still survives in Seville Cathedral, 12
Rests, 94
Rheinberger, rhythmopœia in an organ fugue, 56
Rhyme takes place of ancient balance of periods, 110
Rhythm becomes independent of metre, 22; definitions of, 24; its pleasure-giving quality explained in 19th Problem, 24; must be easy to understand, 25; in vocal melody, 25; arises from division of time, 26; cannot be produced by one note alone, 36; used in various senses, 49; divided between voice and instrument, 67; of comedy, 84 *et seq.*; emotional effects of, 98
Rhythmizomenon, 26; can be arranged rhythmically or unrhythmically, 34
Rhythmoeides, 44
Rhythmopœia, meaning of word, 26; three species of foot in, 37; Aristoxenus' note on, 55
Riemann, *Agogik und Dynamik*, 28
Rising and falling rhythms, 102
Rossbach, 110
Ruelle, 32

Sacadas, 11, 12
Scales the melodic material to which rhythm was applied, 15
Scheme, 37
Schmidt, J. H. H., 2; *Antike Compositionslehre*, 8
Schmidt, Rossbach, Westphal, investigations of rhythmical forms, 110
Schubert, examples of Greek rhythmical feet in, 46, 47; of fifteen-time magnitudes, 67; "Täuschung," 67; "Pilgerweise," 68; D minor quartet, songs, 149; "Erlking," 149–156
Schumann, uses ratio 5 : 1, p. 58; his rhythmical devices, 156–158; Novelletten No. 5, 157; songs, 157
Seikilos, hymn by, 31–33
Semantic trochee, 42
Semantoi, give decision of character, 97
Semeion, the sign of the conductor for thesis, or the down beat, 27; notation-sign, 30
Senkung, 27
Servius, 4
Seventeen-time rhythm, 65
Shakespeare, interlacing rhymes in, 110
Short notes, Aristides on, 95; at end of phrases, 103
Short phrases disapproved of, 94

INDEX

Simonides of Ceos, 19
Simple times, 35
Sixteen-time rhythm, 65
Slow movement, necessity for large number of notes in, explained on Aristoxenian principles, 55
Solo music, 12
Sophocles, leads the dance after Salamis, 12; competes with Aeschylus, 16; alters form of drama, 17; "Antigone," music of, at Bradfield College, 81; "Electra," 89; "Antigone" chorus No. 3, analysis of, 111
South Sea Islanders, music performed at Paris Exhibition of 1889, 173
Sparta, music of, 9 et seq.
Spitta's view of dots in Seikilos Hymn, 32
Spohr's chromatic melos, 100
Spondee, suitable for hymns, 27; derivation of word, 42; major, 43; effective use of by Handel, 43; in Bach's organ fantasia in A minor, 65; induces strength of character, 98
Spondeic anapæsts, 105
Stesichorus, 15
Stigma, 30
Strauss, "Electra," 90
Strongulos, 44
Strophe and antistrophe, 15; and epode, 76; periods in, 110
Style, popular, not approved of by Aristoxenus, 20, 21
Superfluity of sounds produce flat and insipid rhythms, 99
Syncopation, common to all nations, 32; arises from compound arsis against simple thesis, 36; energy of, 54
Systems, the greater and lesser perfect, 13
Syzygy, 50

Telesias of Thebes, 21
Tempo, agōgē, Aristides' remark on, 78 *note*; in tragedy, 83; in comedy, 87
Terpander, 10, 11
Terpandrian nomos, 10
Tetrachordal construction of modern scales, 14
Tetrachords, conjunct, 13; disjunct, 14
Tetralogy, 16
Tetrapody, the normal rhythm of modern Europe, 115
Thaletas, 11, 12
Theodorus, M., 4
Thesis, stress or accent, 25; called *basis* by Aristoxenus, 25 *note*; the downward movement of hand or foot, 27; audibly struck in ancient Greece and modern Italy, 27; Aristoxenus and Aristides apply the word *chronos* to thesis and arsis, 49. See also Arsis
Thespis introduces an actor, 15
Thetic feet, 28
Thrasymachus of Chalcedon applies musical terms to rhetoric, 107
Thyrea, battle of, 12

Time values, Latin grammarians in error, 28; anciently shown by signs, as in tablatures and tonic sol-fa notation, 30
Timotheus, a decadent, 20, 21
Tragedy, origin of, 15; Phrygian mode used in, 15; *tempo* in, 83; dochmiac in, 89; quintuple rhythm in, 89
Transposition, 13
Trent, Council of, views of polyphonic music similar to those of Philodemus of Gadara and Aristotle, 135
Triads, artistic, 24
Tribrach, 42
Trichronos, 35
Trilogy, 16
Trimeres, 11
Trimeter, iambic, 66
Trisēmos, 35
Trochaios semantos, 10
Trochee, derivation of word, and various forms of, 42; used in the pæon, 44; suitable to the dance, 97; described as "warm," 98; performed *prestissimo* in comedy, 104; belongs to the diastaltic and systaltic styles, 105
Twenty-time rhythm, 67
Twenty-one-time rhythm, 67
Twenty-two, and twenty-three-time rhythm, 68
Twenty-four-time rhythm, 67; in Schubert's "Pilgerweise," 68
Twenty-five-time rhythm, 68
Two-time rhythm not approved of, 37
Tzetzes, 6

Uneven relations, Aristides' view of, 94, 95

Varro, 4
Victorinus, Marius, 5; notices that the thesis was audibly struck, 27
Vincent, A. J. H., 4
Violent changes are dreadful and destructive, 98
Vocal music, period in, 108
Vordersatz and Nachsatz, 107

Wagner, R., allusions to rhythm and metre in "Oper und Drama," 7; chromatic melos, 100; function of music in music drama, 159; verse-melody, 159, 160; "Tristan und Isolde," 160, 164-168; rhythm in music-drama, 160; function of the orchestra, 162-164; absolute melody or music, 159, 168; "Preislied," 168
Wallis, 3 *note*
Wessely, Dr, 32
Westphal, R., 2; catalogue of his works, 3; suggests that Aristoxenian teaching may be of interest to modern musicians, 6
Wolf, Hugo, 170; songs, 171-173

Xenocritus, 11
Xenodamus, 11, 12

Cambridge:
PRINTED BY JOHN CLAY, M.A.
AT THE UNIVERSITY PRESS

For EU product safety concerns, contact us at Calle de José Abascal, 56–1°,
28003 Madrid, Spain or eugpsr@cambridge.org.

www.ingramcontent.com/pod-product-compliance
Ingram Content Group UK Ltd.
Pitfield, Milton Keynes, MK11 3LW, UK
UKHW041952230426
12048UKWH00008B/301